"As Wilson and Gislason write, our sector is fac[ing]
nonprofits need to learn how to invest in their top talent, cultivate next-generation
leaders, and share leadership more broadly. Coaching is one very important way they can
do this. This book gives nonprofit managers and leaders a new skill-set to move beyond
the outdated 'heroic leader' model. The authors have done a real service to the field."

—**Heather McLeod Grant,** coauthor, *Forces for Good,*
and consultant, Monitor Institute

"This book presents a compelling case for why coaching is an effective leadership
development strategy. Based on real-life management lessons, this book provides
practical answers to the dilemma faced by the nonprofit sector—how to attract, retain,
and motivate talented people."

—**Cristina M. Regalado,** vice president of programs,
The California Wellness Foundation

"If you believe in collaborative leadership, then coaching is the perfect approach to
developing and supporting it. This book is the total guide to supporting people to make
the highest possible contribution to the mission of their organization. Brava to Judith
and Michelle for sharing such a wealth of practical and specific skills to get us all there."

—**Catherine A. Merschel,** executive director,
Build It Green

"The tools and ideas Michelle and Judith present in this book are the real deal. I know.
They have helped strengthen my leadership and my organization in more ways than I
could have imagined."

—**Aspen Baker,** executive director, Exhale

"Gislason and Wilson combine coaching expertise and practical nonprofit examples that
can be used in real-life situations. Essential reading for anyone interested in developing
the next generation of leaders right inside their own organizations."

—**Linda Wood,** Evelyn and Walter Haas, Jr. Fund

"This will surely be a seminal book about how to use coaching for leadership development, problem solving, and staying sane in one of the most challenging jobs in the
world—nonprofit leader."

—**Carter McNamara,** Authenticity Consulting, LLC

"This book provides valuable tools both for becoming a more effective leader and for
encouraging others to develop their own leadership skills. It provides practical and com-
monsense guidance and also provides 'aha' moments of insight. I know what a gift coaching is. I know I have become a better leader as a result."

—**Ellen Dumesnil,** division director,
Catholic Charities of Santa Clara County Economic Development Services

"*Coaching Skills for Nonprofit Managers and Leaders* not only offers a clear frame and a step-by-step guide to coaching but also shows how organizations can shift their leadership culture and build a dynamic multigenerational leadership."

—**Helen Kim,** Coauthor of *Working Across Generations:*
Defining the Future of Nonprofit Leadership

"Retention is a huge issue facing the nonprofit sector. Most people leave their jobs because of bad managers. This book is a major remedy for this problem."

—**Stephen Bauer,** executive director,
Nonprofit Workforce Coalition

"Wilson and Gislason are experts in the field and provide a contribution that has been sorely lacking for nonprofit leaders seeking to develop their staff. Practical, concise, and full of clear examples of how to coach for greater effectiveness. Well worth the time investment!"

—**Ann V. Deaton,** leadership coach, DaVinci Resources

"Wilson and Gislason remind us that we all can benefit from coaching and give us a model that is clear, interesting, and—most important—immediately useful."

—**Paul Groesbeck,** executive director,
Life Foundation, Honolulu

"As an executive director of a small and very diverse staff, I find that this book provides me with practical tips and helpful tools on how to work with staff to build on their strengths—creating a stronger team, increasing organizational capacity, and developing future nonprofit leaders."

—**Ellen Wu,** executive director,
California Pan-Ethnic Health Network (CPEHN)

"I enthusiastically recommend the principles and contemporary coaching approaches outlined in this fresh perspective on the time-worn dilemma: how to do more with less, while growing nonprofit professionals who truly lead and innovate."

—**Kathy Riggins,** president and CEO, YMCA of Silicon Valley

"Anyone seeking the 'X Factor' missing from their own management and leadership skill toolkit ought to read this book. Wilson and Gislason provide useful coaching dialogues that confront the realities of managing, developing, and retaining talented staff at all levels of an organization."

—**Michael L. Edell,** senior vice president, Netzel Grigsby Associates, Inc.
(former vice president of research for the American Heart Association)

"This book speaks to overcoming the scarcity mentality of nonprofits when solving gaps in talent, training, and resources."

—**Peter S. Crosby,** founding partner, AllTogetherNow Advisors

Coaching Skills
for Nonprofit Managers
and Leaders

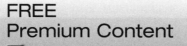

Coaching Skills
for Nonprofit Managers
and Leaders

DEVELOPING PEOPLE
TO ACHIEVE YOUR MISSION

Judith Wilson
Michelle Gislason

CompassPoint Nonprofit Services

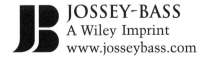

JOSSEY-BASS
A Wiley Imprint
www.josseybass.com

Published by Jossey-Bass
A Wiley Imprint
989 Market Street, San Francisco, CA 94103-1741—www.josseybass.com

Jossey-Bass books and products are available through most bookstores. To contact Jossey-Bass directly call our Customer Care Department within the U.S. at 800-956-7739, outside the U.S. at 317-572-3986, or fax 317-572-4002.

Jossey-Bass also publishes its books in a variety of electronic formats. Some content that appears in print may not be available in electronic books.

Library of Congress Cataloging-in-Publication Data

Wilson, Judith, date.
    Coaching skills for nonprofit managers and leaders: developing people to achieve your mission/ Judith Wilson, Michelle Gislason.
        p.   cm.
    Includes bibliographical references and index.
    ISBN 978-0-470-40130-9
        1. Nonprofit organizations—Management.   2. Executive coaching.   3. Employees—Coaching of. I. Gislason, Michelle, date. II. Title.
    HD62.6.W563 2009
    658.3'124—dc22

                                                                                        2009026289

Printed in the United States of America
FIRST EDITION

PB Printing   10   9   8   7   6   5   4   3   2

CONTENTS

FIGURES, CHARTS, EXERCISES, AND WORKSHEETS

ACKNOWLEDGMENTS

The origins of this book lie in the coaching manual that was created by Judith Wilson eight years ago for a CompassPoint training. Although the ideas and presentation of this material have been put to paper by the two of us, we gratefully acknowledge our debt to the many other coaches, trainers, and friends who have contributed to our learning.

First, we gratefully acknowledge the contributions of our colleague Rich Snowdon, who served as an invaluable adviser as the concept for this book was taking shape.

We also thank CompassPoint's leadership—CEO Jeanne Bell and senior project directors Steve Lew and Tim Wolfred—for their guidance and support for this book, and we offer special thanks to grants and publications director, Cristina Chan, for calmly guiding this book through the writing and submission process.

The official readers of our draft manuscript provided us with extremely important feedback. We thank the following for volunteering their time and insight: Julie Alef, Deborah L. Coleman, Ann V. Deaton, Janet L. Flint, Donald J. Gerard, Susan B. Wilkes, and Julia R. Wilson.

We also thank Prism Coaching for contributing to our thinking on culture, specifically Donald Gerard and Wendy Chiyo Horikoshi, and we thank Melissa Mahoney for the beautiful graphics of the coaching model she created for the book. We have benefited greatly from all the authors whose work we reference.

Finally, we owe a great deal of gratitude to all our clients and workshop participants who have contributed their insight on this topic and who inspire us every day with their commitment and leadership. These contributors include the following:

Angel Barrios, Institute for Human and Social Development

Casey Ryan Budesilich, Breakthrough Collaborative

Percy Campbell, Youth Uprising

Cathy Craig, Bay Area Local Initiatives Support Corporation

Mary Donnelly-Crocker, Young & Healthy

Kristen Dambrowski, Presidio Community YMCA

Michael Dismuke, Eden Housing Management, Inc.

Andrea M. Finley, Child Care Links

Shannon Griffin, 4 C's of Alameda County

Caroline Griswold, National Writing Project

Amanda Kobler, Kobler Development Consulting

Patricia Osage, Satellite Housing

Josephine Pritchard, Coastside Children's Programs

Sara Razavi, Honoring Emancipated Youth (HEY)

Carol Richards, Neighborhood Infant Toddler Center

Susie M. Rivera, Fresh Lifelines for Youth (FLY) Program

Pat Swartz, Girls Incorporated of Alameda County

Meredith Thomas, Neighborhood Parks Council

Julia Wilson, Public Interest Clearinghouse and the Legal Aid Association of California

Luke Woodward, Asian & Pacific Islander Wellness Center

Judith would like to also acknowledge Eiji Hirai, her husband, greatest ally, and dearest friend: Thank you for believing in me as an author and the daily love and support you provided that cheered me on. Thanks for all the weekends we gave up while I made progress. And a special thanks to my friends who offered their help and wisdom along the way and who let me disappear for a period of time to get the writing done.

This book was made possible by the generous funding of the W. K. Kellogg Foundation and The Harnisch Family Foundation.

PREFACE: A NOTE FROM THE AUTHORS

A surprising number of people have asked us why we wrote this book. We've simply told them, "Because we love nonprofits and want to see them thrive." But then they'd ask for more, so here's the why behind the book.

Judith: In 2000, I was sitting in Toronto in the middle of the first organizational coaching conference. I looked around and saw it was all businesspeople, and I asked myself, "Where are the nonprofits? Why don't they get to have this too?" I thought nonprofit leaders could thrive even more if they had access to a coach, and they would benefit greatly from knowing how to coach those who worked with them.

Michelle: At CompassPoint during the late 1990s, we were distressed by what we were hearing anecdotally from nonprofit leaders about their tenure, and we started putting significant new resources into finding ways to provide support for them.

In 1999, we conducted a research study we called "Leadership Lost," and then we did a follow-up in 2001 titled "Daring to Lead." Although the results of those studies weren't completely surprising, they were still shocking. So many leaders told us they were burning out. So many told us they were planning to leave leadership positions sooner rather than later. And given that, how could our sector possibly sustain itself? In 2000, we started working with Rich Snowdon to check out coaching in small ways with small projects. We got interested enough that we decided to test it seriously. We wanted to find out whether coaching could really make a difference for our nonprofit leaders or whether this was just another passing fad.

So we launched the Executive Coaching Project, a yearlong demonstration project in which we provided forty hours of coaching to twenty-four executive directors (EDs). Judith was one of the coaches on that project, and that's how we first met.

We integrated assessment into the project at many points and had it measured and studied by an independent evaluation firm. The results were well beyond what we expected. The overall satisfaction rate was 4.5 out of 5 for the EDs, so that was quite a vote of confidence. But there were many other things we saw that were confirming: increased effectiveness with fundraising, strategic thinking, program design, and sustainability, both personally and professionally.

Also—and especially interesting to me—we saw increased effectiveness in supervising and working with staff. Many of the EDs had started doing with their staff what their coaches were doing with them. And they were getting results that made both them and their staffs much happier and more effective.

In 2003, after the results were published, Jossey-Bass called and asked if CompassPoint wanted to do a book on coaching. We told them we'd love to, but we weren't yet ready. We had more work to do. If we were going to do a book, we'd need to have enough depth with coaching so we could really do it right.

In 2004, Rich and I launched a series called Thriving for Executive Directors, in which we did coaching-style workshops with a group of twelve EDs; we gave them individual coaching sessions as well. Over and over we saw discouraged EDs come back to life. We saw them claim their talents and strengths and remember who they were as leaders. And having gotten a renewed sense of themselves, they were surprised to see how much more easily they were able to clear away problems that had previously been blocking them.

At about the same time, I set up a coaching referral service at CompassPoint. I kept seeing the difference between the moments when someone first called to get a coach and later after several months of coaching. People were doing so much better because of the coaching. They were finding much more satisfaction in their work. And they weren't talking about quitting leadership.

Judith: In my coaching practice, I had started working with leaders and managers in all sectors, but I kept finding myself called to nonprofit work, and nonprofits kept calling me. So, remembering Toronto, I created the class called Coaching Skills for Managers. I offered it to CompassPoint, and they jumped at it.

Michelle: This workshop has been one of our most successful ever and is even more popular today than when it started. To date, through Judith's workshops and the other coaching programs CompassPoint has run, we've trained more than 2,500 managers, leaders, supervisors, board members, volunteers, and foundation staff in using the coaching approach.

One thing people have said to us again and again is, "Instead of just coaching us, you're teaching us how to use coaching effectively with our staff and everyone we come in contact with. And that has made such a difference."

Then in 2006, we got the most amazing call from the W. K. Kellogg Foundation, and we stepped in to manage a national project for them—Coaching and Philanthropy—to test out coaching in even greater depth and to see how it might integrate more deeply into the life of nonprofit organizations. The project has continued to increase our awareness and knowledge of how coaching can have an impact on nonprofit leadership development and organizational effectiveness.

Judith: While this swirl of coaching activity was going on at CompassPoint, people started asking me for a book. They loved the workshop, but they wanted something to take them to greater depth and something they could refer back to when they were trying to figure out a particularly tough situation. I know how repeated review can help lock in new skills and make them second nature, so I wanted there to be a book, too. Then in 2007, I led a session on coaching at CompassPoint's Nonprofit Day Conference.

Michelle: The session sold out fast and was high energy. There was a lot of enthusiasm in the room. Unbeknownst to us, Allison Brunner from Jossey-Bass was there, and she said again, "This should be a book." This time we were ready to go. Of course, there were lots of coaching books already on the market. But we wanted something just for us and our community.

Judith: People ask me what I do all day. Half the time I coach individuals at all levels, in all fields, in many countries. The other half of my time is spent training managers to learn how to coach too. I coach not only because it is my calling to help people be their best; I do it because coaching is the backbone of learning. Coaching helps a person translate thought into action. Coaching is my passion. It's just plain fun pulling out the brilliance in people that has yet to fully surface.

Everyone deserves easy access to the gifts coaching has to offer. No one should have to wait for a special time to learn and grow. I'm personally on a mission to place coaching skills into the hands of everyone who wants them. I imagine a world where everyone will use the coaching approach. Up and down. Peer to peer. All around us.

Michelle: I have a passion for working with leaders of social change. There is nothing I love more than seeing these passionate and gutsy individuals claim their personal leadership style and ask for what they need so they can sustain themselves as leaders. And I love seeing how they first take coaching for themselves and then pass it on to their own staff with a sense of sharing something that really matters.

Margaret Wheatley, in her book *Leadership and the New Science*, talks about "living into" different behaviors, even when—especially when—tested by events and crises. She says, "We slowly become who we said we wanted to be." To me, this is coaching. And this is what managers can support others to do—help them become who they say they want to be. Coaching doesn't need to be a costly resource only a few people in an organization get to have. It's a skill that can live everywhere in the organization. Nonprofits are champions of equity and access. And that's what this book is about too. I'm with Judith—let's get coaching into the hands of anyone who wants it.

Judith and Michelle: Together, we've written this book for you, the nonprofit manager. In the years of doing our work to support the remarkable people who are dedicated to social change, we have yet to find a more useful competency than that of coaching. We believe coaching provides the foundation and platform for enduring change. We believe coaching will help you be of great service to all those around you. Take a moment—and sometimes it just takes a moment—to be someone's thought partner, and together you'll do what you couldn't do alone.

August 2009

Judith Wilson
San Mateo, California

Michelle Gislason
San Francisco, California

The sweetest and simplest thing

that happens to me each and every day

is the man I come home to.

Eiji Hirai, thanks for being

my best friend and forever husband.

—*Judith Wilson*

For my parents, Sandy and John,

who taught me to love words,

to embrace my curiosity,

and to adapt to just about anything.

For Hal, whom I miss.

And for Keenan, who makes me smile every single day.

—*Michelle Gislason*

Imagine you supervise a development director. Let's call him Michael. Michael has just met with a funder on his own. He thinks his performance could have been better and is frustrated because he didn't get the response he was looking for. He comes to you for guidance. Even though he's not new to development, it is tempting to tell him what to do. You are in a hurry. To you it seems very clear. And it is human nature to jump to the seemingly most efficient approach, which is giving advice. This is an option. You could give him advice and send him on his way, confident that he got the benefit of your years of experience. Or you could do something different.

Instead of telling him what to do, you take a couple of minutes to ask some questions. You ask things like, "What went well in the meeting?" "How could things have gone better?" "What outcome were you seeking?" You give him time to think about this. He begins to offer things like, "I didn't really take time to get to know the funder or her interest in the program before I launched into my proposal," or, "Now I realize I needed to spend time practicing beforehand. I was kind of nervous." You ask what else he could have done. He thinks some more, then says, "You know, I should have created a handout to share so things were clearer as I presented our ideas." You ask Michael how he plans to do things differently next time. He says, "I'm going to prepare something in writing, and I'm going to practice my presentation with a colleague before I go to the meeting. I'm also going to take some time to ask the funder what about this program interests her and what she's hoping to accomplish by working with us." You support his decisions and perhaps add a small suggestion for him to consider. You ask what you can do to support him, and he shares that he'd love someone to give him feedback on his next presentation beforehand. You agree and make plans for next time.

This took perhaps five to ten minutes; it didn't require you to have all the answers, and yet it provided an opportunity for Michael to reflect, learn, and make some conscious decisions about what to do next time. This is a coaching approach.

WHY BOTHER WITH COACHING?

As coaches and trainers to nonprofit organizations, we have seen firsthand the many challenges nonprofit managers face. Nonprofits, and those of us who work in them, are under pressure. Resources are stretched thin. We are trying to do more with less. This scarcity of resources is inherent in many nonprofits, if not the majority of small to midsized organizations. And at the time of this writing, an economic recession unlike any we have seen in years is exacerbating this problem. Yet a number of specific trends are occurring in the sector that make it important for nonprofit organizations to consider strategies like coaching to develop and support staff. On a macro-scale, the nonprofit sector is grappling with a leadership crisis. Many of the baby-boom generation are retiring. Talent is leaving. On a micro-scale, we've found that people working and volunteering in the sector struggle with managing, developing, and retaining talented staff.

There are countless articles and studies on nonprofit leadership in the nonprofit sector, and even more in the world at large. Grantmakers for Effective Organizations (GEO) provides a fairly comprehensive literature review on leadership development. We won't overwhelm you with all the research by taking a deep dive into this. However, we do want you to consider some of the typical leadership and management issues the sector is currently grappling with and how coaching may be one way to respond. Specifically, we address the nonprofit leadership deficit and the desire for a new playing field.

THE NONPROFIT LEADERSHIP DEFICIT
The Shrinking Talent Pool

Workforce challenges in the sector have been well documented. CompassPoint's "Daring to Lead" study reports that 75 percent of executives polled plan to leave the sector within five years (Bell, Moyers, and Wolfred, 2006, p. 3). Many of these executives are founding executive directors (EDs) who are of the post–World War II baby-boom generation and who have plans to retire. The baby-boom generation is 76 million people—significantly larger than the succeeding Generation X cohort of only 58 million. "The Leadership Deficit," a report by the nonprofit consulting group Bridgespan, predicts that there will be 640,000 vacant senior management positions in the next decade (Tierney, 2006, p. 26). This poses a mathematical dilemma that has many people concerned that there will not be enough people to fill those positions.

> *"The Leadership Deficit," a report by the nonprofit consulting group Bridgespan, predicts that there will be 640,000 vacant senior management positions in the next decade.*
>
> —Thomas J. Tierney, 2006, p. 26

Moreover, it's not just executives that nonprofits are losing. As researcher Paul Light asserts, one of the nonprofit sector's most valuable resources is its workforce. Light found nonprofit employees to be highly motivated, hard-working, and deeply committed. But he also discovered that "nonprofit employees experience high levels of stress and burnout, and report that their organizations do not provide enough training and staff to succeed" (Light, 2002, p. 1).

Despite the economic uncertainty we all are facing, we cannot ignore the fact that there is a leadership and workforce deficit that will have drastic and long-lasting impact in the sector. This requires us to look at ways to build leadership and management capacity in organizations.

The Need for Internal Succession Planning

Leadership succession is a hot topic. Bridgespan's leadership program, Bridgestar, is focusing on how to move management team members into executive director positions. Public Allies, a leadership organization, is making significant efforts to train next-generation leaders. Nonprofit Management and Leadership Certification Program, American Humanics is working with colleges and universities to steer graduates into the nonprofit sector and organizations that need to increase their leadership "bench strength." All of these activities indicate the need for organizations to expand their internal leadership development programs now.

In his book *Built to Last*, Jim Collins notes that the most successful organizations fill their top spots from within (Collins and Porras, 1994). We believe he's right. Never before has there been such urgency to develop new leaders from within organizations at every level. The good news is that there is evidence of a new cohort of leaders. "Ready to Lead," the CompassPoint research study mentioned earlier, discovered that one in three respondents indicated an aspiration to be an executive director someday. When asked what they needed to prepare for the position, they named such readiness factors as developing external networks, management skills, and an ability to lead, supervise, and manage staff. Surprisingly, 55 percent of all survey respondents believed that they needed to leave their organizations in order to advance their careers (Cornelius, Corvington, and Ruesga, 2008, pp. 20–22). This data point is reinforced by research from Bridgespan, which states that two-thirds of the time, a nonprofit board fills a leadership position from the outside because "there just isn't the strength on the inside" (Duxbury, 2008). We are seeing how coaching helps to strengthen internal leaders and support career expansion.

One of the reasons I left [my last position] is that there was a real unwillingness to share knowledge with me. I felt that I wasn't working to my potential. They weren't allowing me to do the job that I thought I was hired for.

—Unnamed executive director, quoted in Cornelius, Corvington, and Ruesga, 2008, p. 22

The Challenge to Attract and Retain Talent

As nonprofit leaders retire or leave because of burnout, nonprofits will be challenged to find and retain talent. According to American Humanics, the sector has long-standing recruitment and retention problems that are exacerbated by competition with the public and private sectors (Halpern, 2006). As social entrepreneurship and corporate social responsibility continue to gain traction, nonprofit workers may become more and more "sector agnostic" as they seek careers that are meaningful to them. In fact, a survey by the Young Nonprofit Professionals Network indicates that 45 percent of its members intend to pursue for-profit jobs. As Commongood Careers (2008) states, "In the war for talent, nonprofits are poorly matched in terms of financial resources and recruiting expertise" (p. 3).

As nonprofit trainers and coaches, we have come to witness something commonly referred to as a *culture of scarcity* in the nonprofit sector. In *Financial Leadership*, the authors hypothesize:

> When mission perpetually (and heavily) outweighs money, it may be that key people inside the organization are stuck in the 'nonprofits can't make money' mind-set. . . . Symptoms of the culture of scarcity include underpaying key staff. . . . Another characteristic of nonprofits that lean too heavily toward mission is underinvestment in infrastructure [Bell and Schaffer, 2006, p. 8].

It's not news that nonprofits are challenged to operate on extremely tight budgets. However, these budget challenges can affect the ability to invest in, for example, training and staff development. In his article "The Leadership Deficit," Tom Tierney (2006) references this infrastructure component: "nonprofits can rarely afford to make investments in HR, recruitment and leadership training . . . and tend to view such expenditures as wasteful overhead. . . . There is a view that resources devoted to leadership capacity—recruiting expenses, training costs, salaries and benefits. . . . should all be kept to a bare minimum" (pp. 13–16).

Often in the nonprofit sector, because of the scarcity of resources, issues like training, professional development, leadership development are viewed as the most discretionary items and are the first to go in difficult economic times. . . . This is really important to the long-term health of an organization and of the sector.

—Jim Canales, president and CEO,
James Irvine Foundation, quoted in Duxbury, 2008

The culture of scarcity is exacerbated by the reality that many organizations are struggling to stay afloat financially, and this can result in nonprofits failing to invest in needed training and professional development of staff, which can then result in staff retention issues. We all might do well to strategize further about how to maximize the resources we do have, including our human resources. Not only is this smart planning, it will also help us embrace the new dynamic that we are asked to work within: fewer resources and people who expect more than ever.

THE NEED FOR A NEW PLAYING FIELD
New Talent Wants Something Different

Huge efforts are under way to identify, hire, and develop new leaders. And these new leaders are different. Many younger leaders are not interested in the current traditional models of leadership. They want new ways to structure their work. According to *Next Shift: Beyond the Nonprofit Leadership Crisis* (Kunreuther and Corvington, 2007), these new models include shared leadership and participatory structures that move away from the traditional hierarchical structures that were so popular in the 1970s and 1980s. These new structures are more creative and flexible and are not slowed down by cumbersome, top-down decision making. They are also supported by current leadership academics Peter Senge and Joseph Raelin, who promote movement away from "solo or heroic" leadership (Senge, 1999) to "leaderful" organizations, where leadership is spread throughout an organization (Raelin, 2003).

This younger generation also has a different perspective on work. They want a more even balance between work and life, immediate and ongoing feedback, personal connection, and professional development opportunities. Research from the Interchange Group (an organization that works closely with younger employees) indicates that Millennials (born approximately between 1981 and 2002) are not only familiar with being coached (by parents, teachers, counselors, and peers), they also prefer being coached over being told what to do (Deloitte & Touche, 2006). They want timely and frequent feedback. According to the Interchange Group (2006), "[W]e must provide ongoing mentoring and coaching opportunities to offer guidance and reinforce organizational culture" (p. 1).

> *Gen Y employees [also known as Millennials]*
> *welcome coaching. In fact, they expect it. They want*
> *consistent feedback—tons and tons of it.*
>
> —BlessingWhite, 2008, p. 24

Most nonprofits will never be able to compete with a for-profit in salary offered. In the absence of high salaries in the nonprofit sector, newer employees want meaningful work and self-development opportunities. In their book on staff retention, *Love 'Em or Lose 'Em: Getting Good People to Stay*, authors Beverly Kaye and Sharon Jordan-Evans (2008, p. 12) note that providing challenging assignments and opportunities for learning and development were ranked as more important to staff retention than finances. And what's becoming clearer is that those who are coming to work with organizations now want to share leadership. Top down structures may not work for them.

The Solo or Heroic Model of Leadership Is Outdated

> *The term "leader" is typically used as a synonym*
> *for top manager. . . . [I]f leadership is defined as top*
> *management, then it has no real definition at all.*
>
> —Peter Senge, 1999, p. 2

Traditional leadership has focused primarily on one person who has a group of followers. This person is highly visible in the organization, sets the overall vision, and influences others. It is typically the executive director. Sometimes, it can be a member of the management team or even a board member. In fact, most research on nonprofit *leadership* has really meant nonprofit *executives*. This is not surprising, considering that up until the 1990s, most leadership theories focused on individual attributes and organizational charts (Hubbard, 2005). Add to this one of the more distinctive features of nonprofit culture—the tendency for nonprofit workers to put mission above all else—and you have what we call the heroic model of leadership. You may recognize the hero-leader, who looks like this:

A hero-leader is so passionate about the work that she falls into the trap of trying to do it all herself. Or she focuses primarily on the pressing issues of fundraising or payroll (Shepard, 2008). Or she feels that, as the leader, she has to have all the answers and make all the decisions. She does not delegate (or she struggles with delegation) and often ends up doing the work herself because she imagines it would get done faster, smarter, or better. She is always stressed. She can't say no and never has much of a life outside work. She fails to focus on developing staff. As a result, her staff starts to forfeit responsibility and looks to her, the leader, for all the decisions. Staff members don't feel invested in, challenged, or really even supported. Now the hero-leader holds so much responsibility that she starts to burn out. She begins to wonder how long she can keep this up.

Of course, this is merely one leadership archetype. Others include the charismatic leader, who has so much personality and influence that the organization can't survive without her. Another is the leader who suffers from "founder's syndrome" and can't seem to let go of the strategies he used to grow the organization (or the organization itself). As we mentioned in the Preface, much has been written on these archetypes. And we've seen firsthand how these types of leaders tend to burn out and result in turnover.

If you can identify with any parts of the scenario just described, you're not alone. And it's OK because you've done it for good reason, and we're guessing it's probably worked for you. However, as Peter Senge points out, a pattern is emerging in organizations. "Faced with practical needs for significant change, we opt for the hero-leader rather than eliciting and developing leadership capacity throughout the organization" (Hesselbein, Goldsmith, Somerville, and Drucker, 1999, p. 76).

Traditional Management Doesn't Cut It Either

Traditional managers often think of themselves as *working managers* (BlessingWhite, 2008, p. 2). In other words, they're responsible for delivering programs and meeting the needs of the clients they serve, in addition to managing people. In this way, the program can often take priority over the duties of managing staff. In our workshop series Management 101, we ask participants to share what called them to their work in the nonprofit sector. People often share a passion for the organizational mission, an interest in a particular field such as the arts, health services, youth, or education, or a desire to work in community organizing. Rarely do people share that they came into the nonprofit sector because of a desire to manage others. Management Assistance Group, a nonprofit consultancy serving social purpose organizations, echoes this in its article, "Advancing Your Cause Through the People You Manage," stating that "very few people go to work aspiring to be a manager . . . yet they know that mastering the skill of getting the work done through others is crucial to expanding the impact and reach of organizations" (Gross, Mohamed, Katcher, and Master, 2007, p. 1).

Like it or not, we are in an environment of rapid change. Our organizations and the people in them need to be agile and responsive to ever-changing conditions. This requires a new way of engaging, developing, and managing others. This is where coaching comes in.

COACHING: A NEW APPROACH TO DEVELOPING NONPROFIT LEADERSHIP

The mark of effective leadership is not an individual who "does it all"; rather, it's the full leadership team that fuels high performance over the long haul.

—Sylvia Yee, Evelyn and Walter Haas, Jr. Fund

As the nonprofit sector has matured, the prevailing attitudes about management and leadership have evolved. A lone manager at the top doesn't create a stable and sustainable organization. New theories continue to emerge, including an emphasis on shared or collective leadership, which we mentioned earlier. These theories, cited by Grantmakers for Effective Organizations, are described as being "based on the premise that leadership is the product of groups rather than individuals. In other words, leadership can come from many places in an organization or a community" (Enright, 2006, p. 20). Organizational health depends on strong leadership in all positions, which brings us to a new way of looking at the definition of leadership itself.

We define leadership as a process of moving forward an organizational or community agenda, rather than a position of authority.

In other words, leadership is action, not a title. As Jim Collins shares in *Good to Great and the Social Sectors* (2005), the nonprofit sector has complex governance and diffuse power structures that require a different kind of leadership that focuses on the cause, the movement, the mission, the work—not on themselves. This is the kind of leadership we're talking about. Within organizations, there are many individuals who exhibit leadership from where they sit each and every day. They do it by engaging others and posing challenging questions, rather than providing all the answers. Ronald Heifetz, director of the Leadership Education Project at Harvard University's John F. Kennedy School of Government, asks us to "[i]magine the differences in behavior between leaders who operate with the idea that 'leadership means influencing the organization to follow the leader's vision' and those who operate with the idea that 'leadership means influencing the organization to face its problems and to live into its opportunities.' That second idea—mobilizing people to tackle tough challenges—is what defines the new job of the leader" (Taylor, 2007). Mobilizing others to tackle tough challenges, rallying people toward a better future, encouraging contribution or involvement—these are all essential elements of moving an agenda forward. We offer these as definitions of leadership, while recognizing that some may not agree with us. Leadership can be interpreted differently, depending on your own cultural lens. For the purposes of this book, however, we will operate from this definition.

Leadership can be practiced by anyone in any kind of movement, community, organization, or institution. . . . Leadership has little to do with formal authority or where one is in the chain of command, and a great deal to do with forming and sustaining relationships that lead to results in the

*common interest. Furthermore, leaders are not
necessarily the most prominent or vocal members
of a group; they are often quite deferential,
leaving space for others to voice their concerns and
contribute their ideas.*

—Stephen Preskill and Stephen Brookfield, 2009, p. 4

Rather than the traditional top-down process of telling people what to do and providing answers, the goal becomes to engage others and support them to tackle challenges and goals. To do this, we need to focus on a new way of developing leadership. We think this new way includes coaching.

We're convinced the best way to serve the mission is to encourage and develop existing staff. How do we encourage those we supervise? How do we aspire to professional lives that are purposeful, sustainable, effective—and dare we say it—fun? We may not be able to afford big salaries. But we can be more effective, avoid burnout, and attract and retain staff through something we all need. That something is a chance to grow through ongoing professional development, which, as it turns out, is just what this book you are holding is all about.

WHOM THIS BOOK IS FOR

Coaching Skills for Managers and Leaders is primarily for those who manage others in any nonprofit setting. For the purposes of this book, we use the term *manager* or *leader* to describe anyone who supports, guides, influences, has authority over, works alongside, or organizes one or many people. You don't need to hold *positional* or traditional authority to find the coaching skills and framework we present rich in possibilities. Accordingly, we use the words *manager* and *leader* interchangeably.

Coaching is a leadership skill—a skill that applies to the part of all individuals' work where it intersects with the people who report to them or count on them for guidance, or both. We do know that both leaders and managers can use the coaching approach to improve how they develop people.

This book will benefit those in every size organization and every field. In addition to benefitting managers and leaders, it is written for use by funders, consultants, and coaches working with nonprofit organizations, and for teachers and students of nonprofit management.

You will learn about a coaching model and about the skills to use within the context of your managerial job working with nonprofit staff. The skills are simple. You use them in your daily conversations. The question, though, is what impact could you have if you mastered them? The primary objective of this book is to provide you with useful ways to master key coaching skills and practices that will improve your ability to better lead, manage, develop, and support others. It will teach you how to add the coaching approach to almost any conversation you have at work. Feel free to also use this approach outside work, too.

We've seen countless times how learning the coaching approach expands one's development in communication and leadership skills. But coaching is one tool in the vast toolkit of leadership. It's not the only skill or tool you need. As you practice the concepts in this book, you will likely become more confident in your role. Your coaching will encourage others to feel more empowered and to become more accountable and responsible. Using the coaching approach will also support you in growing staff and leveraging their strengths. This book offers ways to become more practical, to know when to give direction or when to support, and when to coach and when not to coach. Knowing how to coach will also make way for more successful delegation. The book provides ways to be better prepared to give feedback and hold performance management conversations. This is not a guide on how to deal with difficult staff, though this book can support you in dealing with difficult situations.

Although it is a resource to provide you with the basic skills of coaching, this book does not attempt to make you a coach on par with those who are certified by programs to be professional coaches. It does, however, give you the level of coaching skills you need to succeed on the job. See Chapter Seven for more information on going further with coaching. The coaching tools in this book have repeatedly demonstrated their worth in thousands of situations. We're confident that if you learn and practice these skills, they'll make your experience easier and more successful. Whether you're supervising line staff or sitting on the board of a nonprofit organization, this book is a pragmatic guide to more effective interpersonal interactions.

HOW TO USE THIS BOOK

This book is organized into seven chapters. We start with a discussion about what coaching can bring to nonprofit leaders and managers. We then define what it takes to become more coachlike and provide you with the skills and framework for a successful coaching conversation, including examples of when and how to coach in specific situations and when not to coach. We end with a discussion on how to create a coaching culture in your organization.

Chapter One discusses what coaching is and what a coaching manager does differently. We also share how to use the coaching approach to manage others and how it differs from other ways of developing staff. We'll even provide an example of coaching, to give you a better sense of what it looks like in action. The final part of this chapter provides examples of opportunities to coach and the specific coaching approach we present in this book.

Chapter Two lays out in-depth instruction for understanding and mastering the four foundational coaching skills. There are plenty of guiding questions to help you coach yourself and exercises to use back on the job. The chapter also offers a sample dialogue using all the skills together.

Chapter Three gives you a conversational framework for your coaching approach. Here we offer you a pathway for productive conversations and tools to support both you and the person you are coaching.

Chapter Four recognizes the importance of knowing how to be your best as a coach beyond the use of the skills and framework. We address the mind-set of a coaching manager and the need to be aware of your coaching lens. You'll gain insight into what the person receiving coaching will need from you to make the best of the coaching experience.

Chapter Five discusses when to coach and when to use other management practices.

Chapter Six offers real-world scenarios that further prepare you to apply your new skills and knowledge in real life. These nonprofit workplace scenarios give you advice and tips on how to handle specific situations and sample coaching dialogues.

Chapter Seven addresses what you can do to introduce and develop a culture of coaching in your organization. It also gives you ideas about how to expand your own coaching approach and how to leverage professional coaching.

Throughout this book, we share what we've discovered and what we've learned as coaches in the nonprofit sector. There are questions you can use to coach yourself and to coach others, indicated in the book by the question mark icon. We also offer insights and the experience of managers and leaders who are using the coaching approach in their work today. This book offers you practical coaching skills to complement other management and leadership approaches, providing examples and case studies that can be translated into real-time application. (See Chapter Six for scenarios and advice for real-world coaching.)

Although this book is one tool to help you become a coaching manager, it may not be the only tool you need. People learn differently. Some people are quite visual and respond well to reading information in order to learn. However, some learn best by listening or by experiencing something firsthand. We suggest you consider how you learn best. Resource B provides a good supply of questions for you to use in specific situations; the other resources provide additional exercises and resources to guide your coaching or enhance your skills. Some of these tools can also be used in the team environment. Take what works and leave what doesn't. And go at your own pace.

Are you ready to get started? Let's go.

What Coaching Can Bring to Your Role

We define coaching as a process that supports individuals to make more conscious decisions and to take new action. It helps them to identify and build on their strengths and internal resources and moves them forward from where they are to where they want or need to be. Coaching supports reflection, awareness, communication, and accountability.

We receive countless requests from nonprofit managers seeking support in managing staff. The requests usually look something like this:

- This person is doing a good job, but how can I get her to step into a larger position of leadership?

- My staff members are asking for more feedback on their work. Some of them say they don't know where they stand. What can I do about this?

- How can I delegate better when I don't have time and it's easier to do it myself?

- I need to have a difficult conversation with someone I manage. What do I do?

- Our organization is flat and doesn't have a lot of career paths available. What is the best way to provide professional development for staff so I can keep them engaged?

• I'm feeling that I need to do everything for this person. How can I help her to stop asking me what to do and take on more accountability so I can get to my own work?

We hear many more questions, but these are some of the highlights. And these are merely the presenting issues. When we dig deeper, we find that nonprofit managers are really struggling with some fundamental skills. They are spending a great deal of their time telling staff what to do so they can get back to their own work (the traditional *working manager* role), but they are spending very little time helping their staff to learn and grow on the job. As a result, they become frustrated because their staff aren't doing anything different.

A central task of leadership is learning to support the growth of others.

—Stephen Preskill and Stephen Brookfield, 2009, p. 61

What we believe has been missing from the equation is coaching. Although working with an external, one-on-one coach has its benefits (see Chapter Seven for more information on this type of coaching), we've seen how bringing coaching skills into an organization can have a much greater impact on staff commitment and the achievement of organizational goals.

According to a study by BlessingWhite, the relationship between a manager and staff is the most critical and reliable option for building strong organizations. "To achieve results and to keep employees engaged, coaching is a practice that requires relatively little investment, is infinitely adaptable, and is inherently personalized" (BlessingWhite, 2008, p. 3). Ongoing coaching is technically a part of any manager's role, but it has yet to be embraced as much as it could be in the sector due to lack of exposure and training.

In this chapter, we discuss

• What a coaching manager does differently

• Using the coaching approach to manage others

• What coaching is not

- How coaching differs from other ways of developing staff

- Opportunities to coach

- An example of coaching (a scenario)

- The specific approach we'll be using

WHAT A COACHING MANAGER DOES DIFFERENTLY

Coaching is unlocking a person's potential to maximize their own performance. It is helping them to learn rather than teaching them.

—John Whitmore, 2002

Managers who use the coaching approach with their staff help them to develop their thinking, find new possibilities, and grow their abilities. These managers support others to learn on the job. Here are some key ways these managers approach leading others:

- They provide a space for reflecting and learning.

- They engage others to solve their own problems or reach their own solutions.

- They identify and build on an individual's internal resources and strengths.

- They use coaching to create accountability.

- They use coaching to support adult learning and the development of others.

Many nonprofit managers we've worked with say they initially thought coaching meant sitting around talking and never really getting any work done. But in our nonprofit work, the focus is on action and results: How many clients did we serve? Did we complete the program on time? How much money have we raised? Nonprofit managers are often so busy they tend to focus on *doing*. To them, coaching can seem a waste of time. Or they may think coaching is about telling and showing people what to do, as a sports coach does on the field. Though getting results is important, and telling people what to do has its place, all this doing and telling can easily lead to the trap of focusing instantly on problem solving or giving quick advice so people will get back to work and do more, more, more. But more *doing* doesn't always mean better outcomes. Managers who use the coaching approach find they attain better results in the long run.

Coaching creates an opening in communication that being directive does not. It invites conversation, problem solving, and a realization on the part of those being coached that they are active participants in the process. The people I supervise ultimately become more self-sufficient. They come to rely on their own judgment and become less dependent on me. They also pass along the skills they learn to the people they supervise. It has contributed to my confidence as a supervisor.

—Pat Swartz, program manager, Girls Inc. of Alameda County

Coaching Managers Support Reflection and Learning

Though we are all here to get the job done, most of us need to learn and grow along the way. A basic assumption of adult learning is that adults have a great deal of life experience and learn best when they can be in dialogue with a person and reflect about that experience. In this way, they will learn new knowledge, skills, or attitudes (Knowles, Holton, and Swanson, 2005).

Remember the example we shared in the introduction about Michael, the development director who thought his meeting with the funder was dismal? He needed to reflect on the action he had just taken. He knew he could do something more or better, but he couldn't figure it out alone. A coaching manager would ask him questions like, "What worked?" "What didn't work?" "What would you do differently next time?" As a coaching manager, you would support him to reflect and to think. From reflection, new realizations are born and learning happens. Learning leads to more successful actions, such as making more time for the next meeting, getting to know the funder, or practicing the presentation with a colleague. This type of critical reflection can also reinforce what Michael did well and may want to do more of. When he knows what he does well and *why* he does it, he will be operating from a place of greater self-awareness. This process of using reflection-based awareness and learning to lead to new and better actions is called *action learning*, and it is graphically represented in Figure 1.1.

More often than not, managers tend to focus exclusively on the action part of this process. That's because all of us are more concerned with results than with what led to those results. When managers focus exclusively on results, they miss opportunities to support the learning and development of the individuals they manage. This focus cuts them off from the reflection and learning process. A coaching approach supports the whole action learning process, not just action. According to Peter Senge, author of *The Fifth Discipline* (2006), adults learn best

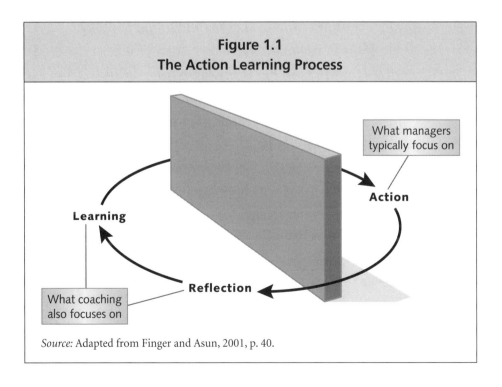

Figure 1.1
The Action Learning Process

What managers typically focus on

Action

Learning

What coaching also focuses on

Reflection

Source: Adapted from Finger and Asun, 2001, p. 40.

from each other. They do this by reflecting on how they address problems, question assumptions, and receive feedback. Grantmakers for Effective Organizations similarly acknowledges these characteristics as best practices for identifying successful leaders: "[Successful leadership development] embraces an 'action learning' or 'learning-by-doing' focus, supporting and creating opportunities for participants to apply acquired knowledge and skills to real challenges facing their organizations" (Enright, 2006, p. 3). When you use the coaching approach, you provide the space and support for reflection and learning to happen.

Coaching Managers Encourage Others to Solve Their Own Problems

"Coaching provides conditions that are ideal for adult problem solving and learning. In the midst of continual change and development, people rarely struggle because they lack some key piece of information or some precise procedure from a course or a book. Rather, they often get stuck in how they think and feel about themselves or their situations" (McNamara, 2001, p. 68).

_____

Reeling in my natural desire to solve my coworkers' problems or offer advice helped me to identify the strengths of my team members, each of whom problem solves in her or his own unique and effective way. I do not have superior problem-solving skills, merely a different methodology. As a leader, it is my responsibility to bring out the best in my team members, not to create carbon copies of myself.

—Michael Dismuke, property supervisor,
Eden Housing Management, Inc.

_____

Coaching assumes that the individual being coached does not need to be given all the answers. In other words, when you use the coaching approach you assume the "person with the problem is the expert on the problem" (McNamara, 2001, p. 2) and simply needs support to find her or his own answers. Leadership coach and author David Rock (2006) stresses this point, emphasizing that the best leaders bring out the best performance in others: "They improve their employees' thinking—literally improving the way their brains process information—without telling anyone what to do. Improving thinking is one of the fastest ways to improve performance" (p. xv).

When a staff member comes into your office with a goal or a problem on an especially busy day, you may think, *What's the fastest way to get her out of my office so I can get back to work? Or perhaps you think, Oh goody, a distraction! Let me solve this for her.* In either case, as you read this, you may think it would be a whole lot easier just to solve her problem or give her some advice. Saves time, doesn't it? If you think this way, you are not alone. Lots of people operate like this. It's so easy to focus on problems and problem solving. In fact, it's natural. As David Rock (2006) points out, neurological research verifies this fix-it mentality. Our brains love to find associations, connections, and links between bits of information. When we do this, our brains give off alpha waves, which have been found to correlate with the release of the neurotransmitter serotonin, a chemical that increases relaxation and eases pain. In other words, it feels good. The upside of this is that it feels good to make connections and learn. The downside is that our brains like it *so much* that we may naturally want to do the thinking and make connections for everyone around us! So we get paid to fix problems *and* it feels good to do so. This may be especially true for nonprofit managers who extend that fix-it orientation to problems in our society such as homelessness, poverty, and civil rights infringements.

Focusing on fixing people's problems can have a number of drawbacks. First, let's look at what it means for you as a manager. When you begin to fix the problem for someone else, whose problem does it become? Yours! All of a sudden, that person's challenge, goal, or problem is sitting in your lap, and you're the one who put it there. We work with many stressed-out, overwhelmed nonprofit managers who can't understand how they ended up dealing with so many problems; in reality, they are the ones who keep taking on their staff's issues. And let's not kid ourselves—most managers are not doing staff any favors by taking on those issues. By letting people think through their own issues, you support their learning (as we mentioned earlier).

Let's return to an example we used earlier. Michael, the development director, knows something is not quite right. He's already starting to think about what happened. If you were to simply tell him what to do, you might say something like, "It's important to our fundraising efforts to get this particular funder on board. You need to really prepare next time." You might also go into problem solving and offer suggestions, like talking to another staff member who knows the funder. These things may or may not be helpful, depending on what Michael has already tried.

When you coach, you pull an individual to a place of possibility. Your questions become, "What will increase your confidence next time?" "What do you need to change to make that happen?" "What else can you do?" Coaching managers attempt to avoid problem solving themselves and telling others what to do. Instead, they focus more on supporting others to process their own experience and find their own answers. Doesn't this sound better?

Coaching Managers Support Others' Strengths

There's a great deal of research suggesting that we are all at our best when we play to our unique strengths and talents. This includes the work of Marcus Buckingham and Curt Coffman, coauthors of the best seller *First, Break All the Rules* (1999), and Marcus Buckingham and Donald O. Clifton (considered the father of strengths psychology), coauthors of another best seller, *Now, Discover Your Strengths* (2001). The strengths-based approach assumes the best way to develop people—and gain the greatest return on investment—is to identify how they most naturally think, feel, and behave as unique individuals. Coaching capitalizes on this assumption, supporting individuals to identify and become more comfortable with their individual talents and strengths. Again, if you were managing Michael, you would already know he's thinking about his deficiencies and how he didn't pull off the meeting as planned. When you coach him, it's good to help him recall the strengths he does bring to the table. Perhaps he's good at organizing data and research. He might be a strong proposal writer. He might have good relationships with other people. As you coach, you remember his strengths and leverage what he can do to support what he has not yet tried to apply to this situation.

Now, let's not kid ourselves. Everyone is responsible for fulfilling a job description. If a program manager hates budgeting but it's part of her job, she still has to deliver. However, a coaching manager would support the program manager to identify what in that job description she is best at and then determine how to manage for the rest (like budgeting) so she can spend the majority of her time doing the things she excels at. This might involve strategies like partnering with a team member who has a talent for numbers or asking a peer to proof her budgets before she submits them.

At first I really struggled with not jumping in to giving advice and directing folks. But when I started asking questions and really engaging with a healthy sense of curiosity, I was truly rewarded by all the wonderful ideas my staff came up with. I realized I had been cutting off a whole source of creative and effective resolutions!

—Julia Wilson, Public Interest Clearinghouse
and the Legal Aid Association of California

The International Coach Federation shares that a primary assumption of coaching should be that the person being coached is naturally creative and resourceful. In other words, people are not broken and in need of fixing. They merely need support to tap into their potential. This could be encouraging a site coordinator to trust her instinct when it comes to working with a client or helping a program manager think through how to put together an advocacy campaign. Not every person can become an expert in all areas of a job, yet each of us has gifts to contribute. Coaching can support staff to reach their best performance.

Coaching Managers Support Accountability

Don't worry. Coaching is not just about reflection and learning, and helping people focus on strengths (although, we feel those are some essentials that are often ignored in traditional supervision). Coaching also supports someone to move from that learning to a new action or behavior to taking responsibility for their actions. As a part of this process, coaching also supports the development of self-responsibility and task ownership—in other words, accountability by the individual being coached. Accountability can be created in different ways. With Michael, you might discuss what his original goal was in this situation. You help him to ensure that goals and outcomes are clear to him and you. Next, you might help him identify a structure to measure his own progress and results. Then you could ask him what he actually feels or knows he will do differently next time. We'll talk about how to do this in Chapter Three, "The Coaching Framework."

At a deeper level, accountability can be created by allowing people to reach their own solutions. When people decide for themselves what to do, they are more likely to actually follow through than if someone else suggests or advises that they do the same thing.

USING THE COACHING APPROACH TO MANAGE OTHERS

Coaching allows time for exploring and getting to know one another on a deeper level so that the supervisory relationship can be stronger.

—Susie M. Rivera, director, High Touch Division,
FLY Program (Fresh Lifelines for Youth)

As we mentioned in the introduction to this book, traditional managers tend to consider themselves *working managers* who are responsible for program delivery and spend far less, if any, time on developing others. Sure, they see themselves as supervisors, but supervisors do have to both get things done themselves *and* get things done through others. Many managers share that they often don't have time to supervise and develop staff when all their time is spent delivering programs. In fact, many managers say that having to do both gets in the way of their "real work" of fulfilling the mission. Typically, those who consider themselves working managers will relegate the management of others strictly to staff supervision, making sure goals are clear, contracting for roles, and conducting evaluations. In Chart 1.1 we discuss the traditional role of the supervisory manager and the role of a manager who is adding the coaching approach to his or her work with others. Compare the difference between the supervisory manager and the coaching manager.

What do you notice about the left-hand side of Chart 1.1? On this side the supervisory manager starts with establishing structure, setting forth plans, delegating, and monitoring the situation. The supervisory manager provides role contracting and evaluation. Role contracting entails communicating clear job

CHART 1.1
Traditional Supervisory Manager Versus Coaching Manager

Traditional Supervisory Manager	Coaching Manager
Role Contracting *Goal: Work and expectations are mutually agreed on and managers know how to capitalize on individual talents*	
• Communicating job expectations • Agreeing on performance goals and standards • Agreeing on time frames and work-loads (often called a work plan) • Establishing professional development goals	*Everything on the left plus* • Discovering what is unique about each person • Knowing and valuing the unique abilities of staff • Turning particular talents into action and performance • Providing coaching support to ensure expectations are clear and needs are met
Check-ins *Goal: Ongoing support and feedback are provided*	
• Reviewing work plan and workloads • Assisting with prioritization	*Everything on the left plus* • Facilitating thought process that leads to new ideas, options, or actions • Giving feedback • Identifying additional development needs and desires
Evaluation *Goal: There are no surprises*	
• Analyzing performance through team feedback and Individual performance review • Compensation review • Discussing potential promotion or added responsibilities • Recontracting role for next period, adjusting job description, or creating new work plan • Career planning	*Everything on the left plus* • Formalizing performance review that has already been provided through ongoing check-ins and coaching support

Note: Duties for role contracting are the same.

(Continued)

CHART 1.1 (*Continued*)	
Traditional Supervisory Manager Versus Coaching Manager	
Traditional Supervisory Manager	Coaching Manager
Traditional supervision can result in this:	**Using a coaching approach can result in this:**
• Focusing only on staff members' actions	• Empowering staff to take better actions
• Driving behavior; feeling that we have to babysit or micromanage staff	• Eliciting best thinking; challenging staff to step into greater responsibility
• Expecting staff will be dependent on us	• Creating an interdependent environment
• Spending time pointing out what staff did wrong	• Working to develop the strengths of staff; asking challenging questions and engaging staff in the answers in order to identify their unique abilities and learn how best to integrate them
• Solving staff problems	• Helping staff to solve and prevent problems
• Taking on staff's work if it's not up to our standards (it's easier to just do it ourselves, right?)	• Supporting staff to think and grow in order to do their own work

Source: Adapted from CompassPoint Nonprofit Services and Coach U, 2008. Copyright by Coach U, Inc. (www.coachu.com). All rights reserved. Reprinted with permission.

expectations, performance goals, and workloads, and establishing a professional development plan. Evaluation entails analyzing your staff member's performance. This usually happens in some form of annual or twice-yearly performance review. When you focus solely on these two things, you are sitting squarely in the traditional working-manager role. When managers have engaged in this type of supervision, they have shared challenges such as, "My staff are too dependent on me," or, "I feel like I have to solve their problems or micromanage them." Some managers have shared that they often end up taking on the work of the other staff member because it's either not up to their standards or it's simply easier to do it themselves. And we've also heard from a number of people about the tremendous tension that surrounds evaluating staff performance. In some situations, the outcome can be a lot of confusion or a very uncomfortable conversation when it comes time to evaluate performance. At worst, it can be a human resource nightmare when the staff member is surprised by the performance review.

Coaching is a process that fosters self-reliance rather than dependence on me.

—Workshop participant

Now let's go to the right-hand side of Chart 1.1. The coaching manager starts by assessing who's on board, identifying their strengths and talents that can be leveraged, and focusing on achieving growth and performance for reaching goals. Next, the coaching responsibility is added to role contracting and evaluation. Ongoing coaching and feedback support the individual to achieve results. And—this is very important—this ongoing attention ensures that by the time you get to performance evaluation, there are *absolutely no surprises.* Investing time and attention in ongoing coaching not only supports staff but can prevent potential disagreements. Notice how the actions change when a traditional working manager shifts to being a coaching manager.

By adding the coaching approach, you also pay attention to where the manager and the staff member can partner. We're not suggesting you ignore your positional authority or role as boss. You must always be clear about roles. However, coaching calls on you to become a *thought partner.* Most people actually want another person to think with. When you coach, you can become the thought partner who provides this service. For this moment in time, you are parallel in your relationship. Two of you are thinking for one.

This is not about the old notion of empowerment, where you, as manager, have power and can dispense it to those who don't. You do have positional authority over those you manage. However, when coaching you stand shoulder-to-shoulder in equality. Instead of only dispensing your expertise about the situation, you learn to develop a new set of tools to bring forth the unique talents of the person you are coaching. This is about partnering with, supporting, and encouraging staff to step into their professional potential.

And coaching is not limited to those you manage. You can coach peers and those you report to. We'll talk more about that in Chapter Six. If you think this whole process sounds very collaborative and highly facilitative, you're right. It is. According to *The Coaching Manager: Developing Top Talent in Business*, "Managers who coach want to help, as opposed to fixing or changing others . . . they show less need for control . . . they believe that most people really do want to learn . . . they show empathy in their dealings with others . . . they are open to personal learning, and to receiving feedback" (Hunt and Weintraub, 2002, p. 42).

WHAT COACHING IS NOT

Before we dive fully into this book, we need to say a little bit about what coaching is *not*. Coaching is still relatively new to the nonprofit sector and is therefore difficult to fully define. However, we can describe some things that coaching *isn't*:

- Coaching is not therapy.
- Coaching is not punitive or just for performance problems.
- Coaching is not a replacement for good human resource systems.
- Coaching differs from mentoring and training.
- Coaching is not a cookie-cutter approach, and it's not for everyone.

Coaching is not therapy. Traditional therapists focus on healing pain, dysfunction, and conflict within an individual or a relationship between two or more individuals through a variety of methods that usually focus on a client's history. As Jeff Kaplan (2007) says, "Therapy often asks, 'Why?' and concerns itself with the client's past. . . . Therapy seeks to fix unresolved issues. . . . Coaching often asks, 'What?' and concerns itself more with the present and future" (p. 1). Kaplan also describes coaches as "collaborators rather than experts." The International Coach Federation (2008) describes traditional therapy as focusing on resolving difficulties arising from the past which hamper an individual's emotional functioning in the present, improving overall psychological functioning, and dealing with present life and work circumstances in more emotionally healthy ways. The primary focus of coaching is on creating actionable strategies for achieving specific goals in one's work or personal life. The emphasis in a coaching relationship is on learning, action, accountability, and follow through.

Coaching is not punitive or just for performance problems. Coaching is not meant to deal with the ongoing performance problems of a staff person. Coaching is an investment in the development of an individual. Many

Figure 1.2
Planet 501c3 Cartoon

management books focus solely on working with difficult situations or people. Our approach is different. This is not a book to help you fix your "broken" or "problem" staff. We are starting with the assumption that you are working with people you want to invest in and develop (if you're not, you may want to take a look at the scenarios for coaching an exit in Chapter Six). There is a huge difference between a staff person who has a learning gap that is coachable and a staff person who has ongoing performance problems that require an HR response. This leads us to the next thing coaching is not.

Coaching is not a replacement for good human resource systems. It is meant to complement *good* human resource systems. In other words, if you don't have good HR policies in place, like how to deal with volatile workplace issues, ethical layoffs, or other termination issues, then coaching might only be a Band-Aid for something.

Coaching is not a cookie-cutter approach, and it's not for everyone. In other words, one size does not fit all when it comes to coaching. Coaching is very much about getting to know the individual sitting in front of you. As we mentioned earlier, the best managers identify what is unique about each individual, and they capitalize on it. Staff don't want a manager to throw a cookie-cutter approach at them. They need someone to adjust to their individual needs. But coaching is not for everyone. The person you coach needs to be fairly open to learning and growth. If that's not the case, this could be an uphill battle. We share a way to deal with this in Chapter Six.

HOW COACHING DIFFERS FROM OTHER WAYS OF DEVELOPING STAFF

When it comes to developing others, there are lots of choices. Training is probably the first resource managers look toward to develop staff. We happen to be big fans of training and see it as a wonderful resource for sharing knowledge or modeling procedures to increase proficiency. However, it's not for everyone or every situation. As the American Society for Training & Development (ASTD) puts it, "Training is something that is done to others. It *pushes* knowledge, attitude, and skills that are essential to successful work performance" (Rothwell, 2008, p. 3). Coaching *pulls* knowledge, attitude, and skills from a person. This helps implement what was learned in the classroom. The odds of achieving behavior change in a one- or two-day workshop are fairly slim. In fact, Princeton University shares that only 10 percent of learning and development should come from formal training. The rest should come from on-the-job experience, problem solving, and feedback (Office of Human Resources, Princeton University, 2009).

Coaching often happens after training to provide the opportunity to practice and obtain constructive feedback regarding the subject matter. This is where behavior change can start to take hold. Nonprofit consultant and trainer Carter McNamara (2005) shares that even if a person goes so far as to get a master's degree in business administration, it will be of little use unless he or she can apply that learning. "In order for the learning process to succeed, the individual must be willing to be open to new ideas, be able to share doubts and fears about new information and situations, apply the new information to current and real-world challenges, and then learn, especially by asking themselves and others powerful questions about their experience" (p. 218). This is where coaching comes in.

Mentoring is another development resource for staff that we absolutely encourage, particularly for emerging leaders in the sector. The purpose of mentoring is to groom an individual to fill a role by teaching proven methods and to introduce the person being mentored to a network of contacts that will help him or her succeed. In *Working Across Generations*, Frances Kunreuther, Helen Kim, and Robby Rodriguez (2008) describe a mentor as "someone who gives a sense of perspective and history, offers advice, and shares contacts and influence" (p. 129). We're big fans of mentoring, but be aware that it is not synonymous with coaching.

We've heard people describe a mentor as someone who walks through the door *before* another person, whereas a coach walks through the door *with* that person. Moreover, a coach doesn't necessarily need to have formal experience in the role of the person he or she is coaching in order to be an effective coach. Given the changing nature of how people need to work, the construct of mentoring could be expanded to consider a more participative opportunity. You can add coaching to the mentoring experience by supporting people to translate your advice into real action for themselves. You can listen to how they think about things, give them questions to ponder, help them figure out where to go for resources, and give them feedback as necessary.

Staff are at the heart of mission delivery,
so it pays to invest in their development.

—Peter Brinckerhoff, 2007, p. 19

If you are responsible for supervising staff, you are also responsible for developing them. We all have opportunities to help others develop, whether they report to us or not. And coaching will give you a simple tool to use in many conversations to expand what you have to offer those who work with and for you.

OPPORTUNITIES TO COACH

Coaching opportunities are everywhere. Coaching can be done informally in the hallway, during a phone call, or just before a meeting with funders. It can also take place in a more formal, regular one-on-one meeting or quarterly development conversation. It may take a few minutes, or you may be able to put aside an hour. Coaching may occur once or on an ongoing basis.

Here are some examples of potential opportunities to coach:

- You know the person who reports to you has been excited for weeks about standing up to speak in front of your major donors. Right before she goes on, she says her confidence is shaky. You step aside with her to help her regain confidence. This is a time to coach.

- Your program manager says he'd like to promote his new idea to help three other programs. You set aside time to help him figure out how. This is a time to coach.

- Your coworker is not working well with other team members. You really want him to find new ways to work better within the group. You ask to help him think through possibilities over lunch. This is a time to coach.

- It is the middle of the year. You're meeting with your team to review progress to date and to plan for the next successful six months. This is a time to coach.

- You have your regular one-on-one meeting with each of your staff members. You listen to what their key concerns and opportunities are, and guide them as they develop how to manage in the weeks ahead. This is a time to coach.

- Although you don't have authority over the team you've been asked to lead, you see that the group could do with more thinking about the program. The team needs support. This is a time to coach.

- Someone in your group has just had some bad news from a community partner. You want to be there to support her as she works through her disappointment and figures out how to proceed. This is a time to coach.

- One of the resource center volunteers seems to be brash with the distressed parents who call in for help. You ask the volunteer to talk with you about how to optimize support for the parents. New behavior is going to be required. This is a time to coach.

- Someone has just started at your agency. It's time to learn what she knows and doesn't know and how to leverage her strengths for the first few months. This is a time to coach.

For a list of additional coaching opportunities, see Chapter Five, "Knowing When to Use a Coaching Approach." The following example presents a more detailed scenario of a spontaneous coaching moment.

AN EXAMPLE OF COACHING: A MOMENT IN THE HALLWAY

Nisha is nervous. She's new to the team at Active Compassion Now, and she's starting to get frantic about her first meeting tomorrow with Tough Philanthropy International (TPI). She bumps into her manager, Terri, in the corridor.

Terri: What's the hurry?

Nisha: Tomorrow is the first meeting with TPI. I've heard how they want people to be brilliant and be done quickly. I'm trying to get thoroughly prepared. I want to do a good job.

Terri: Good for you. What is the one thing you want to walk away from this first meeting with?

Nisha: [Thinks: "I don't want them to think I'm new and don't know what I'm doing. That's why I have way too many confusing

	slides."] I want to know what the funder values more than anything.
Terri:	How are you going to find that out?
Nisha:	[*Thinks: "I don't have time for research. I have to tell our story. But wait a moment, I have an idea."*] I could talk to Pascal. He's worked with them.
Terri:	Yes, using your network makes sense to me. Is there anything else?
Nisha:	Yes. I'm wondering if thirty-three slides are too much for a half-hour presentation.
Terri:	How many do you really think you can go over in half an hour?
Nisha:	More like ten slides. I'm going to go back and prepare them differently.
Terri:	Anything else that will help you?
Nisha:	No, thanks for your help.
Terri:	It's your idea to call Pascal and change your slides. And don't let TPI intimidate you; they mean well. It's just their style. I have every confidence in you. Let me know how it goes.
Nisha:	I will.

What Just Happened?

This is what we mean by a coaching moment. It only took a moment. Who had the answers? Who was taking responsibility? Who has developed a new way of working? Who is being more effective? With successful coaching, it is always the individual being coached.

Hard-working Nisha wanted to show TPI that she knew her stuff. She was preparing to tell them everything about Active Compassion Now. But would they have been prepared to listen? If they're known as a group that demands getting to the point, they wouldn't have happily sat through a long-winded presentation. She was really more focused on what they thought of her than what she needed to understand about them. It's easy to get focused on a task. But it's important to take the time to step back and see if it's the right task. Coaching gave her clarity. And it took only a few minutes.

THE APPROACH WE'LL BE USING

Figure 1.3 on the following page illustrates our approach to coaching. This approach involves three factors: (1) developing and using some basic foundational skills, (2) applying those skills to a framework as you coach someone, and (3) embracing the mind-set of a coaching manager.

Pivotal to this coaching approach is the core value of staying curious. The significance of using this inquiry-based methodology will become apparent as we unfold the four primary skills and the framework. The central theme of curiosity will also keep you true to the coaching mind-set, which we discuss later in the book. The goal of this approach is to stay attentive, interested, and open to helping others develop to achieve the mission.

In the next chapter, Chapter Two, we unfold each skill in depth. The coaching framework presented in Chapter Three will give you a structure for your coaching conversations. And the coaching mind-set in Chapter Four will ask you to look at your capacity to coach in terms of how you come across as you manage others.

To get you thinking, you will find a coaching manager self-assessment in Resource A to help you determine your awareness of coaching and how you currently may be using the foundational skills, framework, and coaching mind-set, as you develop other individuals. The score will help you determine what you might want or need to strengthen as you read through this book. Notice where you are already strong and where you might need to put more attention or go deeper. This assessment is specifically for individuals, supervisors, managers, and directors who influence others, whether they have authority over those people or not.

Now that you have some background on what coaching could offer you as a manager and the path we will take to prepare you to coach, let's move on to Chapter Two. In that chapter you will learn and practice the foundational skills of coaching.

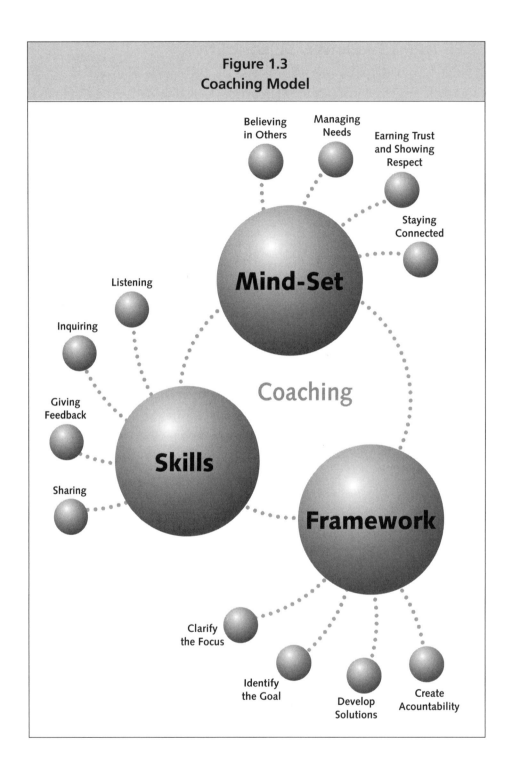

Figure 1.3
Coaching Model

Believing in Others

Managing Needs

Earning Trust and Showing Respect

Staying Connected

Listening

Inquiring

Mind-Set

Giving Feedback

Coaching

Sharing

Skills

Framework

Clarify the Focus

Identify the Goal

Develop Solutions

Create Acountability

Foundational Coaching Skills

Coaching skills can be learned. In fact, you use these skills all the time. The question is, Have you mastered them so they are of maximum benefit to those you coach? Although there are many skills a manager can fine-tune in order to coach, four foundational skills are critical to coaching. In this chapter, you'll learn everything you need to know about the four skills you need to coach effectively:

- Listening
- Inquiring (the skill of inquiry)
- Giving feedback
- Sharing

We'll help you determine the most effective mode of listening so you'll really hear what people are saying—the first time. You'll know where the conversation is going. You'll discover how to listen with full focus, so the person you are coaching gets understood.

You'll learn the skill of inquiry by asking stimulating questions. The key here is to understand the importance of putting your advice on hold during the inquiry stage. You'll give the people you coach time to respond so they can do their best thinking. Your goal is to forward their thinking, help them take ownership of solutions, and be better prepared for a self-directed future.

You'll develop your ability to be straightforward with your feedback and get acquainted with the difference between appreciative and developmental feedback, and when to use each.

Finally, we'll discuss ways to appropriately share information, how to reflect back in the moment what you see or hear, and when to share to best help the person you are coaching.

Let's start with the first skill, with listening (see Figure 2.1).

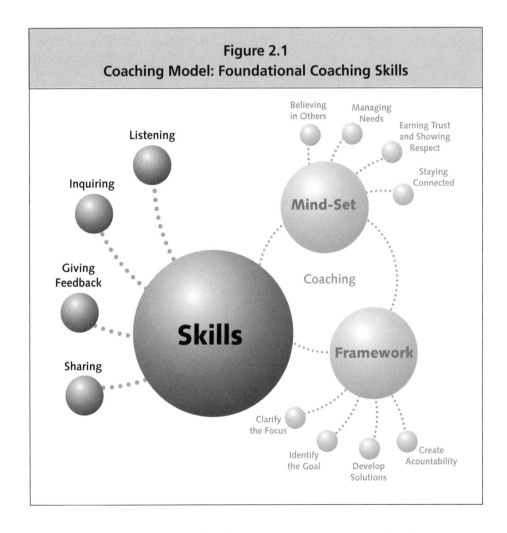

Figure 2.1
Coaching Model: Foundational Coaching Skills

SKILL 1: LISTENING

If someone asks you if you have a minute, and you say, yes, I do, from that moment on you are in a verbal agreement to actually listen for that minute.

Listening is the skill of really hearing what people say, what they mean, and what they want to say. Believe it or not, there are four different modes of listening. Everyone uses all of them some of the time. Yet one mode of listening works best when coaching. Let's look at the four modes.

The Four Modes of Listening

Here's the short version:

1. *Superficial listening*: I'm listening to you but I'm distracted with my own thoughts. I don't hear you. In this situation, it's really all about me.

2. *Self-referential listening*: I'm listening to you, but I will nudge the conversation. So now it *becomes* all about me.

3. *Fix-it listening*: I'm listening to you but I want to fix your issue by myself. In this situation, it's still really all about me, in relation to you.

4. *Engaged listening*: I'm listening to you with full attention. I want to understand better who you are and what this experience is like for you. In this situation, it's all about you.

If you guessed engaged listening is the mode we use when coaching, congratulations! Your inner coach-manager is alive and well. Engaged listening is the bedrock of coaching. It is full-attention listening with a focus on the person you are coaching, without reference to yourself. It is respectful and purposeful. It goes beyond trying to understand what people say. Its focus is on what they mean, and sometimes even more important, what is meant by what is left out of the conversation.

It's a sad fact that few of us really get listened to. In the hectic pace of our work-life, it seems we're all just too busy. If you don't develop adequate listening skills, miscommunication abounds, mistakes mount, and people say of you, "She just never listens to me." Listening at a deep, intentional level can be extremely challenging. Every day, we have things that get in the way of really paying attention to someone. Those things can be as simple as work deadlines or background noise. Or they can be as complex as personal agendas, past experiences, or conscious or subconscious prejudice about someone's age, gender, race or ethnicity, or sexual orientation.

On those rare occasions when you give—or get—full attention, it can have an enormously positive effect. It helps you think more clearly. It creates the space to say things that don't usually get said. It tells you that someone cares enough to heed what you have to say. Listening is a gift—a gift for you to give.

Let's look at a graph to see how the progression of your focus on the other person increases as you advance through the four modes of listening. As you concentrate your attention toward engaged listening, you increase your value and usefulness as a listener to others (see Figure 2.2).

On the left-hand side we have scattered attention and superficial listening. Here attention is not on the speaker at all. As we move toward the right, attention becomes increasingly more focused on the person doing the talking.

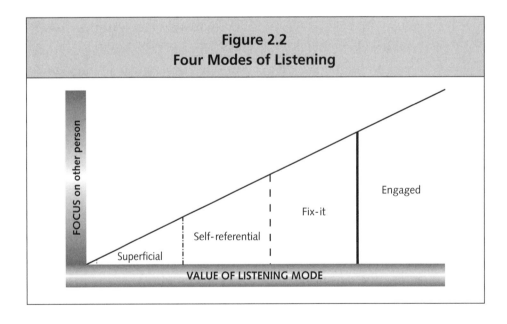

Figure 2.2
Four Modes of Listening

FOCUS on other person

Engaged

Fix-it

Self-referential

Superficial

VALUE OF LISTENING MODE

Now we'll take a look at each of these modes of listening in more detail.

Listening Mode 1: Superficial Listening (I look like I'm listening to you, but I don't hear a word you're saying. *You may think I am listening to you. But I'm not. I may be nodding my head in the right places, although really my attention is elsewhere. In fact, I'm not even looking at you. I'm texting under the table. See how efficient I am! I'm thinking of all the things that I must do. There goes my instant e-mail response. I have to get my grant report out, pick up the kids, and prepare my comments for International Women's Day. The thoughts in my head are far more pressing than what you have to say. My attention is scattered. I'm a fantastic multitasking manager. From my perspective you're just a distraction. Really though, I'm distracted by my own minutiae. I'd much rather you just leave me alone. I haven't a clue what you are saying. I say, "Sorry, what did you just say?"*

At some point most people listen at this superficial level because so much is going on in their environments. Take it from us, this mode really doesn't work for coaching. There's no intention, no focus, no attention on the other person.

At this level, it is all about me, the so-called listener. Let's look at a situation involving a manager we'll call Corinne and Alfredo, a supervisee.

SUPERFICIAL LISTENING IN ACTION

Alfredo: Hey, have you got a minute?

Corinne: [*Thinks, "No! I have a funder deadline today!" But actually says:*] Sure, what's up?

Alfredo: I'm feeling kind of overwhelmed with the housing project right now. I don't know what to do.

Corinne: [*Thinks, "Where did I put those budget actuals from Kevin? I'll need those for the report."*] What's going on?

Alfredo: Well, I've been dealing with the event and managing the volunteers. And then when Jeremiah left, I got the housing project. Now, there's this deadline for the project and I'm worried that Agnes isn't going to make it.

Corinne: [*Thinks, "I must call Lisa and tell her I'm going to be late." Nods at Alfredo.*] Uh-huh.

Alfredo: I guess I could ask if someone else can back up Agnes. The fact is, I'm overwhelmed. I am thinking of asking Frank if his team could help, but he . . .

Corinne: [*Interrupting as she thinks, "I haven't got time for this. What's the fastest way to get him out of my office so I can get back to work?"*] Sure, I guess that makes sense.

What Just Happened?

Corinne became so distracted by her own agenda that she missed some pretty valuable information. Let's look at the impact on both parties. Alfredo doesn't really know if his idea makes sense. Corinne goes away before Alfredo can even finish his thought. He doesn't have specific steps to take. Later, Corinne may not remember agreeing to Alfredo's suggestion to ask Frank for help. And because Corinne wasn't listening at a deep enough level, she will probably question Alfredo sometime later about his problem. Neither party is communicating. Alfredo didn't get an answer, and he comes away with a feeling of not being cared about. He is still stuck, unsupported by Corinne, and not knowing what to do.

> *Westerners speak first, listen second, and observe third. Eastern cultures observe first, listen second, and speak third.*
>
> —Rebecca Shafir, 2000, p. 21

Listening Mode 2: Self-Referential Listening (I am listening to you but I will nudge the conversation to focus on how it relates to me.) *I am initially listening to you because you have caught my attention. Soon my attention ricochets, reminding me of the time I had a similar issue. I am engaged in what* *you are saying only because what you are saying relates to me. If you mention your experience, my first reaction is to think of how I had an experience like that. I'm not sure if I should share my story, but I go ahead anyway because it's so interesting (to me). I think I am connecting with you. I'm not. In fact, I am competing with you. Self-referential listening is all about me, me, me.*

Have you ever had one of those conversations where someone said something to which you had a strong emotional reaction? At that point you stopped listening. You started imagining. Of course, this happens to everyone once in a while. What is going on here is that you are distracted by your own thoughts. You are no longer present. You are interpreting the conversation entirely in terms of yourself.

Many of us love to tell stories, especially about ourselves. There is a time to share examples, but not now. You may want to teach someone and you feel your story is instructive. However, what you want to do here is to maintain the conversational agenda. Be careful not to steal the conversation with your own self-reference. Good listening keeps your attention on the person you are listening to. You know when someone is using self-referential listening because when she stops talking "at you," she says something like, "I'm sorry, what was your point?" She has been making so many points of her own, she has forgotten the original issue.

SELF-REFERENTIAL LISTENING IN ACTION

Alfredo: Hey, have you got a minute?

Corinne: [*Thinks, "Not really, but oh well."*] Sure, what's up?

Alfredo: I'm feeling kind of overwhelmed with the housing project right now and don't know what to do.

Corinne: How come?

Alfredo: Well, I've been dealing with the event and managing the volunteers and then when Jeremiah left . . .

Corinne: [*Thinks, "That sounds familiar!"*] I know what you mean about managing volunteers. [*Corinne genuinely thinks she is connecting—being empathetic and helpful.*] Last year, I had three of them drop out! You can imagine how that caused problems. Still, don't worry. We hired a temp. We did work longer hours, but in the end we got the project done. In fact,

> it turned out to be fun making our deadline. Get a temp. It worked for us.

Alfredo: I don't think we have the budget for a temp.

Corinne: Well, maybe we were lucky because we did. It was such a help. Why don't you see what you can do?

Alfredo: OK.

What Just Happened?

Corinne did listen to Alfredo. But soon she lapsed into memories of her own heroic effort to work with fewer people. Corinne failed to help Alfredo think through a better solution. It was as if getting a temp was the only solution. Getting a temp to replace a volunteer is an emergency measure. It may well not be repeatable. One size doesn't necessarily fit all. Alfredo didn't get much help. Yet Corinne thought she was being helpful.

Listening Mode 3: Fix-It Listening (I am listening to you but for a skewed purpose.) *I know what to do! I am a results-oriented manager, and I want to fix problems as fast as I can. I listen to you in reference to my agenda and my solutions. You come to me because I have answers. I feel valuable.*

Unlike the superficial listener, the fix-it listening manager's attention is narrowly focused on the conversation. This is a good thing. However, he filters as he listens. He listens for problems and issues. In this mode he is paying attention, and he *means* to hear what the person has to say, but he may not hear everything. Halfway through, he is already contemplating his own perfect solutions. He says, "Now, let me tell you how to fix this. First you should do this, second do that, and third do the other thing. And don't forget to try doing it this way and then that way. Listen to my solution." If this sounds like a micromanaging nightmare to you, we agree.

The problem is, fix-it listening doesn't allow the other person to explore her own ideas and develop self-reflective thinking. It fosters dependency (some would say irritation too) on you, the manager. Fix-it listening will mean you often take the first thing a person says, even if there were more important points she wanted to make. It's impossible to give your full attention to everything that's being communicated in fix-it listening mode. You can miss an opening to listen to what else of value might emerge from the conversation. You might miss something that's being implied, yet not actually being expressed in words. A person's body language may be telling you something that you don't see. You are so quick to share your solutions that you don't really notice nonverbal cues. You think all these people need is another way to do their tasks—and do you have solutions for them!

FIX-IT LISTENING IN ACTION

Alfredo: Hey, have you got a minute?

Corinne: [*Thinks, "I'm sure I can help."*] Sure, what's up?

Alfredo: I'm feeling kind of overwhelmed with the housing project right now and don't know what to do.

Corinne: So what's the problem?

Alfredo: Well, I've been dealing with the event and managing the volunteers, and then when Jeremiah left, I got the housing project. Now, there's this deadline for the project and . . .

Corinne: What if you asked Agnes to help you?

Alfredo: I tried that already. She's so busy I'm worried about her too.

Corinne: Did you check to see if there are any volunteers available to help? You should be able to recruit a few for this.

Alfredo: I've tried that and . . .

Corinne: If you called Frank, he would be able to help you out. I've got his number here.

Alfredo: I guess I could do that.

Corinne: Great! Call Frank and he'll help you out. Anything else?

Alfredo: [*Thinks, "Well, this was a waste of time."*] No, I suppose not.

What Just Happened?

Corinne was eager to get Alfredo out of there. She wanted to get on with her own work, so she kept throwing solutions at him. Instead of Alfredo's agenda, Corinne focused on her own solutions. Corinne failed to see that Alfredo was really struggling. Poor Alfredo left, frustrated.

Answers have their place. So does information sharing. Most of the time, however, we need more than quick-fix answers. Many managers see themselves as emergency responders. Rushing around, putting out metaphorical fires can make you feel appreciated. However, our advice is, if you want to be a firefighter, join the fire department. (You get to have a siren, a big red vehicle, and a cool uniform.) If you want to be a good coach-manager, though, you'll need a different level of listening: engaged listening.

Listening Mode 4: Engaged Listening (I am listening to you with full attention.)

It's very easy to fall into superficial listening, which can limit your ability to engage and draw on your team's expertise. Since finding out more about the four modes, I have consciously tried to be an engaged listener.

—Sara Razavi, executive director,
Honoring Emancipated Youth (HEY)

At last, we come to listening that is not about you, the manager. In engaged listening, your full attention is on the person being listened to. Let's look at the characteristics of this type of listening from the perspective of the coach-manager.

You have my full attention. It's about you (the person being listened to). I'm listening with genuine curiosity. I am listening without an agenda. I listen with patience to hear you out. I don't have to rush in and fill any gaps in the conversation. I am listening to what you are saying and what you are not saying. I am aware of the context of our conversation, the impact of my attention on you. I notice your gestures, emotional tone, energy, and body posture. I'm aware of my responses, beliefs, and attitudes, yet my focus is on you. I am listening to understand you, so you feel heard. I am listening with respect. I am staying curious about your level of awareness, your situation, and your finding your own solutions.

Listen deeply. Listen with intent to hear, beyond the words for the entire content and what is behind the words. Engage heart and mind—beyond "hearing." Listen with alert compassion.

If you are listening to a person by phone, you listen attentively to the tone of voice, the pauses, the words, the atmosphere, the feelings, the mood, and the heart of the matter. If you are listening to someone in front of you, you listen with a keen ear and a keen eye. You'll notice body posture, eye contact, and all the other nonverbal cues that give you information about what is and isn't being said. You are listening for what might need to be said. And in either situation, you don't allow distractions.

Engaged listening also allows space for silence when someone is thinking. It may seem unnatural, but two people can have a conversation without filling every moment with words (see the section titled "Silent Listening," later in this chapter). Engaged listening lets you really hear the essence of what is being said. And from this listening emerges knowing what to say next.

Now let's see Corinne and Alfredo in a much better interaction.

ENGAGED LISTENING IN ACTION

Alfredo: Hey, have you got a minute?

Corinne: [*Thinks: "No! I have a funder deadline today!"*] Actually, I have to get this report to the funder by 3 P.M. today. I want to give you my full attention. Is there any way we can talk after that time?

Alfredo: Sure thing. How about 3:30?

Corinne: Sounds good.

Later that day . . .

Corinne: So, what's up?

Alfredo: Well, I've been dealing with the event and managing the volunteers, and then when Jeremiah left, I got the housing project. Now there's this deadline for the project, and I'm worried that Agnes isn't going to make it.

Corinne: [*Checks to makes sure she understands.*] It sounds like you're dealing with a lot of projects right now, especially since Jeremiah left. How is this all going for you?

Alfredo: To tell you the truth, I'm feeling pretty overwhelmed.

Corinne: [*Thinks: "Oh no, that is NOT good . . . uh-oh, I'm getting distracted. This isn't about me, it's about him."*] I'm sorry to hear that. What's overwhelming?

Alfredo: I've never done a project like this before. I'm nervous I'm going to mess it up.

Corinne: [*Thinks: "What does he mean by mess up?"*] Mess up how?

Alfredo: I'm juggling so many projects, I'm afraid I'm going to miss an important deadline. I've never had to work with the board before. I'm nervous.

Corinne: [*Thinks: "I need to be quiet and let Alfredo continue." Doesn't say anything.*]

Alfredo: And well, to tell you the truth, I'm kind of worried about staff morale since Jeremiah left. He was so great at this project and everyone really liked him. Since he's been gone, it seems like everyone's stressed out.

Corinne: And how does that impact your work?

Alfredo: I get stressed and worry that it won't be as good.

Corinne: So, what would support you most right now?

Alfredo: I would love it if I could meet with you to check in on the project.

Corinne: Absolutely. Is there anything else that's on your mind right now?

Alfredo: Well, it would be great if . . . [*They continue talking.*]

What Just Happened?

Corinne was too busy to talk when Alfredo first came to her. Corinne was straightforward and told him she couldn't give him the attention he deserved just then and requested another time. When they did talk later, Alfredo had Corinne's full attention. Notice how Corinne allowed for pauses in the conversation. At one point, she didn't say anything, and this allowed Alfredo to more fully engage with his own problem solving. Corinne paid attention to Alfredo's nonverbal cues—expressions of his feelings—which helped Corinne ask the right questions.

Finally, consider this useful warning: stress can prevent engaged listening. It's much easier to listen when things are going smoothly. In *The Zen of Listening*, Rebecca Shafir (2000) points out that listening can break down when a situation becomes uncomfortable or when a stressful situation occurs: "During heated arguments and confrontations, the listening demands are much greater. The challenge is to process not only the words and emotions behind the words but to avoid becoming defensive. . . . To do this you need to unconditionally accept the reality of the other person as legitimate" (p. 172).

Silent Listening

Silence is the element in which great things fashion themselves.

—Maurice Maeterlinck, Nobel Prize–winning playwright, poet, and essayist

Can you stay silent when the time calls for it? Let's face it, some of us are comfortable with silence, and some of us have to bite our tongues to make ourselves silent. But silence has great value. It is worthwhile to cultivate. You may be thinking that not saying anything may make others feel ill at ease, but we are not talking about the silent treatment where someone doesn't talk because she is in a huff. We are talking about quiet, full attention on the other person.

Now, there are people who just love to hear the sound of their own voices, and even when they try to be silent they make some strange noises. They make sounds like this: "Um-hmm." "Hmm . . ." "Yep!" "Oh! Oh!" Or they insert words that have no real value, such as "No way!" or "Oh my God!" Other noises imply agreement, "Yes!" "Wow!" "Right!" Are those noises really needed from the point of view of the person being listened to? They may just be distracting. (Judith's first coaching teacher suggested that the noises she made to make sure people knew she agreed with them sounded like a cow mooing!)

Exercise 2.1 is one we do in our popular workshops to experience silent listening. You can try this at work or home. It's a good activity to practice in staff meetings or team-building workshops. You can do it with anyone around you in order to see whether a person can possibly move toward a solution if given just a minute to share his or her thoughts without interruption. Try it. You'll be amazed at how much you can do for someone by the simple act. Thinking blooms when you don't immediately talk back and fill every space. Unhindered by the pressure to come up with fast answers, those you coach can develop their own ideas.

EXERCISE 2.1
Silent Listening Exercise

1. One person is the listener (the coach), and the other does the talking (the person being coached).

2. The person being coached talks about a current issue, challenge, or opportunity.

3. The listener uses engaged yet silent listening without any vocalization to support the other person. The listener uses only gestures and body language to show that he or she is listening. In this silence a lot is going on. When you are the coach practicing silent listening, you help the people you listen to because you

   - Allow them to express everything they need to say.

   - Make a space for them to think all the way through something without interruption.

   - Encourage more of their best thinking by nodding your head in a curious, encouraging way.

   - Use your facial expressions to show support for what they are saying, giving them the confidence to keep on talking out their concern.

- Use your body language to show you are engaged and open to what they are saying. (Be careful not to exaggerate your gestures or they'll become unauthentic—or unintentionally comic.)

- Don't interrupt their process; let them finish their thought so that it leads them onto the next thought. This paves the way for new ideas and behaviors.

- Listen for at least a minute to see what happens.

- Jot down your thoughts on the following questions:

  How hard or easy is it for you to stay quiet?

  What is the benefit to you from staying quiet?

  What is the benefit to the other person when you stay quiet?

  What do you need to do to strengthen your ability to stay quiet when appropriate?

When we do this exercise in our trainings, we ask those being listened to how they felt about having a minute to speak without interruption. These are some of the common responses we hear:

"I don't think I've ever had a whole minute to get my thoughts out."

"Given a minute to think out loud without interruption actually let me voice what I thought was in my head."

"I felt more listened to because I had a little time to say what I needed to say."

"Given a minute I have actually started to solve my own problem and feel I can take the next step."

Silent listening is not the only kind of listening you need to do, yet it is called for more often than you might think. We suggest this silent listening exercise to give you a perspective on your natural conversational style. You'll discover how much you might need to temper your engaged listening skills. We are not saying you should never respond verbally with noises. We all do. But be aware of what you're doing. At times it's necessary to respond with questions or statements too. Learn what balance works best for the person being listened to.

Guidelines for Engaged Listening

Create the space for engaged listening by using the following guidelines:

- If it is not the time for a conversation, be honest and say so. Arrange another time, or say something like: "I only have ten minutes now."

- Put aside all distractions.

- Look directly at the person who is speaking. No, looking at your computer won't do. If you are on the phone, try to imagine seeing the person on the other end. It will help you keep your attention focused on the conversation.

- Notice when your thoughts turn back to yourself. Gently turn them back to the other person.

- Stay aware of your internal chatter and practice making it still.

- Listen with empathy. Put yourself in the other person's shoes. Listen to understand his or her perspective.

- Use your intuition to sense when to talk and when not to. Allow there to be silence.

- Notice your level of comfort or discomfort if you hear something that triggers an emotional response in you. Put aside your emotional response for that moment.

- Listen for what's not being said.

- Allow people to express a wide range of emotions in order to clear the way for the coaching conversation. Don't take these emotive reactions as venting directed at you personally.

- Listen for the heart of the matter.

- Stay silent when the occasion calls for silence.

 ## Questions to Ask Yourself About Listening

Coach yourself with the following questions as you continue to master the skill of listening.

Are you in the right frame of mind to listen?

Are there some people you listen to more attentively than others?

Whom do you listen to most?

Whom do you listen to least?

Who needs to be heard even more?

What does it take to give your full attention to someone?

Is the environment distracting you from your ability to listen?

In what mode do you usually listen?

What is the impact of your listening on the other person?

If there is something you need to get off your chest before beginning, do you do that?

What is going on for you right now as you listen to us or yourself?

What will it take to master engaged listening?

Now that you can give your full attention, you can use the next skill to partner with the person you are coaching to develop his thinking and problem solving. By prompting with solid questions, you discover what is really being said and bring out the person's best thinking. Let's get more curious and move to the next skill: inquiry.

SKILL 2: INQUIRING (THE SKILL OF INQUIRY)

Learning how to question is one of the foundational skills of leadership.

—Stephen Preskill and Stephen Brookfield, 2009, p. 127

Inquiry is the ability to ask useful questions. Its purpose is to stimulate another person's thinking and to help elicit from that person new behaviors, actions, goals, or solutions. Although many managers ask a lot of questions about the status of work in progress, this is not coaching. This is simply a status update. Questioning what has been done and why is for the benefit of the manager. However, the skill of inquiry is used for the benefit of the person being coached.

How inquiry benefits your staff. Questions can act as a springboard to a whole new level of thinking and experience. By mastering the skill of inquiry, your attentiveness will create connection and space for meaningful dialogue. You will stimulate useful, pragmatic thinking in people. We showed the action-learning process to you in Chapter One. Questions can be the catalyst that sparks valuable new thinking—possibilities that lead to better actions.

How inquiry benefits you. Inquiry helps you, the coach-manager, too. It helps you understand the perspective of the people you coach. You realize what they know or don't know. You grasp what they can or can't do. You see whether they are willing or not. With inquiry, you are not burdened by the responsibility of thinking through solutions and delivering your take on what must be done. The other person gets to do the thinking—at least about the topic you are focused on in coaching. Your life becomes easier because the more you coach others, the more they coach themselves. Wouldn't you rather people think through their own issues before they come to you?

 ## Be generous. Let the other person own the solution.

Inquiry is a gift. It encourages self-reliance by allowing the person being coached to make connections by doing his or her own thinking. You want to give people these opportunities for self-development. Recall a time when you had an aha! moment, a flash of insight in response to a question. That flash of insight is actually your brain creating new neural connections based on your thoughts and experience. When this happens, it is a learning moment, and it's all yours. When you actively problem solve, you own the solution. You thought of it. Well done!

All of us remember events when an emotional attachment is formed. We remember how we felt. When we come up with the answer ourselves, we feel a sense of accomplishment. This is an emotional event. So when you use inquiry, you help others tap into their own insights.

Here are some things to keep in mind as you guide others with inquiry:

Detach from the outcome; be open to possibilities. Even if you see an obvious solution, it is still better to ask questions so the people you coach can develop their own responses. Their path may be different from the one you would take. And this is a good thing, because when we all think the same way, we all suffer from the same blind spot. Diverse thinking creates more and varied options.

 ## Ask questions for the other person's sake—not yours.

Put your advice on hold. As mentioned earlier, when you actively engage in problem solving, you make the outcome your own. You attach more meaning to something you have had to work at. Activity or work makes you remember better. You want the people you coach to engage their own thinking. You want them to take ownership toward better thinking and better performance.

Be empathetic. Put yourself in the other person's shoes. Imagine what it is like trying to think through uncharted territory with *your* supervisor. In most cases, the staff member you are coaching will be aware of your positional authority, so be particularly sensitive to how you ask questions. Keep your manner neutral and respectful (see the discussion of empathy in Chapter Four).

Use inquiry to coach strengths and promote learning. It's common for managers to approach a situation from the perspective of identifying a problem that needs to be solved. Asking what is going right or what the person is doing well sets the tone for a positive interaction. Then use questions to help the person think about how to leverage his or her strengths or learn to support future actions or needs.

Three Types of Questions Used in Inquiry

Three types of questions are used in inquiry:

1. *Open-ended questions*, which require a longer answer than a single word or two. Use these 90 percent of the time when inquiring.

2. *Closed-ended questions*, which can be answered with yes or no. Use these 9 percent of the time when inquiring.

3. *Why questions*, which require an explanation or justification. Reserve these for 1 percent of the time when inquiring.

Before we discuss these questions in detail, here are the differences in a nutshell. Open-ended questions prompt a response that moves a conversation, an action, a thought, or a behavior forward. Closed-ended questions request the status of something. Answering a closed-ended question leaves you in the same spot as before. Most problematic of the three categories—and least useful in coaching—is the question "why?" This question often evokes a defensive response; people feel they need to provide a reason. The question "why?" is least likely to help a person move forward.

INQUIRE WITH CURIOSITY

Tylana is a family advocate manager who has a history of success running programs to keep abused children out of danger. She has always built solid relationships with the parents. However, as her workload has increased, some parents are becoming distant. Some of them are hostile. She's not clear why or what's going on. Tylana goes to see Sandra, her manager.

Tylana: I don't understand this change in the parents' attitudes. You know, I wonder what I am doing wrong.

Sandra: Let's not rush to blame yourself. What do you think could be causing this attitude change that doesn't have to do with you?

Tylana: It could be the new program-reporting requirements the courts have just imposed.

Sandra: And?

Tylana: I now have to ask for more detailed information than before.

Sandra: So, what does that mean?

Tylana: No one wants to give it, but they have to.

Sandra: Who needs what?

Tylana: The parents need to know they aren't at risk disclosing more information.

Sandra: Anything else?

Tylana: They need to have confidence in our team.

Sandra: And what do you need?

Tylana: Oh! I've never really thought about that. I need them to trust me.

Sandra: How are they going to be more trusting and confident?

> *Tylana:* I've been rushed. Perhaps I need to take more time explaining how confidentiality works.
>
> *Sandra:* That sounds like a good idea.
>
> **What Just Happened?**
>
> Sandra asked simple questions that helped Tylana think about her situation. The questions were short, to the point, easy to grasp, and open. The pivotal question emerged as "Who needs what?" This allowed Tylana to change her perspective and think about what she needed, as well as what the parents needed.

 Question Type 1: Open-Ended Questions   At their best, the most effective open-ended questions open up the mind. They stimulate creative thinking, problem solving, and cognitive growth. They encourage a full, meaningful response relying on a person's own knowledge, feelings, perspectives, and ideas. They are the heart of good inquiry. Open-ended questions generally start with the words *what, when, who, how, where,* or *which.* Effective open-ended questions look like these examples (also see Figure 2.3):

> What is most important to you about all of this?
>
> How can you make that happen?
>
> What are the steps to get you there?
>
> What do you want?
>
> Who can support you?
>
> Which option seems most viable?
>
> How do you see that happening?
>
> Where can you take this from here?
>
> When can you start doing this?
>
> What does that mean to you?

Notice in Figure 2.3 that on the spectrum of open-ended questions, there are questions that are more effective and less effective. Stay aware that even the questions on the left of the spectrum are indeed open-ended questions; these questions

Figure 2.3
Open-Ended Questions Continuum

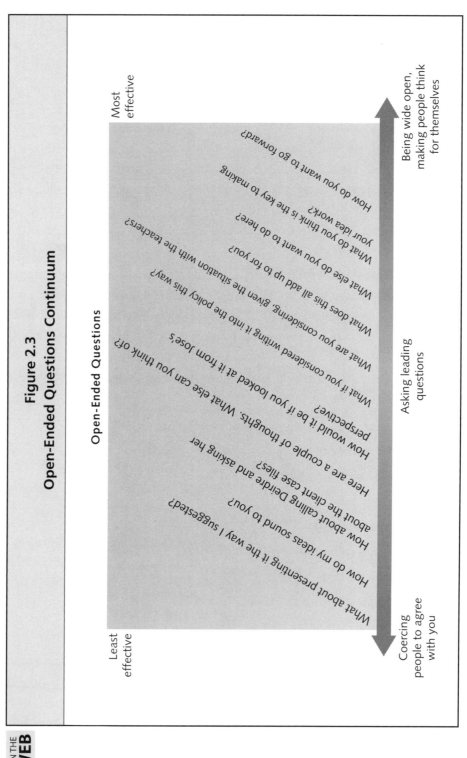

Open-Ended Questions

Most effective

Being wide open, making people think for themselves

How do you want to go forward?

How do you think is the key to making your idea work?

What do you want to do here?

What does this all add up to for you?

What are you considering, given the situation with the teachers?

What if you considered writing it into the policy this way?

How would it be if you looked at it from Jose's perspective?

Here are a couple of thoughts. What else can you think of?

How about calling Deirdre and asking her about the client case files?

How do my ideas sound to you?

What about presenting it the way I suggested?

Asking leading questions

Coercing people to agree with you

Least effective

can be misused to coerce someone into agreeing with you. Use these very sparingly. Move more toward the center of the spectrum for better impact.

When I ask open-ended questions, I do not have to pry so much or have to make assumptions. I just sit back and the staff comes up with their own next steps. They are able to come up with what they are doing or what they need to do better.

—Susie M. Rivera, director, High Touch Division,
FLY Program (Fresh Lifelines for Youth)

Beware of leading questions. But what if you do have a thought you want to share? We are not saying you can't share a quick idea or something useful (read the section titled "Sharing Ideas, Information, and Examples," later in this chapter, before you do, though). To do so, you might use a leading question, that is, one that attempts to steer the respondent's answer or has the information you want someone to use inserted into it. Leading questions may limit options. And beware: those who use *only* leading questions do not master the skills of a solid coach. Here are some examples of this type of open-ended question:

What if you asked the clients first?

How does adding a green circle to the graphic update the look of the flyer?

How about asking the city councilwoman to introduce the new ED?

We recommend that you master the more general, wide-open questions and manage how often you pose leading questions. Be careful that they take into account the needs of the other person and not just your thoughts and your needs. Stay with questions that help the other person expose his or her best thinking. If your question is not working for the person you're coaching, let it go; drop your line of leading questions and let that person lead the way.

Keep your questions short and to the point. You have probably noticed that our sample questions are not long-winded expositions. This is a case of less is more. "The dumber the better," Henry Kimsey-House, a grandfather of the coaching profession and cofounder of the Coaches Training Institute (CTI) in

Marin County, California, used to tell his students. He was adamant that questions should be simple and short. Henry was right. Shorter questions are easier to grasp and give more opportunity for a full response:

What do you want?

What does that mean to you?

What could you do?

What else is possible?

What's next?

Some questions can even be one or two words. Let's say you are coaching a man who tells you he has stopped trying to do something. You ask, "Because?" Or maybe you are coaching a woman who is thinking about how she will try adding something new to her process. You ask, "Then what? What else?"

Try it. Open-ended questions just beg to stimulate thinking. Make sure you use an appropriate tone. Think about the words *and* and *so*. If you add question marks to them, you have the perfect prompts. Let's take a look at this in action.

EFFECTIVE INQUIRY DOESN'T NEED TO BE WORDY

Sue: I'm fed up with those two team members.

You: And? [*Your one word, in a curious tone, implies you are asking what she wants to do.*]

Sue: And I think something should be done.

You: So? [*The implication is a request for what she thinks should happen next.*]

Sue: So, I think I should talk to them to get things straight. I'm not going to let this go on anymore.

You: That's a very good idea.

Sue: Thanks for helping me think through this.

You just used seven words for a fully engaged conversation!

Forget it! Don't be attached to your question. Once in a while, you will get a blank stare or a puzzled expression in response to your question. Give the person a moment, just in case she is still thinking. However, if she is baffled by your question, you can ask her to forget that question and quickly ask another. Don't try to explain your question; move on. Even if you think your question was particularly clever or insightful, just let it go. This may be difficult because we can get attached to our own brilliance, but guess where the focus needs to stay? Yes, you guessed it—as much as possible on the other person.

Coaching has changed how I approach conversations. Taking the time to ask a few questions rather than offer my thoughts directly has resulted in better long-term working relationships.

—Casey Ryan Budesilich, national growth director,
Breakthrough Collaborative

Be aware of the intention of your questions. As discussed, good open-ended questions cannot be answered with a simple yes or no. When you engage in inquiry, a vast majority of your questions will be open-ended. However, the fact that a question is posed using the open-ended format and requires more than a yes or no answer doesn't necessarily mean that the question is effective.

Open-ended questions should focus on the needs of the other person, opening up new learning; they should not be a crafty way of getting your own agenda met. If you keep this in mind, your open-ended questions will be productive. Sometimes, you do need to take a little more time. Just be sure your focus is on helping the other person think and not on coercing him to answer the question.

Be careful when inquiring. As you can see from Figure 2.3, not all questions carry the same weight. Some questions asked out of context or said in the wrong tone of voice may send a negative message rather than help the other person to think clearly. Then there are some questions that are just too close to being obnoxious and need to be reworded.

Try saying some of the following questions in a reasonable voice and then say them in an obnoxious tone:

How on earth did you come up with that?

What were you thinking?

Where is your head at?

What have you been up to all this time?

Have you lost your mind here?

Did you really say that?

How come you haven't done it yet?

Can you hear a difference? With a small shift in tone, even a completely sincere inquiry can insult a person's mannerisms, opinions, or intelligence. Do your best to reword these types of questions, and make sure your inflections are in the right place.

Consider this question: What was a pivotal or best moment in your leadership or in your life, a peak experience—a time when you were feeling confident and challenged in a good way? When you have that moment in mind, use

EXERCISE 2.2
Asking Open-Ended Questions to Build Your Inquiry Skills

What?	**When?**
What was the moment?	When was this?
What happened?	When else have you experienced something like this?
What happened next?	
What were you feeling?	When do you remember this event?
What did you discover?	

Who?

Who inspires you to be in the flow or at your best?

Who recognizes when you're at your best?

Whom do you have for company at those times?

Whom do you inspire to be at their best?

Where?

Where were you when this happened?

Where is it easiest to get in the flow?

Where is it the hardest?

Where do you want to go next in your leadership or your life?

How?

How did this happen?

How consciously did you create the event?

How accidental was it?

How did other people respond to you?

How did you respond to yourself?

How did you see yourself differently afterward?

~~Why?~~

For the sake of this exercise, we suggest practicing without using the question "Why." We'll explain this more on page 52.

Source: Copyright © 2008 CompassPoint Nonprofit Services and Rich Snowdon.

the questions in Exercise 2.2 to see how much you can help the person you are coaching share about this event.

 Question Type 2: Closed-Ended Questions Closed-ended questions elicit a dichotomous answer: yes or no, true or false, or a statement of fact. This type of question controls the response you'll get. It is restrictive. Limit your use of closed-ended questions, because too many of them will keep the person you are coaching running in place. That's a problem because coaching is about moving someone from point A to point B.

Generally, closed-ended questions start with the following words: *do, did, have, is, are, can, will,* or *should.* Closed-ended questions sound like this:

Is it possible?

Are you finding it difficult?

Did you try doing it like this?

Can you put this book into use today?

Will you make sure you do?

Should you try telling him?

Do you understand what I'm saying?

Could you ask her about it?

Have you spoken to him?

Figure 2.4 shows a continuum for closed-ended questions.

At best, closed-ended questions are useful for understanding or updating the status of things. At worst, they are used to make someone rank, rate, choose, or respond quickly. On the far end, these closed-ended questions give you the history or backstory of a situation, yet don't necessarily help the other person move forward. You will not go far using only this type of question. In our classes, most participants say they revert to the "did you," "have you," "will you" questions about 90 percent of the time before they learn to ask the other questions.

If you really want a response beyond yes, no, or maybe, or true or false, reword your closed-ended question. Here are some examples:

Closed: Do you understand what I'm saying?

Open: What do you understand by what I'm saying?

Closed: Did you ask her about it?

Open: What do you need to ask her?

Closed: Have you tried doing it like this?

Open: What approach might work best?

Closed: Is it possible?

Open: What is possible?

Figure 2.4
Closed-Ended Questions Continuum

Closed-Ended Questions

Most effective

Are you saying that we need to look at these three things first?

Are there any other questions you have?

Is this OK now?

Do you have what you need to proceed?

Have you finished your employee reviews?

Did that conversation yield what you needed?

Are we up-to-date with our grant proposals?

Have you tried disciplining the people involved?

Would it have been better if you had called the program officer and asked if she'd talk to you?

Did you try delegating the tasks as I told you?

Can you tell me what happened?

Least effective

Checking for understanding—yours and theirs

Questioning for status update

Getting filled in on the back story

Closed: Are you finding it difficult?

Open: What, if anything, is difficult for you?

Closed: Can you put this book to use today?

Open: How can you put this book to use today?

Closed: Will you make sure you do that?

Open: What will it take to be sure to do that?

Closed: Should you try telling him?

Open: What would happen if you told him?

The closed questions in each example are not bad. They can help you understand the current situation. But if you want to encourage a more conversational or creative process, switch a few words and—voila! You are on your way to mastery.

Now here, you see, it takes all the running you can do, to keep in the same place.

–Lewis Carroll, *Through the Looking Glass*

Question Type 3: Why Not "Why" Questions?   If closed-ended questions keep a person running in place, the question "why?" can send a person backward. And backward is not the direction we want to go.

Who benefits from asking "why"? Is it you or the person you are coaching? When you ask why, you are asking the other person to explain her reasoning or decision-making process to you. It can send the person into the past to search for reasons or an explanation for a current situation. Although her answers may make you more learned, the person being coaching has not moved forward an inch.

Be aware of the impact of asking this question. At worst, it's a potentially inflammatory question that can produce a defensive response—not always, yet often. It can be like lighting the blue touch-paper on fireworks. Stand back and—whoosh! (See Figure 2.5 for a continuum of why questions.)

Figure 2.5
Why Questions Continuum

Why Questions

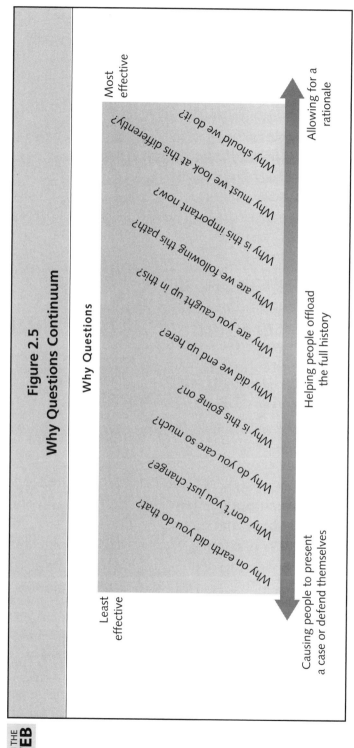

Most effective

Allowing for a rationale

Why should we do it?

Why must we look at this differently?

Why is this important now?

Why are we following this path?

Why are you caught up in this?

Why did we end up here?

Why is this going on?

Why do you care so much?

Why don't you just change?

Why on earth did you do that?

Least effective

Helping people offload the full history

Causing people to present a case or defend themselves

On one end of the spectrum of asking why, your question may help a person present the full history of a situation, but how does this help that person move forward? If recounting the backstory will help him learn something new, then by all means, ask what happened, then manage the amount of time given to his account. Also notice whether you are the only person benefiting from his answer. If you are, this is not coaching. This is status updating.

The most reasonable motive for asking why is to allow a person to explain the rationale for moving forward (see the questions in Figure 2.5 that may prompt this). However, be cautious about how much time is spent on the rationale; perhaps much more of that time could be spent on forwarding the agenda or new thinking. A small spin on one or two words can change the level of thinking elicited by your question.

Here are some ways to move from why questioning to more open-ended questioning:

Why question: Why is that happening?
Alternative: What do you make of what is happening?

Why question: Why can't you format it properly?
Alternative: What do you need to format it properly?

Why question: Why do you use that tone of voice with her?
Alternative: How does your tone of voice help you engage with her?

 The question "why?" is often asked by professional therapists to deepen understanding of emotional issues. This is not our job as managers. Inquiry is not an emotional inquisition. Keep in mind that you are helping the other person move forward through better or new thought, better or new behavior, or better or new action.

There is no definitive list of questions for managers to fall back on. There are literally thousands of questions that might be appropriate for a situation. Is there a right question or a wrong question for each situation? It depends. The question to ask yourself is this: *What is the question that will promote the best thinking in the person I am coaching?*

As coaches, we have found it useful to familiarize ourselves with certain questions that work for many situations. In Resource B you will find numerous questions for various situations, and in Chapter Six you will find many scenarios applying the questions in on-the-job situations. To get you started, here's a list of questions that Judith keeps in her back pocket (so to speak).

Judith's Back-Pocket Questions

What's most important for us to talk about right now?

What do you really want?

What do you mean by that?

Where should we go with this?

What's the bottom line?

What options are you looking at?

Which option seems most viable?

What have you not yet tried that might work?

What else? What else? What else?

What's next then?

What support will you need?

Now, create your own list of simple questions that can be used in a variety of circumstances and then start using them in various coaching moments (use the form in Worksheet 2.1 if you wish).

Questions to Ask Yourself About Inquiring

In Worksheet 2.2, you'll take a moment to think about your current level of awareness, competency, and confidence when it comes to using the inquiry process effectively. As you answer a series of questions about your own approach to inquiry, look for trends and themes that will identify where you need to focus in your own development as a manager-coach.

Mastering the skill of inquiry will make you a solid thought partner. You will see how the people you coach bring about their own decisions to try on new behaviors, move into new actions, set higher goals for themselves, and, through finding their own solutions, take more initiative.

| WORKSHEET 2.1 |
| Create Your Own Back-Pocket Questions |

1.

2.

3.

4.

5.

6.

7.

8.

9.

10.

Is coaching all about questions? No. In the next two sections, you'll learn about providing feedback and how to best share thoughts and observations while coaching.

WORKSHEET 2.2
Inquiry Self-Assessment

Use this assessment in two ways: (1) right now and as needed later, to determine where you need to focus in mastering your inquiry skills, and (2) after a coaching conversation, to determine how well you are progressing in your inquiry skills.

1.	When someone comes to me for support, do I suspend my agenda and stay genuinely curious?	☐ Yes	☐ No
2.	Do I keep my questions short and to the point?	☐ Yes	☐ No
3.	Do I ask (mostly) open-ended questions to move the conversation forward?	☐ Yes	☐ No
4.	Do I limit my closed-ended questions to getting current status?	☐ Yes	☐ No
5.	Do I use the question "why?" with extreme caution and understand its impact?	☐ Yes	☐ No
6.	Do I hold off on giving advice or imposing my own solution?	☐ Yes	☐ No
7.	Am I patient? Do I allow space for a thoughtful response?	☐ Yes	☐ No
8.	Do I ask questions for the benefit of the person I am coaching?	☐ Yes	☐ No
9.	Do I ask myself, "What does this person need right now?"	☐ Yes	☐ No
10.	Do I detach from outcome, stay present, and pay attention?	☐ Yes	☐ No
11.	Do I attempt to see the other person's situation?	☐ Yes	☐ No
12.	Do I respect a different perspective from mine?	☐ Yes	☐ No
13.	Do I avoid interrupting, offering advice, or proposing solutions?	☐ Yes	☐ No
14.	Do I let the other person own the solution?	☐ Yes	☐ No
15.	Do I make space for responses to my questions?	☐ Yes	☐ No
16.	Am I sensitive to how my questions could be misinterpreted?	☐ Yes	☐ No
17.	Do I let go of or reframe my question when it isn't understood?	☐ Yes	☐ No
18.	Am I empathetic?	☐ Yes	☐ No
19.	Do I stay with the other person and the subject under discussion?	☐ Yes	☐ No

SKILL 3: GIVING FEEDBACK

Feedback is information about past behavior delivered in the present which may influence future behavior.

—Charles N. Seashore, Edith Whitfield Seashore, and Gerald M. Weinberg, 1992, p. 3

The purpose of giving feedback is to let people know how they are doing, with an ultimate goal to encourage positive behavior or improve performance. According to the authors of *What Did You Say? The Art of Giving and Receiving Feedback*, feedback is "information about the past delivered in the present which may influence future behavior" (Seashore, Seashore, and Weinberg, 1992, p. 3). Feedback is always for the benefit of the person being coached.

We teach two types of feedback in our coaching skills workshops: (1) appreciative feedback and (2) developmental feedback. Appreciative feedback acknowledges and encourages existing positive behavior. Developmental feedback addresses the need for alternative, more effective behavior. Both are positive and constructive and aim at supporting, encouraging, or improving performance. They are always for the benefit of the person being coached.

Both types of feedback require you to call on your listening and inquiry skills, which, we hope, you've started to get comfortable with. Feedback also starts with observation—specifically, the important skill of *objective* observation. In the context of coaching, you observe someone's behaviors and simply articulate what you saw without adding your interpretation, evaluation, or judgment. It should be as if the person being coached is looking into a spotless mirror in order to reflect and think more about his own actions or behavior. As you call your observation out, you also ask a question to confirm it.

Prepare well and keep your feedback straightforward, genuine, specific, and personal. Avoid general statements. Say what the consequences (positive or negative) of the behavior are for your organization. Remember to choose an appropriate time and place to give your feedback. In this section, we cover the following:

- Objective observation
- Appreciative feedback
- Developmental feedback

Let's get started with objective observation.

Objective Observation

Before you can provide any feedback to the person you are coaching, you need to build the skill of objective observation. Practicing objective observation is an amazing discipline. It teaches you to know when you are seeing without judgment and when you are interpreting. There is a big difference, and many people confuse the two. Indian writer and philosopher J. Krishnamurti (1970) notes that we all have fears, prejudices, and past experiences that shape our opinions about what we see in front of us. In this way, we are not really seeing but merely coming to conclusions and making judgments based on our past experiences. At best, these conclusions and judgments can lead to misunderstanding or confusion about another person's intentions. Or they can lead to simply making generalizations (often known as *labeling*) about that person. At worst, they can lead to marginalizing, dismissing, or disregarding others.

By the time you have read through this section, you will have noticed how often people are judging other people's actions rather than objectively observing. If you can master the art of observing without judgment, you are ready to practice the two key essential coaching skills we are discussing in the last half of this chapter: giving feedback and sharing.

If all the people in a room could agree on what they see or hear, they would be practicing objective observation. If Beatrice is sitting on a chair looking out the window, and all the people in the room can see her sitting there, that is an objective fact. Their opinion of *why* Beatrice is sitting there looking out the window (she's bored, she's worried, she's daydreaming, she's pensive) is not objective observation. That is interpretation.

To observe without evaluating is the highest form of human intelligence.

—J. Krishnamurti, 1970

Have you ever heard someone describe another person like this?

"He really knows what he's talking about."

"She is extremely professional."

"She did an excellent job on that project."

"She is such a bulldozer. She just runs right over people."

"He talks too much."

"She is obviously upset."

These examples are not observations. They are subjective interpretations and a form of evaluation or judgment about another person. What you think is professional and what someone else thinks is professional can differ. For instance, one person may think talking nonstop for two minutes is too much, while someone else may consider it perfectly fine to go on for a good ten minutes before the line is crossed. Interpretation can lead to misunderstanding, so why burden the other person with trying to understand what you mean? Yet most can agree on objective observations: what we saw and what we heard.

Look at the first three examples again. They are positive statements, yet even praise is a form of judgment. Now, don't get us wrong—praise can be a positive motivator. However, let's also acknowledge that praise is actually a form of judgment if you add your interpretation.

Here is the problem: most of us rarely stop and pay attention to what's going on around us, especially what other people are doing. When we do, it's almost second nature to start analyzing, making judgments, and attaching meaning to what we see someone else do. So how can you observe and accurately capture what someone is saying or doing, without evaluating? Here's how:

Spend a few minutes simply paying attention to what you see and hear.

Focus on the person's behavior.

Pretend you are videotaping a movie of that person and then playing it back. What did you actually see or hear?

Ask yourself: "Would other people see or hear what I saw or heard?"

Get specific: note exactly what the person did or said.

Say what you observed without judgment.

Avoid labeling ("unprofessional," "lazy," "eager," "smart")

Be aware of your language ("you never," "you always")

Chart 2.1 illustrates what objective observation looks like when it is used to give feedback.

CHART 2.1 Using Objective Observation in Feedback		
Observable behavior	**Observable data**	**As part of feedback**
Language	Hearing someone say things such as "Never" "Always" "I'm not sure" "I was so stupid" "I can't do this" "This deadline is really stressing me out"	Last week I heard you say this deadline was really stressing you out. How are things going for you now?
Body language	Seeing someone do things such as Laugh or smile Cry or tear up Sit with her arms crossed Roll his eyes or look away	I always see a smile on your face, even when you are dealing with hard deadlines.
Action	Seeing someone do things such as Miss a deadline Invite volunteers to a meeting Turn a report in early Volunteer to stay late for a client intake	I saw how you invited all of the volunteers to attend the planning meetings leading up to the event. You shared a lot of information with them and made sure they knew their roles and responsibilities.

Objective observation can be used to give feedback to someone about past behavior. It can also be used to share or reflect back to someone what you are noticing about her when you are coaching her. We'll talk about this particular practice a little more in the section on the fourth skill, sharing, which appears at the end of this chapter.

Examples of the Difference Between Evaluation and Observation of Behavior (Without Evaluation)

Evaluation: Suman did an excellent job managing the Transitional-Age Youth Retreat.

Observation without evaluation: Suman arranged for the travel of every retreat participant. She confirmed that the facility was booked and that all the materials were delivered to the site well in advance of the training. She asked questions when she wasn't sure about something. She followed up within the day to every request for information from group members. Participants mentioned that when they called, Suman was very friendly and she made sure they had the information they needed.

Evaluation: Harriet has been talking too much and taking up too much time in meetings.

Observation without evaluation: Harriet spoke five times during the last staff meeting, in comparison to other staff who spoke once or twice. I also noticed that she spoke an average of four minutes while other comments were a minute or less.

Evaluation: Stephen is slacking off at work.

Observation without evaluation: Stephen came into work after 10 A.M. three times this week and left before 5 P.M. twice. He also took two days longer to complete the client survey. Each time I walked by his desk on Tuesday and Wednesday, he was checking his Facebook account.

You can practice observation for a moment by completing Exercise 2.3.

ON THE
WEB

Now that you're comfortable with making objective observations, you have a sound foundation for giving feedback. Remember, there are two kinds: appreciative and developmental. Let's look at appreciative feedback first.

Feedback Type 1: Appreciative Feedback

According to David Rock, author of *Quiet Leadership: Help People Think Better—Don't Tell Them What to Do!* (2006), people get on average only a couple of minutes of positive feedback *each year*, versus thousands of hours of negative feedback. What's wrong with this picture? If we want someone to do more of something, why spend so much time talking about what she's *not* doing? Wouldn't it be easier to reinforce what she's doing right?

Managers who offer feedback only when something goes wrong miss opportunities to connect with staff and strengthen what is working. Appreciative feedback helps people identify what they're good at. It focuses their efforts in the right direction. It supports and encourages existing beneficial behavior. People are rarely aware of their own talents, skills, or qualities. As a manager, it is your job to observe, understand, and reflect back to them what you see. When you acknowledge team members, you tell them: "Look! This is the person I see. This is what I saw you do."

Focus on talents and strengths in giving feedback. As reported by Buckingham and Coffman in *First, Break all the Rules* (1999), the Gallup Organization interviewed eighty thousand effective managers to find out what made them so special. This comprehensive study showed that regardless of socioeconomic and racial groupings, people who did best invested in their strengths. And this is where appreciative feedback comes in. People rarely notice what they do well. It's your job to point it out. This may be their first time seeing themselves positively the way you do. When you appreciate them for the first time, it may be hard for them to hear your encouraging words. They'll say: "Yes, but that's just something I do." It takes a moment for it to sink in. It's a revelation to some people that they may have a talent for something that other people do not. By appreciating people, you can make them more aware of their unique talents or of accomplishments that they might not have noticed before. This new self-knowledge boosts confidence and productivity.

How to Give Appreciative Feedback   When you acknowledge people, you are recognizing the qualities that they displayed in any given moment, interaction, or situation that made them be successful. You acknowledge their positive actions, behaviors, or demonstrated qualities and say what you noticed. Then you communicate your appreciation of those positive actions, behaviors, or demonstrated qualities.

[I]t dawned on me that just as people do not always know when they are doing something wrong, they may not reflect on what they did right or why their approach to a project was good. By going beyond just thanking an employee to specifically reinforcing a job well done, I am building capacity in that individual and the organization.

—Meredith Thomas, deputy director,
Neighborhood Parks Council

Here are the steps to giving appreciative feedback:

1. Start with the observation. What positive action, behavior, or demonstrated quality did you observe?

2. Reflect back your observation, based on facts. When you put steps 1 and 2 together, you have created acknowledgment. Acknowledgment says, "I see you," or, "I see what you've done."

3. Communicate what that behavior means to you or the impact that it has made. This adds appreciation to your acknowledgment. When you add appreciation, you give meaning to the person's behavior from your point of view. You share the impact it has made.

Chart 2.2 illustrates what appreciative feedback looks like.

CHART 2.2 Appreciative Feedback		
Observation	**Acknowledgment**	**Appreciation**
Seeing someone smile while working on project deadlines	I always see a smile on your face, even when you are dealing with hard deadlines.	I sense the whole team is more at ease because you seem so calm under such stressful deadlines.
Seeing someone invite volunteers to a meeting and share information with them on roles and responsibilities	I saw how you invited all the volunteers to attend the planning meetings leading up to the event. You shared a lot of information with them and made sure they knew their roles and responsibilities.	I appreciate how you've managed your time, and I know that helps the team stay on track. It sets a good example for anyone who wants to move into the project manager role.

Keep It Sincere Generic or vague recognition can feel insincere. According to Kouzes and Posner, authors of *The Leadership Challenge* (2007), one of the common complaints about recognition is that "far too often, it's highly predictable, routine, and impersonal. A one-size-fits-all approach to recognition feels disingenuous, forced, and thoughtless. Over time it can even increase cynicism and actually damage credibility" (p. 331). Elissa's story shows why.

I've become more honest and more specific in this realm. It leaves me feeling more authentic. It leaves staff knowing for sure I saw the good thing they did.

—Patricia Osage, director of resident services,
Satellite Housing

ELISSA'S STORY: WHY "GREAT" ISN'T SO GREAT

In our workshop Thriving as an Executive Director, Rich and Michelle demonstrate the distinction between generic praise and acknowledgment based on true observation, as follows.

Take 1: The Generic Acknowledgment

Toby is a director of an after-school program, and Elissa is a student coordinator. Toby wants to acknowledge Elissa for her work, so she presents Elissa with a certificate of appreciation.

Toby: Elissa, you're great. You do such a great job in this program. In fact, you're so great at being great I've decided to give you this Certificate of Greatness. Thank you for all your great work.

What Just Happened?

Toby didn't actually say anything about what Elissa did really well, so if we were to ask Elissa what she thought she was being recognized for, she probably couldn't really say. Of course this example is an exaggeration. However, we do this to show how easy it is to default to generic descriptions of people. Be specific when acknowledging someone. It means a whole lot more to say, "You really engaged the board in that meeting and gave them a lot of useful information," rather than, "That was a great meeting."

Now consider our demonstration of a different way to share an observation.

Take 2: The Personalized Acknowledgment

Toby: Elissa, when I see you walk into the room, I notice all the kids run up to you with smiles on their faces, all clamoring to talk to you. I also see you greet them immediately with a smile, and you make it a point to say each child's name and give him or her individual attention before going to your desk.

What Just Happened?

This is Toby's observation. She described the behaviors that she observed. It was almost as if she held up a mirror so Elissa could see herself with those kids. Notice how specific this was. Also notice how objective it was: anyone could have walked into that room and seen the exact same thing.

Acknowledgment is not just your basic compliment. Compliments are generic and easy. Compliments are basic forms of flattery. How much thought does someone have to put into comments like these: "Great meeting yesterday!" "Good job on that proposal!"? Not much. The kind of acknowledgment we're talking about goes deeper and takes more effort.

 When you catch people doing something well, tell them!

Now that you've seen acknowledgment in action, let's focus on appreciation. Appreciation is a way to make your feedback personal. Say what the behavior you've observed means to you. Situate your feedback in the context of your organization. Tell people of the consequences of their behavior among other team members. (Yes, a behavior can have positive consequences!) Let them know how they have contributed to the organization's mission. Hold up that mirror again so they can see themselves in a positive light. Appreciative feedback often inspires people to new levels of performance.

To see this in action, let's go back to Elissa's story, in which Toby is the director of an after-school program and Monica is the student coordinator.

ELISSA'S STORY CONTINUED

Take 3: Personalized Acknowledgment with Appreciation Added

Toby: Elissa, when I see you walk into the room, I notice all the kids run up to you with smiles on their faces, all clamoring to talk to you. I also see you greet them immediately with a smile, and you make it a point to say each child's name and give him or her individual attention before going to your desk.

Again, this is Toby's observation. It is an example of acknowledgment. However, she then goes on to give appreciative feedback about what she sees by sharing how her observation has meaning for her.

Toby: When you connect with the kids with such genuine joy, it meets my need for this program to be a place where kids not only learn things but where they feel welcomed and safe. When I see you with them, I know they are getting what they need. I appreciate it. Thank you.

What Just Happened?

In the first instance, anyone in that room could have seen what Toby saw. She was specific about what she observed. When she came to add her appreciation, she attached her own meaning to what she saw. She then went on to communicate what that meant for the organization. In this case, the positive impact was that the kids' needs were addressed. She made it personal, and that created meaning. Addressing the kids' needs is congruent with the greater mission.

When people feel that you've paid attention to them, they understand that you value them. So many relationships within our organizations are held at a distance. But when you provide appreciative feedback that includes a level of acknowledgment and appreciation, you bring the relationship closer. You connect on a deeper level.

Genuine feedback is precise and personal. By attaching specific meaning, you avoid generalized statements. Be straightforward. People need to know they are on the right path. Don't make them guess.

Giving appreciative feedback (like any skill) takes some practice. Yet learning this skill is worthwhile because it can be a powerful springboard to coaching people to new and greater challenges.

Follow up with coaching questions after giving your feedback. In this way, you'll help the person think through previously hidden options. In many areas of work, star performers seek out feedback and use it to improve their performance. People need to hear that they are doing what is expected of them. And if what they are doing is exceptional, they need to know that too. Point out what is right, useful, or going well, and do it appropriately. We think *appropriately* means *often*. Why? That's because it supports and encourages useful behavior.

Later in this section (Worksheet 2.3), you'll find some questions to ask yourself. These will help you think through your own acknowledgment approach. Try to pay attention to how you may be judgmental. This is difficult because it is often unconscious, and the best of intentions sometimes go awry. The idea is not to avoid praise but to go for something more specific, personalized, and meaningful.

 How people respond to appreciation varies. What is acceptable in one culture may be embarrassing or too subtle in another. Ask the people you supervise how they like to receive feedback.

Look for opportunities to coach after giving feedback. Get started by thinking about some questions to stimulate new ways of thinking. Here is an example:

> I noticed that you spent time over the past three weeks reaching out to our volunteers to assist with fundraising. I spoke with several of them, and they've shared how excited they are and how much they appreciate the time you spent with them to prepare them to make calls to donors. It's wonderful how you brought them all together

and prepared them. I'm confident this group will help us reach our fundraising goal for this quarter.

 Here are some examples of follow-up questions:

How can you use your experience with volunteers to help our team?

How can we bring this same enthusiasm to our staff?

What could you share about the volunteers that would encourage our staff to get more involved?

What can you do now to help volunteers stay involved with fundraising?

Who can support you with this program moving forward?

Was there anything you enjoyed the most about working on this project?

As you prepare to give appreciative feedback, take a moment to answer the questions in Worksheet 2.3.

Questions to Ask Yourself About Giving Appreciative Feedback

Coach yourself with the following questions as you continue to master the skill of giving appreciative feedback.

How do my team members like to be acknowledged? What do they need to hear?

What impact does it have on me when someone clearly demonstrates understanding of my situation or issue?

What does it feel like to be understood when I am experiencing difficulty?

What helps me acknowledge others?

What hinders me from acknowledging others?

How do I make choices about whom I acknowledge?

In what way do I acknowledge some people more fully or frequently than others?

How do I know or learn what is important to each person I work with?

Do I only acknowledge what I care about?

Can I put my agenda aside and acknowledge what others care about?

ON THE
WEB

WORKSHEET 2.3
Appreciative Feedback Preparation

1.   What did you actually observe?

2.   When did you see that happen?

3.   What were the consequences of what you saw, and what did it mean to you or other people?

4.   What will you include in your personal statement of gratitude or appreciation?

5.   If you will offer coaching after the feedback (to boost strengths, actions, or behaviors), what questions will you ask the person being coached?

How did better listening and inquiry skills help me acknowledge from a place of understanding?

How did better observational skills help me acknowledge from a place of recognition?

How am I committed to acknowledging others?

We feel good when we are recognized for our behaviors or actions. Most of us feel motivated when someone has paid attention or noticed our accomplishments. In the best of all possible worlds, acknowledgment would be commonplace at work. But it isn't. Think about how many times you were acknowledged in the last seven days. How many times did you acknowledge someone in the last seven days? There's room for more.

Now that we've grounded ourselves in observation, acknowledgment, and appreciation, let's move on to developmental feedback.

Feedback Type 2: Developmental Feedback

Admit it, this is the one you've been dreading. Happily, it isn't a critique of a person. This type of feedback is a learning opportunity for improving performance. This type of feedback positively addresses a need to help the person you are coaching toward an alternative way of acting or thinking.

The big secret to this kind of feedback is to start by commenting on the *behavior* and not the *person*. Go back to the section on observation if you missed the discussion of this approach. Be straightforward, precise, and accurate with your feedback. And make sure the person understands that you are not criticizing him or her as an individual. This is all about a person's behavior and the impact it has had, or is having now. All of us at some time or other need guidance to improve what we do. We'll show you some examples. (See Chart 2.3.)

Why Bother with This Type of Feedback?   Most managers don't give feedback until forced to do so at performance reviews. This is why performance reviews are rarely looked forward to with fanfare and enthusiasm. However, you are not like most managers. Ongoing feedback helps eliminate surprises when it's time for the official employee evaluation.

Consistent feedback helps people develop their ability to catch problems on their own. It helps them identify learning gaps. Developmental feedback is a positive way to address a need for change.

Why Aren't We Straightforward?   Many nonprofit managers are uncomfortable giving feedback that is intended to change ineffective behavior. Often problems exist because no one will take the responsibility to challenge what

CHART 2.3
Developmental Feedback

Type	In a nutshell	In more detail	Sounds like . . .
Developmental	Let's talk about X because there is an opportunity to have a more positive outcome.	Be specific and straightforward about the exact topic to be discussed.	*Notice the factual observations:*
		Help the person see the situation now, the consequences of current behavior, and the way to move toward more effective behavior.	When I asked you how many calls you've made, you said none. You need to call our donors and arrange meetings. So far, you haven't had a single meeting. This has set us back by several months. Can we do some thinking together about what it will take to get those calls going now?
		Stay with the issue at hand that must move from A to B.	I've had three complaints that the information was late in the last two weeks. Complaints are unusual. This late delivery will cause further delays in the audit corrections. What do you think is causing the delay? What can we do about it?
		Leave out judgmental words like *always, never,* and *every,* because they expand perceptions of behavior beyond the specifics of the topic under discussion.	
		Allow the person the space to fully think through the feedback and decide what to do with it.	Each time I walked by your desk this week, I saw you staring out the window. And during the staff meeting, you didn't speak once. Our meeting lacked energy without your usual lively participation. How are things going for you?

needs to be challenged. In the nonprofit world, there is the idea that we are all friends. We don't want to rock the boat. We want to be nice. We want to be liked. We don't want to upset anyone. When we avoid being straightforward, problems persist. We may tell ourselves that if we do nothing we won't upset the person. But what if this inaction is a disguise for avoiding our own uncomfortable feelings of not being liked? Inconvenient truths are, well, inconvenient. But they are necessary. For some people it is easier to avoid a disagreement than be candid about feedback. We feel this is a mistake, because it only causes more problems as time goes on. And what if the truth really does set some people free? Many of us don't know the impact we have on others—until someone tells us.

We're big fans of strengths, that is, focusing on what people are doing well. However, focusing on strengths does not give someone permission to ignore weaknesses. According to Tom Rath and Donald O. Clifton, authors of *How Full Is Your Bucket* (2004): "[P]ositivity must be grounded in reality. A Pollyanna [naïve] approach, in which the negative is completely ignored, can result in a false optimism that is counterproductive—and sometimes be downright annoying" (p. 57).

Being straightforward communicates clarity of purpose. It lets the other person know what the issue is. We are not talking about rudeness or being blunt. Respecting feelings is essential. Accurate feedback must tackle the issue head-on.

 You may have heard this tip before: Hide the negative or constructive feedback in between two types of positive feedback. We suggest this is outdated and ineffective. It can actually do more harm than good. People are smart. They can usually see what's going on and interpret it as manipulative.

Be clear about your position. Are you really advocating for the person you are coaching? The coaching stance is, yes, you are. This doesn't mean you let them do whatever they want. By coaching, you support. Conversationally, it sounds like this: "I see you are capable of achieving. If you want to go there, I will go there with you."

To use a biological metaphor, feedback supports the health of the system. You will often need to challenge people to develop their level of responsibility and behavior. You could say, "I want you to do it and make a real decision to own it." As a manager, you will sometimes need to evoke your positional authority. However, you can still advocate for the person. This is a commitment to being straightforward. (See the section titled "Coaching in Difficult Situations" in Chapter Six.) Remember, most feedback is not about imposing behavior on the unwilling; it is about advocacy, partnership, and development.

Essentials of Developmental Feedback   Here are a dozen essential things to do for successful developmental feedback.

1. *Prepare.* Be thoughtful (even if it takes just a minute). Consider what you are going to say, how you are going to say it, and how you expect your comments to be received. Practice saying your feedback aloud, or write it down so you can organize your thoughts.

2. *Check your attitude.* Are you prepared to be this person's advocate? Are you prepared to be helpful? Or are you angry, frustrated, or ready to launch into a list of what the person is doing wrong? Only give feedback when your emotions and attitude are in check, and you are prepared to detach from outcome and support this person.

3. *Do it now.* If not right now, give your feedback as soon as you can. This is important because people are more likely to be responsive to feedback given soon after the event. Also, observations and reporting of facts can become less clear as time goes on.

4. *Find an appropriate place to give your feedback.* It may be proper to give some feedback in private. Think about who you are giving feedback to. Understand how this person wants to receive feedback and what the likely response will be.

5. *Ask permission to give your feedback if the situation allows.* Courtesy costs nothing.

6. *Address one issue at a time.* Get to the point. And, again, be specific. Keep your comments based on facts and observations. Have a concrete example of behavior you are addressing. Separate the feedback from any other conversation.

7. *Add impact.* What are the likely consequences of behavior on you, others, or the organization?

8. *Do not give your opinion of the person's character.* Avoid using words such as *never, ever*, or *always*, which refer to chronic behavior or perceived habitual character traits.

9. *Do not blame.* Don't allow the feedback to degenerate into fault finding. Focus on what is now and what you hope to achieve in the future. There is no blame or shame. The idea is to foster change. Focus on behavior, actions, and their consequences.

10. *Stay on track.* If the conversation starts to slide onto another topic, gently but firmly bring it back to the topic under discussion. Useful question: How does what you are now saying relate to the issue we are talking about?

11. *Check it out.* Does the person understand the feedback you are giving? If not, reframe what you are saying. If you expect difficulty, think through some alternative ways of couching your feedback so it will be more likely to be understood.

12. *Help the person move forward.* Use the coaching skills of listening, inquiring, and acknowledging to take your feedback from describing the situation now (A) and what that means, to helping the person move toward a more effective future (B). Moving from point A to point B is the purpose of coaching in the workplace.

Now it's your turn to think through giving developmental feedback.

Giving Developmental Feedback Appreciative feedback supports and encourages current behavior. Developmental feedback's aim is to change behavior for the better. Use Worksheet 2.4 to prepare for giving developmental feedback.

The following example exhibits a good developmental feedback conversation.

ON THE
WEB

WORKSHEET 2.4
Developmental Feedback Preparation

1. What did you actually observe?

2. When did you see that happen?

3. What was the meaning to you or others? What are the likely consequences of this behavior?

4. What is required in the future? (What is point B?)

5. What is your request?

6. Which coaching questions will be useful to ask?

GOOD DEVELOPMENTAL FEEDBACK FOLLOWED BY STRONG COACHING

This example of developmental feedback is from CompassPoint's Thriving as an Executive Director workshop series. In this scenario, Sarah is an executive director, and Jacob is the new development director.

Sarah: Thanks for agreeing to meet with me Jacob. I want to talk to you about your development responsibilities. You've been with us for six weeks now, and I love having you here. I really do. AND we have a problem.

Jacob: A problem?

Sarah: Well, it is a problem. But not to worry, we're going to fix it right now. It's going to be OK. In these weekly check-ins, when I ask about the number of calls you've made to possible major donors, you tell me you haven't made any. You haven't made a single call to a major prospect, and you haven't had a single meeting with a major prospect.

Jacob: Yes, that's true, but that's because I've been so busy with grant writing and developing PR materials to give to potential donors. I just haven't had the time to make the calls. I promise I'll get to it soon.

Sarah: Every time I pass your office I see you hard at work, and I appreciate your diligence. I've also seen you working late, I'd say probably three nights a week I see you here till 6:30. And I appreciate your commitment to our organization. AND there's something else we need more. What we need in the development director position is someone who will go out and ask major donors for money. Actually go out and ask.

Jacob: I'm doing the best I can. There's just so much to prepare. And I'm thinking that maybe getting more grants is the way to go. Major donors are so uncertain.

Sarah: May I tell you what I'm seeing? I ask that because I'm seeing a big disconnect. And I'm thinking that you could be having a whole lot more satisfaction in this job and a whole lot more fun.

Jacob: Disconnect? What do you mean by that? Yes, tell me.

Sarah: One the one hand I see you doing everything but asking for money. And you have an assistant who does a great job at grant writing. We really have that down to a system. And we have materials coming out of our ears. As I said in your job interview, our last two development directors, who we had to let go, stayed in the office and developed materials rather than going out and asking. That's on the one hand. On the other hand, you have an amazing talent for connecting with people. I remember when you walked into the job interview, instead of us putting you at ease, you put us at ease. Last week when the staff all went out to lunch, you made friends in the first five minutes with the host and two waiters, and then before we got our orders you were chatting with the owner of the restaurant like you were old friends.

Jacob: Well, that's just something I do.

Sarah: Yes, and I love it. How can you be like that with major donors?

Jacob: I don't know if I can.

Sarah: We believe you can. You have a great spirit. How can you energetically tell our story and create relationships?

Jacob: Well, I'm not sure I'm well prepared.

Sarah: What if you don't need any major preparation, no tricks, no strategies, just heart. How can you just speak from your heart?

Jacob: Well, speaking from my heart, I do feel I have a lot to say.

Sarah: In the interview, I saw you speaking with passion, from your heart. And after six weeks of seeing how you relate to people, I believe you've got what it takes. What do you need to connect with our major donors in the same way you connect with everyone else?

Jacob: Oh gosh. I guess I just need to show my true feelings and not get caught up with so much preparation. I just need to get out there and do it. I'll either succeed or fail.

Sarah: Here's what I want you to do. I want you to fail.

Jacob: What?

Sarah: Let's get the prospect list. I'll give you three names, and you go out and talk to them about the organization and whatever you do, don't come back with a check.

Jacob: That's crazy.

Sarah: What will that give you?

Jacob: No pressure.

Sarah: Yes.

Jacob: OK, let's do it right now. Let me make the calls right away before I get too scared. No money you said? Just get out there and get over myself.

Sarah: Yes.

Jacob: Wow! I like that picture. I like it a lot. But I have to see if I can step into it. Let me go and get started making my calls.

Sarah: Great.

Source: Copyright © 2008 by Rich Snowdon. Reprinted by permission.

 ## Questions to Ask Yourself About Giving Developmental Feedback

Coach yourself with the following questions as you continue to master the skill of giving developmental feedback.

How do I set the context for giving feedback?

Can I put my personal agenda aside in order to provide feedback?

Do I offer as much appreciative feedback as developmental feedback?

How can listening, inquiring, and using observational skills help me be effective in giving feedback?

How do I prepare myself to give feedback?

How comfortable am I with being straightforward?

What can I do to overcome any fears I have about how others will receive my feedback?

How do I avoid criticizing the person and instead focus on the behavior?

How often do I notice people doing things well?

How often do I offer feedback so people can go home feeling good about their organizational contribution?

In what way am I selective about whom I give feedback to?

What is the impact of appreciative feedback?

Do I make myself available to hear other people's suggestions about how I perform?

How can I become even more open to feedback?

What do I need to hear to be receptive to my own performance improvement?

Two ways of encouraging behavior are giving developmental and appreciative feedback. Make sure your feedback takes place in the right context. Keep in mind that your feedback is for the benefit of the person being coached. Keep your feedback straightforward, genuine, specific, and personal. Feedback starts with factual observation; *then* you acknowledge behavior and say what the positive or negative consequences of the behavior are for your organization. Although we have separated out the first three foundational skills, you can probably see how they relate to one another.

Most people jump to conclusions based on what they've observed. Mastering observation without judgment sets you up to be more readily objective in both your appreciative and developmental feedback. When you stay objective, feedback can be a gift of recognition and a gift to help someone develop, by helping him know what is real *and* to think about what to do with the feedback. As Kevin Eikenberry (2006) states:

> When our intent is clear and pure; when we really are giving feedback and coaching with the very best for the other person in mind, it will be more successful. This remains true whether the feedback is to appreciate the person's contribution or behavior or if the feedback is to help the person continue to develop even better contribution or behavior [p. 1].

The key is to stay with them and stay curious in order for others to use the feedback for growth and development.

SKILL 4: SHARING

OK, we're almost there! And we could stop with feedback. However, when we teach these coaching skills in the classroom setting, nearly all managers and leaders want to know the following:

If I notice something they're doing or saying that I think is important, can I bring it up?

I think I have a hunch about something. Can I say it?

I've been through something similar. Can I share my example or a story?

I have some ideas or information that might be useful to the person I'm coaching. Can I share it?

The answer is yes, you can share in the moment. *And* there is a skill to doing it. The skill is in setting the stage to share, sometimes getting permission to share, knowing when to share, and checking the relevance for the other person.

Although coaching is mostly about asking good questions, listening deeply, and providing objective feedback, there is also a time when providing your personal thoughts and advice within a coaching conversation is not only appropriate, it can be extremely helpful. There is an absolute benefit to sharing observations and information to help others become more aware and more informed as they progress through the coaching process, especially if you know something or are aware of something that might support their development.

 Make sure you only do 10 percent of the talking and 90 percent of the listening.

One important flag before we go further: when we say *sharing*, we mean sharing to support the process. Remember back to our discussion of self-referential listening? We don't mean self-referential sharing where you talk, talk, talk, and make it all about you—in fact, make sure you do only 10 percent of the talking and 90 percent of the listening. The questions we will always come back to are, Will this add value to or support the person being coached? and, Is this the right time to share?

In this section, we discuss how to get ready to share, how much to share, and when to hold back. Specifically, we show examples for

- Sharing observations
- Sharing a hunch
- Sharing ideas, examples, and information

The Steps to Sharing

The four basic steps to sharing look like this:

1. I observe (I see or I hear) or I think or I feel something based on what I've just seen or heard, or I have an idea, example, or some information that could be useful.
2. I ask if it's OK to share, to see if this is the right time and to gain permission.
3. I share with you what I observe (what I've just seen or heard), feel, or know.
4. I check it out by asking key questions.

Sharing Observations   The ultimate goal of any coaching conversation is to help someone move to a new awareness, action, or behavior. However, sometimes it is difficult for the person you're coaching to be completely aware of his or her *current* actions or behaviors (or even language) and how those actions or behaviors might be affecting results. When we notice actions, behavior, or language and ask more deeply about them, we ask others to look below the surface.

In the context of the coaching conversation, you notice something someone has said or done and reflect it back to the person you are coaching. You are mirroring back to them what you just saw or heard. We do this because often people say or do things in the moment that they are not even aware of. Does this all sound familiar? This is the same kind of objective observation we talked about in our discussion of feedback. You might ask how it's different. It really isn't. The skill of objective observation is just as useful here, with one exception: rather than using objective observation to give someone feedback about *past* behavior, you are using objective observation to share with someone what you are noticing about their *current* behavior in that moment, while you are coaching. You notice something, reflect it back, and bring it to the attention of the person you're coaching right then.

Remember, be objective. You are not sharing your evaluation of what you see in the moment; you are objectively reflecting what you see. In the examples that follow, notice how to shift from evaluation to objective observation.

> *Evaluation*: You are not listening to me.
> *Observation without evaluation*: You are looking out the window while I'm talking to you.
>
> *Evaluation*: You seem upset.
> *Observation without evaluation*: You are tearing up.
>
> *Evaluation*: You find this situation funny.
> *Observation without evaluation*: You're laughing right now.

Now, add the skill of inquiry as you share your observation. Pose a question to help others think about what you said. Once you've done that it's up to them to decide what to do about it. Here are three examples that go into a little more depth:

1. Erik is meeting with his supervisor about a project deadline. While he's talking about next steps, he says, "I'm not sure," several times. His supervisor notices this and brings it up: "Erik, what I'm noticing right now is that you're saying you're unsure. Is that really true?"

By asking in this way, Erik's supervisor shares her observation and uses it as a springboard into a conversation about whether or not Erik really is unsure. Erik really may be unsure and in need of guidance. Or he may actually know what to do but is second-guessing himself. Or he simply may be seeking validation from his supervisor. The only way to know is to check it out.

2. Kyra is upset about a colleague and complains to her manager: "Jackie always does this! She always tries to take over things when we're working together." Her supervisor says, "You just said she always does this . . . what does 'always' mean? How often does she do this? Are there times when she hasn't?" Here, Kyra's manager questions a generalization Kyra is making by using the word *always*.

3. Felix is meeting with his manager to talk about his progress with the Chinatown food program. As he talks about his experience working with the tenants, he begins to smile. His manager notices this and shares an observation: "Felix, did you know that you've been smiling the whole time you were talking about working with the tenants? What do you make of that?" By calling this behavior to Felix's attention, his manager

opens up the conversation to other possibilities. It may be nothing (Felix may be simply recalling something funny about his experience). Or it may be that this is something he really loves to do. There could be any number of reasons that Felix is smiling. What's important is that his manager noticed and called it out.

 Don't get attached to what you're sharing. It may be something or nothing at all.

Remember, you share something only if it will benefit the person you are coaching. Keep your statements short. Stay curious with him. Allow him to reflect on what you are saying. Don't get attached to what you're sharing. It may be something or nothing at all.

Sharing a Hunch   When you share your observation based on something you see or hear, it's fairly easy to be objective. So what about sharing something you detect based on feeling? What if your gut is telling you something? Should you say it? Here we will touch on sharing a hunch because it is not uncommon for managers to observe something and have a hunch that something might be going on. For instance, you're coaching a volunteer coordinator about his promotion that will start next week, and you sense that he's not as excited as he was when it was announced last month. Your gut makes a quick assessment and says, "I think something is up here. Let me check it out." Notice that you've now moved from observation into some level of *evaluation*. It's OK to share what you think or feel. Just be mindful not to move there too quickly. And be sure to ask if it's OK to share your intuitive thought or hunch.

Because you are expressing a thinking or feeling state, which has no objective data, you are not reflecting back something you have observed. You are *reacting* to something you've observed. If you really feel something may be going on and want to share it, the trick is to check it out immediately. None of this is the truth until you check it out to see if your feeling or gut instinct is correct. If you are not correct, let it go and move on. If you sense the person feels uncomfortable talking about your hunch, allow time, now or later, to think it through and get back to you. The goal is to not be attached. Here are two examples:

1. Ginny's tone is monotone. Her face is blank. I haven't seen her laugh or smile for at least three weeks. My gut says she's unhappy and not speaking about

it. I say, "Ginny, I see that you have not been as cheerful as usual. I haven't seen you laugh or smile for the last few weeks. My gut says you may be unhappy. What is true for you? What do you think?"

2. Jose is in training to become an affordable housing social worker. He has shadowed two social workers to prepare for working with the tenants. He has practiced and been observed completing the tenant intake process. When you talk to him, he says he's nervous about stepping into the role. Yet when you ask him questions, he clearly understands the protocol. He also knows whom to talk to if he has questions. You say, "I'm just going to try this out on you. I think that you're ready. What comes up for you when I say that?"

Are these examples the truth? Not really. They are simply the evaluations you've made from your observation.

Sharing Ideas, Information, and Examples   We agree that ideas and examples can be very useful. As we said earlier, the skill in sharing ideas, information, or examples is knowing and asking if this is the right time to share, keeping it short and to the point, and checking the relevance for the other person (see the list of steps for sharing earlier in this section).

Let's say Chan is getting some coaching from you about the student focus groups that don't seem to be going very well, and she doesn't know what to do. You remember when you had a similar challenge. You want to share that experience with her, your story, because it might help. Wait just a moment though. Just because she said she doesn't know what to do, doesn't mean that it's true. It might simply be an expression of hopelessness. Help her think through her problem as far as she can go.

If she seems stuck, you might say, "Based on what you are saying, may I share a quick story about how I handled it in the past?" You start by acknowledging what you heard, and then you find out if this would be a good time to share a quick story. Notice we said quick. Keep it quick. Thirty seconds or less into your story, ask something like, "Is this relevant to your situation?" before going on. Check again thirty seconds later by asking, "Is this still making sense?" When you are done telling your story (a minute or two should do it), then ask, "How might this be useful to you?" This way, if your story is not relevant, or if the person has tried what you did, then you can stop your story and get back to asking more questions.

The process is similar for sharing ideas. First, remember that sharing an idea is different from telling someone she must use your idea. So stay open and

Acknowledging the Tough Stuff

Sometimes during a coaching conversation, you may notice or sense that a person is feeling down, being self-critical, or afraid to take the next step. You might notice or sense his fear, doubt, anxiety, or concern. It shows up in what he says or in his body language. At times like these, you can share what you've noticed and show you understand. You might say, "I know this might feel tough and we will get through it." Sharing your understanding of someone's feelings can help to neutralize an emotional situation. It can also help the person feel more at ease; this, in turn, makes talking and thinking easier.

You can also help normalize the situation by reminding the person that many others have similar reactions. This can help avoid a sense of isolation, unworthiness, or feeling abnormal. You might say, "It's normal to feel the way you do, given what's going on now. Anyone faced with this would probably feel this way, too." You might say, "It's perfectly OK to feel afraid of speaking in front of five hundred people. Most people have stage fright to start with." When you use these kinds of statements during a coaching conversation, they help calm a person's distracting emotions.

People have a profound need to be understood. At the very least, we want to know we've been heard—even if someone disagrees with us. At best, we want to know that someone grasps what we are really saying. When you acknowledge with understanding the other person's perspective of difficulties, challenges, and the effort to achieve, you make a stronger connection. This type of acknowledgment is about communicating your understanding of what someone might be experiencing. In other words, "I get you."

don't get too attached to your great idea. Also, realize that if you have positional authority over someone, she may feel pressured into using your idea. Who wants to tell the boss that his or her idea is not so great? Start by brainstorming with Chan (brainstorming is discussed in Chapter Three). If she is really out of ideas, you might ask, "Would it be helpful if I shared an idea?" If she says yes, there's your permission to share. Then say, "This is just one idea. We can also think of others." This gives her the notion that if this idea doesn't sound great, you can both keep thinking it through. Then share the idea and again, thirty seconds in, ask, "Is this sounding OK?" If yes, carry on and keep it brief. You might end by asking, "Are there any other ideas that have come up for you now?" The reason to ask this is that your idea may have generated new thoughts for Chan. It also gives her permission to grow ideas from yours or create a new idea. Remember, the more she comes up with, the more she will own it.

Some people ask whether they can offer information up during a coaching conversation. What if you are coaching, and you realize that this person needs to know what you know about a situation or they don't have the complete data? Then offer it to them. Notice, we said *offer*. You might say, "I think this piece of information might help you. May I?" If the person says yes, then you share the information. Again, check that your information is making sense and is helpful in this situation by asking questions along the way. Be careful not to tell the person exactly how to use your information. If the information is useful, that's good. If it's not useful, again, let it go.

 ## Questions to Ask Yourself About Sharing

Coach yourself with the following questions as you continue to master the skill of sharing.

How willing am I to tell a person what I saw, if it will be helpful?

Do I see the benefit of helping people see something about themselves?

How often do I take time to pay attention to what my staff is actually doing?

Am I accurately capturing behaviors and actions of staff, or am I adding my own interpretation?

Am I willing to check things out and be willing to be corrected if I'm off base?

What about observation is difficult for me? What is easy? What do I need to work on?

Can I speak the simple truth?

Am I aware of how much information or how many ideas and examples I share with people?

Do I check the relevance of my sharing stories with people's actual situations?

Can I succinctly share examples, or am I long-winded?

Can I share an idea and not be attached to having others use it?

Do I ask permission to share my thoughts while coaching others?

When you are coaching, you may want to share what you notice about the person being coached, or you may want to share stories, ideas, or information related to the person's situation. There's nothing wrong with any of this, as long as it really helps others to know, realize, or become aware of something that would be of value to them that they don't already know. The skill requires that you use your listening and inquiry skills as you share, being sensitive to the interest and receptivity of the person being coached and intermittently checking the relevance of what you are sharing.

Congratulations! Now you have the foundational tools for beginning to coach other people. You learned that everything in coaching comes from the ability to listen to others effectively. And you learned about the four modes of listening. However, just reading about these things is not enough. Practice is essential. Fortunately, you have ample opportunity to practice your awareness of which type of listening you are doing at any one time. Awareness is the first step. You can practice engaged listening with just about anyone, anytime. The main point to remember is that your attention is firmly focused on listening to the other person.

For many managers, holding off on giving advice is one of the most difficult skills to master. In the inquiry section, you learned how to ask questions by keeping them short and to the point. Your curiosity helps the other person open up his thought processes in a shared environment of trust. You learned to ask questions with empathy and to stay away (as much as possible) from the why question—a question that most likely keeps us running around in circles. Open-ended questions lead to free-ranging responses, while closed-ended questions can stop conversations, which is very frustrating.

Your ability to objectively observe, by reflecting what you see or hear, leads to the skill of giving solid appreciative and developmental feedback. And as well meaning as you might be, there is a skill to sharing your thoughts when you are coaching others. Know the right time, ask permission, and check the relevance. With these skills, you can now advance many more of your conversations and help people learn and grow in-the-moment.

Next, we move on to Chapter Three and a discussion of the coaching framework, which will show you how to get to the point of the conversation quickly, confirm the direction it is heading, identify steps to move to the desired outcome, and create commitment to a course of action.

The Coaching Framework

Great things can happen in coaching conversations. The key to good coaching is to keep the conversation on track and moving. In this chapter, we offer you a framework to keep your conversations as constructive as possible. This framework will create a path for you and the person you are coaching to follow as you identify a clear picture of what's possible, find solutions to the challenge, process anything that gets in the way, and develop a plan for getting where you want to go. By effectively structuring your conversations, you can coach people to think, learn, act, and take more initiative more often. We'll address the four main activities of this coaching framework (also see Figure 3.1):

- Clarify the focus.
- Identify the goal.
- Develop solutions.
- Create accountability.

Use this framework to focus your conversations toward results, and use it as the basis of a coaching approach conversation. This framework will change the way you start, develop, and end your conversations. Use it as a template for any

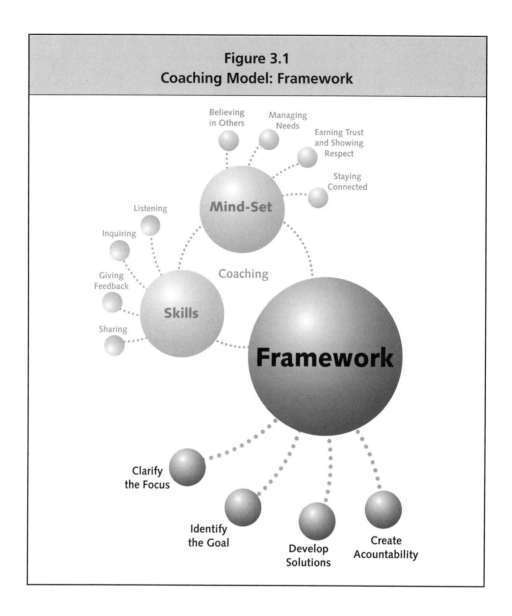

Figure 3.1
Coaching Model: Framework

Believing in Others

Managing Needs

Earning Trust and Showing Respect

Staying Connected

Listening

Inquiring

Giving Feedback

Sharing

Mind-Set

Coaching

Skills

Framework

Clarify the Focus

Identify the Goal

Develop Solutions

Create Acountability

conversation toward new learning or action. You'll notice how you demonstrate a deeper sense of caring. Conversations become more efficient and effective.

THE FRAMEWORK: SHORT VERSION

First, clarify the focus. Get to the point of the coaching conversation. What do you and the other person really need to talk about? What does the person you are coaching really need or want? This isn't always obvious. You may need to take time listening to understand a person's current reality and help him think about what he is trying to achieve.

Second, identify the goal. Know where the conversation is heading. Help the person you are coaching to name the end goal. What does a good job look like? What is the end result? Identify this first before going to solutions. Once you both have a clear picture of where the person is now (point A) and where he is heading (point B), only then is it time to problem solve.

Third, develop solutions. Identify what is needed or required to move from point A to point B. Help the person identify options for getting to the end goal or to the next milestone. Notice we didn't say that this is the point to give people advice. You may have some. Just hold on to it until it's needed or wanted. Once you both understand the gap between A and B, you can think together about the desired outcome and create a path for getting there. Here you partner with the person you are coaching to find a way forward together.

Finally, create some accountability. Call forth commitment and ownership. Review actual steps the person can and will take to progress. In this way the person being coached develops accountability, self-responsibility, and ownership. The goal is to gain agreement about what will happen next and who will do what and by when.

Here are two sample coaching scenarios in which applying the framework will be important. Then, in the next section, we cover each step of the framework in greater depth.

COMPARISON OF TWO COACHING SCENARIOS

Scenario 1

Someone drops by your office and starts talking about ten different things at once. She wants help with something she wants to work on. She brings in an agenda and she has needs, but they aren't clear. You don't have much time, and it leaves you wondering what on earth you will do with all this information and emotion. You realize it's a great opportunity to help. You want this person to leave with a solution because you don't have any more time to deal with a situation later. Yet at the same time, you realize the conversation might not go anywhere. You think: *What's the point?* Then you think: *The point is that this person needs some coaching.* Your charge is to help this person clarify the focus of the conversation, see what's possible, figure out the options, and leave with a plan of action.

Scenario 2

You call a supervisee into your office to talk about how he needs to enhance the curriculum for the preschool kids' class. Some parents have recently commented on the lack of innovation in this class. You know he needs to include more program elements to maximize the creative learning process for the children. You realize that coaching would be helpful to him. This is not personal. You are bringing something to light that must be addressed. To help this person develop in this situation will help the organization and improve the work he does with the children. You bring in an agenda. You have needs to address within the organization. Your charge is to let this person know what needs to be talked through, invite him to find new solutions together with you, and create next steps.

Although one scenario is initiated by the staff member and the other by the manager, the coaching framework still applies in both situations. The person you are coaching may simply need a partner with whom to think things through and make sense of the next steps to take. The coaching framework creates an efficient track to new ideas, new actions, and new results.

The coaching framework offers a useful and well-organized path for either coaching conversation. The goal is to partner with the person to think things through and make sense of the steps to take to greater results. (For more on coaching driven by the manager's agenda, see Chapter Five.)

1. CLARIFY THE FOCUS: GET TO THE POINT

What You Need to Know to Clarify the Focus

- Slow down and take your time to find out what the point of the conversation is.
- Don't jump to conclusions. Clarify the point of the conversation before moving on.
- You need less information than you think. Understand the situation, but don't spend too much time there.
- Be clear about whose agenda it is—yours or that of the person you are coaching.
- Seek to understand the type of issue.

 Slow down to go fast.

When a colleague comes in and tells you she has a problem, you may get the urge to problem solve immediately. Resist the temptation! Don't jump to conclusions. What might at first look like the real issue, on further investigation may turn out not to be. So, first, clarify what the real issue is or what the focus needs to be. Taking your time at the beginning to clarify the focus can save you a lot of misunderstanding (and time, energy, and money) later. Even if you use 80 percent of your time to identify the real issue, it will allow you to go faster as you and your colleague take the next steps together. Once it is clear, it frees the way to better solutions. Your aim is for an effective and efficient interaction that will encourage the other person to do her own thinking and be responsible for her own self-directed behavior. So take your time. It's time well spent. Remember, if you focus anywhere other than on the core issue, you'll miss opportunities.

Remember that coaching is about bringing out someone else's best thinking, not moving people from A to B on the manager's conveyer belt of best advice. As a manager, should you offer your advice and share your ideas as quickly as possible? Well, yes, sometimes, and no, a lot more often than you think. And you definitely shouldn't share your ideas before you fully understand what's going on (see Chapter Five for discussion of when to coach).

Coaching has a simple, conversational format that helps others come up with their own answer, while learning and growing. Interrupting with your first thought could easily end up wasting time. It may seem that you are being efficient. However, the other person may not have made the main point yet. Clarify first; only then help the other person to a solution.

Keep News Reporting Brief (Just the Facts, Ma'am)

When we watch an episodic TV show, we want to know what happened in the past to make sense of what is happening now. It's the same at work. It's usual for us to want to know the details of what led up to the current situation. However, when people you're coaching start talking about what's happening now (point A) or what happened on the way to point A, it is not necessary to know all the details of the past. Repeating them may help you as the coaching manager but not the person being coached; she already knows the details. You need far less information than you think. When someone launches into telling you the complete history of her situation, ask yourself: *How does knowing detailed background information help the person move forward?* If it doesn't, you can simply say, "I appreciate how much you have been through. What is most relevant in your current situation?" In other words, acknowledge the person for wanting to elaborate and then swiftly coach on just the point in question. Otherwise, the conversation can become directionless. Use some of these questions for clarifying the main point:

What exactly is of most concern?

What's most important about this?

What's most clear to you about this?

If you could sum up the past issues in one sentence, what would you say?

What's the greatest need in this situation?

A good solution to a well-posed problem is almost always a smarter choice than an excellent solution to a poorly posed one.

—John Hammond, Ralph Keeney, and Howard Raiffa, 1999, p. 16

Clarify First, Then Narrow It Down

Think of the process of clarifying as being like a funnel. It starts wide and gets narrower and narrower. People may present in an unfocused way. However, you'll find it easier to sort out what's important if you narrow the scope of the conversation. At the top of the funnel all the conversational content gets poured in. Your questions act as a filter to help define the reality of the issue, challenge, or need (see Figure 3.2).

What is the person talking about? Use your listening skills to hear what is really being said. What is her real concern? She may be saying one thing but mean something else. She may be talking aloud simply to process the situation because it's not yet clear what she needs. Your task is to strike a balance between hearing what is being said and knowing when to help the person get to the bottom line.

Use your inquiry skills to prompt the person to discover the main point. Keep your questions short and on track. Ask one question at a time. If the focus of the conversation starts to become blurred, sharpen it again by asking one or more of the following.

Questions to Use in Clarifying the Focus

How does what you are saying relate to this issue?

What is this conversation really about?

What do we need to pay special attention to, based on what you are saying?

What is the issue?

What's the bottom line here?

I've heard you mention three different things—which one do you need to work on?

What's most important out of everything you are saying?

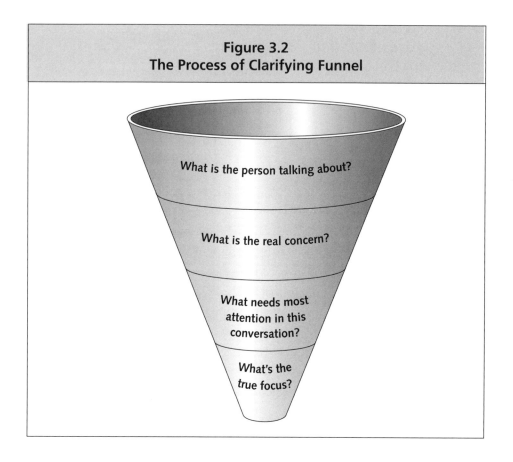

Figure 3.2
The Process of Clarifying Funnel

What is the person talking about?

What is the real concern?

What needs most attention in this conversation?

What's the true focus?

Periodically, you may need to reflect or summarize what you thought you heard. However, summarizing isn't just repeating everything you heard back to the speaker. Here's what summarizing sounds like: "So what you are talking about, Frank, is your perception of Diana's attitude to completing the grant writing project. And what you need to focus on is how to approach Diana to get the project over with. Is that right?" Be careful not to overdo this. No one likes a human parrot.

When you ask a question like, "Is that right?" you verify what you heard. If it's *not* right, stop! This is not about what you think the issue is—it's about what the other person thinks the issue is. Closed-ended questions (that you learned to be cautious about earlier) are helpful when summarizing. They let you know you are on track. Use your follow-up questions skillfully to uncover what's really going on. Help the other person focus on one piece of the conversation at a time.

In the summarizing example, the manager is not concerned with Diana. He or she is focused only on Frank, the person being coached. It is Frank's perception of Diana's attitude that is of interest, not Diana herself. You can only coach the person in front of you. And remember to coach only one person at a time.

More Questions to Use in Clarifying the Focus

What do you want to focus on?

What's going on right now?

What are you currently experiencing?

What do you want from this conversation?

What do you need to get out of this conversation?

What does this all add up to?

What's most important here?

What should we be talking about that will help this situation?

What is the bottom line?

Where must we focus to get some different results?

What does this actually mean?

What do you really mean?

What are you essentially saying?

What do you want most out of this situation?

What's the true point?

If you are unable to identify what the real issue is, ask the classic coaching question, "What is the big question in this situation?" (See the discussion of inquiring in Chapter Two for additional examples of questions.)

The goal in the first part of the framework is to clarify the focus and purpose of the conversation so your time spent on coaching is efficient and effective. Once you and the other person are both clear about the need, the focus, the bottom-line issue, you both then move on to find a path to take you there. The next step will be to make sure you have a picture of a positive outcome so you know where you are heading.

2. IDENTIFY THE GOAL: KNOW WHERE THE CONVERSATION IS HEADING

What You Need to Know to Identify the Goal

- First, help the person determine what the end goal is and then how to get there.
- Don't get distracted. A clear picture of the outcome keeps the person on track.
- Aim for ownership. When people set goals for themselves, they are more likely to make them happen.
- Current reality (point A) is important but not as important as the destination (point B).

If you don't know where you are going, any road will get you there.

—Based on Lewis Carroll, *Alice in Wonderland*

When people set specific goals for themselves, small or large, they are more likely to make those goals happen. Similarly, when you coach a person to create a vision of what the destination (point B) will look like when he gets there, he is more likely to stay on track. (See Chart 3.1 for examples.) Having a clear picture of the outcome narrows attention and helps the person establish targeted tactics. A goal doesn't have to be large, but it does have to be clear. Often people jump quickly to how they will get things done and miss confirming what they are aiming for in the first place.

Coach people to be specific about their goal, keeping the following steps in mind: (1) give people the freedom to describe a concrete future outcome; (2) let them add details; (3) coach them to spell out exactly how to get there. Only then add your own perspective of what point B looks like. Point A is the current reality. Point B is the ideal outcome. Make sure you both understand exactly what point B is before coaching toward it and don't spend too much time talking about point A. This is a great time to ask such questions as, "What does success look like?" or, "If this was to come out as you need it to, what would have happened?"

Say More Than "Do Your Best"

In an article in *American Psychologist*, Latham and Locke (2002) have summarized thirty-five years of empirical research on goal-setting theory and the relation of goals to satisfaction. They found that when most people were told to do their best, they wouldn't. "Do your best" is not specific enough. When you coach, you must help the individual you're coaching to set a goal that is easy to imagine, with clear steps to get there. Specific goals direct behavior. Vague encouragement from management doesn't work.

GET THE PICTURE; BE SPECIFIC

Knowing what you don't want is useful. It tells you what to avoid. But it isn't as actionable as knowing what you want. Imagine you are coaching Ginny, a recently promoted manager in her organization. One of her new responsibilities is planning the annual staff retreat. She is not shy about telling you her dislikes. Things are going to be different now that she is in charge. The staff retreat cannot be a repeat of last year. She doesn't like all that dull and boring lecturing by managers. There is going to be more interaction and fun this year. (Exactly how this will happen she is not telling you at the moment.) The community hall is out. She wants to hold the event in a better place. Ginny is enthusiastic but lacks a positive direction.

As you listen to all this, you can feel Ginny's passion for a successful retreat. Ginny knows what she *doesn't* want. Now you must help her see what she does want.

You: Ginny, we both want a really successful retreat.
Ginny: I agree that a successful retreat is the focus.

Now you need to help Ginny get a clear picture of the perfect outcome. Only then can she establish specific actions toward it.

> You: Ginny, what's your vision for this retreat?
>
> Ginny: A lively, interactive, valuable retreat that everyone will want to go to next year.
>
> You: What does that look like to you? [*You listen to her answer and then you say:*] So, what needs to happen to make this retreat a success?
>
> You are now well on your way to helping Ginny realize new actions that will culminate in a specific outcome. Ginny starts to realize what she does want as the final outcome.

Chart 3.1 provides examples of moving from a vague description of a person's current reality (point A) to a clearer picture of her desired outcome or destination (point B), and the following list contains further examples of preferred destinations.

CHART 3.1
Moving from Point A to Point B

Point A	Point B
My reports don't get in on time.	My reports are in on time every time.
I lose people when I talk about the educational resource program.	I keep people engaged, even when giving people the fine details of the educational resource program.
My case files are left open all over my desk.	I understand and honor confidentiality, storing documents in their right place.
I'm concerned about being a new manager.	I feel confident in my ability as a manager.
I don't think the crisis intervention process is working.	I've identified and instituted critical changes to the crisis intervention process to make it as effective as possible.
My team members are not getting on very well since the changes.	I'm leading a collaborative team that makes good things happen even during change.

Case reports are now orderly, complete, and submitted on time.

Now the retreat is a fun mix of creative process, discussion, and learning.

The resource center will serve three hundred additional people by December.

My relationship with Harriet is genuine, pleasant, and conducive to getting work done.

My staff member Jilly is taking greater initiative with her program oversight.

I'm able to clearly communicate my expectations and standards.

Understand the What and How of a Goal

When coaching, it is useful to separate the coaching conversation into the *what* of the goal, which is the outcome, and the *how* of a goal, which is the path to the goal—in other words the *to-dos*—as illustrated in Chart 3.2.

Use the inquiry process to prompt the other person to confirm the goal before getting going on the details. Listen as he unfolds his vision of what could be. Acknowledge the person for establishing a picture of what he needs to see, experience, or create before he acts. Use the following questions to help you coach the person to confirm the outcome.

CHART 3.2 The What and How of a Goal	
What the Goal Actually Is	**How to Accomplish the Goal**
To be fit and healthy by June 3 (so I have more energy at work).	Establish and follow a good eating plan. Lose two pounds a week for ten weeks.
To build a searchable Web directory of health-related philanthropic organizations, within budget, by end of December.	Research all health-related philanthropic organizations.
To raise $25,000 above expenses by end of fiscal year through one key event.	Market the 5K walk-a-thon to an extended audience outside our city.

Questions to Use in Identifying the Goal

Where are you really heading with this?

What will it look like when you get there?

What is the goal of this whole situation?

What is the desired end goal?

What does success look like?

What change do you want?

What will change bring about?

What are you hoping to achieve?

What impact can you have?

What do you think is possible?

Choice of action depends on the goal. When you coach people, help them see the outcome clearly first. Only then are you ready to coach them on how to achieve it.

3. DEVELOP SOLUTIONS: IDENTIFY WHAT'S NEEDED TO GET FROM A TO B

What You Need to Know to Develop Solutions

- Use coaching to move the person from analyzing the reasons to finding new solutions.
- Understand the path. That is the space between the current reality (point A) and the pictured outcome (point B).
- Recognize perceived obstacles in the path and help the person to generate solutions or alternatives.
- Focus on realistic choices; recognize and avoid unrealistic ones.

Figure Out How to Get There

Good news! Now we know where point B is. We have helped the person identify the desired outcome. Some managers will pat themselves on the back and head for the exit knowing they've done a good job. If you have helped the person identify point B, we congratulate you. But wait, all is not over yet.

The next step is to develop solutions. There is the all-important process of getting there, so don't leave the employee to figure it out alone. As you and the other person travel the path together toward the goal, you look at how the person can dissolve obstacles, define options, and make choices. On good days, the path will be smooth. But sometimes issues are complex. When they are, obstacles will need investigation to see whether they are real or imagined, relevant or irrelevant, and whether they can be removed or avoided. The focus here is on encouraging behavior, actions, or practices that will help the person get safely to point B.

Who knows what's lurking in this space between A and B? Your job is to be brave and find out. It's likely you'll sometimes need to coach along the path from A to B. Here are some typical challenges or items you may encounter that may need attention:

- Increased technical skills are required.
- More information or knowledge is needed.
- A strength may be used to leverage an opportunity or to manage a weaker spot.
- A change in behavior may be needed to enhance relationships or engage others more.
- Better time management may be needed so things can get done within a reasonable period.
- More leadership of people, projects, or situations may be needed.
- Relationships with those up, down, and around the person or with clients or funders may need to be improved.
- A better attitude toward a situation, person, or even the organization may be required.
- It may be necessary to manage weaknesses that affect the job.
- Overcoming a lack of confidence may be an issue.
- Better understanding of others and the ability to see others' perspectives may need attention.
- More openness to possibility or future achievement may be needed.

In just a few minutes, coaching can help a person generate one new thought or a small perspective change; it even can help a person identify the best new solution or one not thought of before. The more time you can take, the better, because you can concentrate on generating more options, and you both can look at alternatives more thoroughly. Focus on what behaviors, actions, or practices the person you are coaching is planning to use. You don't want to hear just about the current situation. Be sure you are guiding the conversation toward point B.

Problem with Focusing on Problems

When the person you are coaching spends too much time focusing on difficulties, as coaches we call it *jumping in the hole*. It sounds like this: "I don't know why this happened. I'm so frustrated. I'm not good at this. It's not my responsibility. It isn't working."

Don't jump in the hole with the person (there isn't room for you both). If you jump in the hole, your questions will focus only on the problems. Those questions will probably sound like this. "Why do you think this happened?" "Why is it a problem?" "Why isn't it working?" Notice that they are all why questions. And notice whether this is helping to forward the conversation to new outcomes (most likely not) or just digging the conversation into a deeper hole.

As a coaching manager, you have the job of leading people toward possibility. There may be holes on the path that need to be stepped over. Keep moving the conversation toward answers and solutions. You may stop momentarily to process feelings, yet the key is to move closer to a better outcome or resolution. When you do this, your questions become: "What do you want to achieve?" "What do you want to do differently?" "What would it look like if you *were* good at this?" "Who can best achieve this?" Ask questions about the thinking itself rather than the issues.

Brainstorm to Illuminate Choices

Coaching staff has taken some of the weight off of me. The pressure for me to know a single "correct" solution is no longer there. Being able to brainstorm about options is far more enjoyable and productive (especially in the long run).

—Patricia Osage, director of resident services,
Satellite Housing

Sometimes people feel they are out of choices. This is rarely the case. Your role as their thought partner is to help them regain their sense of choice. Brainstorming is an effective way to stimulate ideas and generate options. This technique is helpful when the situation calls for new ways to approach a challenge, to break out of established patterns of thinking, or to improve on what has already been created. When brainstorming, we want to bring forward many ideas and then help the person being coached to choose the best option. You may offer suggestions, but make sure your main intention is to encourage the person's best thinking. Ask a few of the following questions.

Where are you coming from as you look at this situation?

How else might you look at this situation?

What would you choose to do about this if anything was possible?

What are the options? What else?

Which option seems to be more relevant?

How are you making this decision?

What other factors come into play as you choose to act like you do?

What other way is there?

What if there was another way, would you take it?

What if you came from outside the box? Where would that be from?

Which option seems to be less obvious but might actually work out?

Brainstorming Dos and Don'ts

Brainstorming Dos
- Define the problem, need, or goal. Use the first two steps in the framework, clarifying the focus and confirming the outcome, to help the person become clear about the outcome.

- Welcome all ideas. Create space for "anything goes"—at least for right now. Have fun. Don't worry if what the person is saying sounds wild or unrealistic. Now is not the time for criticism.

- Add a couple of your own ideas.

- Try to stimulate even more choices. Suggest one or two wild options that the person might say no to, then come up with better ideas. Lay out all the generated ideas. Look at all the options before coaching too much on any one of them.

- Hold off on analysis. And that goes for both of you. Let go of judgment and evaluation until all options have been revealed.

- Keep building on ideas. Expand on one option to generate even more options. Help people think broadly and big.

- Set the criterion for selecting the most useful option. Ask, "What will choosing this option serve most?" Help the person define the reason for the choice.

Brainstorming Don'ts

- Don't accept the first idea and make that the focus of your coaching.

- Don't give people your two best options and ask them to pick one.

- Don't see things from your perspective only.

- Don't look at what can't work or state things in the negative.

What to Do When Things Come Up

Delicate matters come up while coaching. As we said earlier, coaching is not therapy. It's not counseling. Show empathy (as discussed in Chapter Four), but be careful not to jump in the hole with the person you are coaching. Be objective. Something personal could be affecting his work. It's possible that his feelings are hurt, preventing him from achieving his goals. Fear makes it hard to believe things are possible. Be willing to process issues that will help him close in on the goal. You may simply need to listen a little longer. Avoid making assumptions or adding any meaning of your own to what the other person is saying.

Listen to where the conversation needs to go. What is the person telling you that guides you to your next thought or question? Use your inquiry process for follow-up questions. Try to bring the person's process to a conclusion in an appropriate amount of time. However, be sure to aim for at least a small next step along the path from A to B.

Questions to Use in Developing Solutions

Where must you start with this situation?

How do you see the path to where you want to go?

Where are you in relation to what you want to achieve?

What needs to shift for something different to happen?

What have you not yet tried that might help?

What options can we look at?

Which option seems best right now?

What are the possibilities as you see them?

What other perspectives could there be?

What are other ways to get there?

What attitudes and beliefs do you need to adopt or let go of?

What skills and abilities must you acquire?

What are the obstacles in the path?

How will you move beyond the obstacles?

How would it look if you tried that?

What must we talk about that we haven't talked about so far?

How can you break that into manageable chunks?

What support do you need from your manager, coworkers, family, and friends?

A coaching conversation is effective once the goal, big or small, of the conversation is clear, when the picture of success is in view, and new and different ways to achieve the goal have been identified. The next key element in a solid coaching conversation is to make sure both parties leave with clear agreements and accountability.

4. CREATE ACCOUNTABILITY: CALL FORTH COMMITMENT AND OWNERSHIP

What You Need to Know to Create Accountability

- Leave the conversation with an agreement, so both people are clear about what is going to happen.
- Establish a goal: by the end of the conversation the other person should have a better path or idea, with reasonable actions to take.
- Make requests, when necessary, that will challenge the person to new levels of achievement.

You both know what the goal is, and the person you are coaching is now clear about which solutions to use to get there. Now it's time to create accountability. The ultimate goal of coaching is to help someone move to a new action or behavior. However, this won't happen if the person doesn't take personal responsibility to do the task or make the change. You both deserve to leave the conversation with a clear agreement about what actions or steps the person will take next.

Accountability is determined by three questions:

What are you going to do?

When will you do this?

How will we know it's done? (What's the evidence?)

Once you make sure that goals and projected outcomes are clear, the next step is to identify a structure that will help the person measure progress. We call this process *contracting for action*. But let's not overdo it. It's unlikely you'll want to hold a person accountable for every single phone call made or e-mail sent. When contracting for action, ask what it will take to commit to getting the task done. This might mean including an item on her next status report or reporting on an action in her next one-on-one meeting. She may even want to loop back to you to think things through again. Some people will need more accountability than others, based on their level of competency with the task. Agree on what support she needs to succeed, and contract for action accordingly.

Make Requests

If at the end of the conversation the person you are coaching has not identified a next step or there is more to come, you may find it necessary to make requests that will challenge her to new levels of achievement. It's completely acceptable to call for an action or a behavior shift or to request that she stretch herself. If you are supporting her leadership development, you may want to challenge her to take more responsibility or exercise greater initiative. This may involve assigning or delegating tasks that will foster her own professional development and help her meet the needs of the mission. Here's our checklist for making effective requests (adapted from Marshall and Friedman's *Smart Work: The Syntax Guide to Mutual Understanding in the Workplace*, 1995):

- Be clear about who is asking (that's you, the coaching manager).
- Be clear about who is being asked (that's the person you are coaching).
- Be clear about what is being asked.
- Clearly define the end result.
- Set firm timelines (as in, When will this be done?).
- Provide the context for the request or item to be delegated (why you are making the request).
- Be sure to provide sufficient resources and appropriate authority (if needed).
- Talk about any anticipated problems. (Only some surprises are pleasant!)
- If necessary, put ongoing monitoring and evaluation in place.
- Check for understanding.

Yes, No, or Negotiate

When you make a request, the other person can accept, reject, or modify your request. The other person has a choice. She can negotiate. Ultimately, you are thinking things through together. You are simply challenging that person to take responsibility for her commitment, to change a behavior that will move her forward in the task or to perhaps give something else a try. You are negotiating for new or different action. You are negotiating for her ownership. Ask what support she needs. Agree on the support you will offer, if any. Ask what success might look like on her next status report. Again, remember to keep listening and inquiring. You can also ask for feedback about the coaching conversation.

We create accountability by getting commitment to an agreed-upon course of action. It could be as simple as agreeing to show up at a meeting or as complicated as completing a task vital to the existence of the organization. The secret to getting commitment is in asking the right questions and encouraging the person to review what she has committed to before leaving the conversation. Let her summarize the conversation. Let go of summarizing it yourself. Then you'll see the difference in what can happen next.

Note that if you are directing, showing, or telling someone what to do, there is likely no need for a request. If you are delegating a task, you probably expect the person to own that task once you've assigned it without negotiation. Make sure to communicate your expectations clearly and let him know if he *can* negotiate. The person may be OK with owning most of it but may not want to take all of it. Here's a place for negotiation. Later in the book, we'll also discuss what to do if people don't respond or take responsibility. In such cases, repercussions for noncompliance may become necessary (see Chapter Six). There are many opportunities to make genuine coaching requests aimed at the other person's well-being. Remember to be clear if negotiation is an option and be sure to use your listening and inquiry skills along the way.

 Questions to Use in Creating Accountability

What are you going to do?

When will you do it?

How will we know this has been achieved?

How will this benefit you?

How will this benefit your coworkers?

What's in it for the organization when you complete this course of action on time?

How motivated are you to achieve this?

How will you feel when this is done?

What does it mean to be responsible for this project?

How confident are you that you can follow through on your commitment?

What will you lose or gain by doing what you say you will do?

What made you feel you could take on this responsibility?

Being accountable for specific actions helps employees take ownership of their work. It encourages self-management and gives them a perspective on the contribution they make to the larger nonprofit mission.

Creating an environment of individual responsibility not only will lessen your stress, but it's likely to boost morale because individuals now have a chance to develop their own skills. You'll find it easier to maintain your boundaries and avoid falling into the trap of taking on work that should have been done by someone else. Accountability is essential for employee and organizational effectiveness. It keeps everyone moving to achieve the mission.

PUT IT ALL TOGETHER

Now that you've learned the foundational skills and the framework for coaching, let's take a look at how you put them into action in a coaching scenario. This next example shows you how.

SEE THE FRAMEWORK AND SKILLS TOGETHER

Tam has worked with Leaf City Food Bank for two years. She's in charge of several programs, including the work of volunteers. Recently, she's been feeling bad about a lack of volunteers. She wants to talk to her boss, Jin, about the situation.

> [*Tam enters Jin's office.*]

Tam: Jin, do you have a minute?

Jin: Yes. [*Jin has a moment of panic as he says yes. He has a lot of work on his desk. If he invites her in, he knows it will be more than just a minute. Then it will be an agreement to listen, an actual contract. He hopes Tam won't stay long. He says:*]

Ah, just a moment. I need to send this e-mail. [*Jin sends the e-mail. Then he imagines the lunch meeting he has to get to in thirty minutes. And then there are the donor letters he is expecting from Hanna. He hasn't even seen those yet. He says:*]

I've got about five minutes. [*Jin is clear with Tam about his time boundaries. He takes a second to self-manage, clears his mind,* and commits himself to listening to Tam instead of planning his busy day ahead. Then he says:]

What's on your mind, Tam?

Tam: Jin, I'm going to be honest with you, this issue with the lack of volunteers for the food drive is making it hard. I'm not sure I know what to do.

[Jin assumes he knows what the volunteer problem is and is about to tell Tam what he did the last time he had to deal with a similar situation. He decides, though, not to share his advice just yet. He knows Tam is very responsible and capable. He continues to listen.]

Tam: I feel like we've tapped out everyone we've got on our list. I know there are more people out there, but I'm not sure why they aren't signing up.

Jin: Go on. [He leans into the conversation to show Tam he's really hearing what she's saying.]

Tam: I guess I'm just fed up. I'm not sure who else to call. And what's happened to everyone's excitement? It's like we dropped off their radar. I have eighty-five names and only seventeen want to help. School is out, so what's the problem? It's like they forgot who we are. I feel like no one is interested anymore. What am I going to do?

[Jin is now engaged in listening. He listens for the heart of the matter. He hears Tam's complaints and sees how drained she is about keeping people engaged between projects. He acknowledges her feelings.]

Jin: The situation does sound frustrating. What's the biggest issue you face? [Jin starts to use inquiry skills helping Tam think through her situation and to clarify the most important challenge.]

Tam: I don't think I've overused our volunteers. Some of them are newly committed. It's just now that we've actually got an event, they're disappearing or not showing up.

Jin: What do you think is causing them not to show up?

Tam: Loss of interest. They're busy. I really don't know.

[Jin lets the comment "I really don't know" pass. He believes in Tam and how much she does know.]

Jin: What's most important for you and me to talk about right now?

Tam: How to keep them with us. [*Tam becomes clear on what she really needs to think about.*]

Jin: What's your real goal with our volunteers? [*Jin knows that before they go any further, it would help Tam to have a clear picture of her goal to support her needed outcome.*]

Tam: Hmm. Good question. I guess I'd like to see the volunteers active on an ongoing basis. They would be highly engaged, asking what they could do each quarter. A solid corps of volunteers would continue to enroll more people every year. We'd have a year-long calendar so they would know what they were going to be doing.

Jin: Are you saying you want engaged volunteers who are truly committed to our organization?

Tam: Yes. We go on these campaigns to get people to join us, and then when it's time for them to do the work, many of them are gone.

Jin: What do you think keeps them with us? [*Jin knows he must help Tam work toward what she can change in order to engage the volunteers.*]

Tam: They like what we're up to. We give them something good to do in the community. Who knows? I feel so disappointed.

Jin: I hear your disappointment. May I offer a thought? [*Jin acknowledges her disappointment and requests that they work together on a plan to change the situation. He doesn't want Tam to stay in the negative. Jin can see she wants direction.*]

Tam: Yes.

Jin: Could it be that the volunteers need us to offer them something more than just a great cause?

Tam: I guess I'm trying to figure out what it takes to retain the volunteers we do enroll.

[*Jin realizes that Tam has found an even more important focus that will get her closer to her goal.*]

Jin: That's very smart to be thinking about keeping volunteers. You were a great help to the human resource team when you created the employee retention program. Your program really reengaged our staff. What could you take from the program that might work with our volunteers? [*Jin acknowledges Tam's strengths to help her learn from them and move closer to the goal.*]

Tam: Thanks. That's a really good question. I'm not sure we've ever looked at it quite like this. Retention as a key part of our volunteer program would make so much sense. [*Tam feels better and starts thinking about the bigger possibility. She says:*]

I know it's all about engaging them over time. We could survey our volunteers and ask what they need for the long run. We did that with the staff.

Jin: What else? [*Jin helps Tam look at all the options before building tactics around any one.*]

Tam: I'd like to know their motives by screening them up front, and I want to recognize their contributions.

Jin: That makes a lot of sense. What else?

Tam: Listen, I'm going to call the people we've had on our list for a while and ask them to help us with this information. Also while I'm on the phone, instead of saying what we need done on the drive, I'm going to ask what skills they'd like to use. I'm going to see what motivates them about this drive before I make any requests. I'm going to do that right now.

Jin: Excellent. Before we work out an action plan, what else can be translated from our employee retention program into the volunteer program? [*Jin realizes that Tam has lots of great ideas. He also knows her ability to balance priorities may be an issue. He notes this as something to bring up later.*]

Tam: We might want to think about some ongoing training that keeps them involved and shows how we can use these people to provide trainings in the future. What's your thought on training?

Jin: If training is focused and valuable, it's worthwhile. How can we find out what training they need and want most? [*Jin shares his opinion and follows it up with coaching.*]

Tam: I can ask when we survey them.

Jin: Good first step. I need to go in a minute. First, though, how are you feeling now?

Tam: Something shifted. I feel like I'm less in a panic. I realize I haven't done a very good job of identifying what people wanted to give when they volunteered four months ago. Keeping them involved between events is really important.

Jin: You're now looking clearly at where we can improve. What's one thing you can start doing before we meet again on this? [*Jin creates accountability for Tam to help her prioritize before their next meeting.*]

Tam: First, I'm going to create a few good questions to ask the volunteers about what they want, their strengths, and so on. Then I'm going to make twenty calls today and take a really different approach with them.

Jin: Great. What support do you need?

Tam: I'm going to share our conversation with Helen and get her to take the same approach.

[*Three days later Jin and Tam meet again. Jin has been thinking about Tam's situation. He wants to offer some feedback that might help her develop the program further.*]

Tam: Jin, thanks for making time for me again.

Jin: I'm glad we can meet. How are things going with the volunteer program?

Tam: I've laid out four more strategies that will help retain the volunteers. I'm calling it the Volunteer Management System. I called two agencies that have great programs and asked them about what they do. [*Tam briefly tells Jin about the ideas.*]

Jin: Very good process. All six components will add up to a really solid program, Tam. I know you want to ensure that your Volunteer Management System remains high quality and that everyone is benefiting a great deal from their work with the organization. Can we talk together about how you're balancing your priorities with this program and the events in general?

[Jin sets the context to give feedback and use agenda-driven coaching to help Tam develop her skills.]

Tam: Hmmm. Sure. Is something wrong?

Jin: It's not about being wrong at all. *[Jin creates a place free from criticism for Tam to step into. He continues:]*

You show such passion in all your work. People want you to succeed, and they all need your attention. This seems to be an opportunity for you to set even better priorities around events so you have a balanced amount of time for the volunteers. *[Jin is specific about what he'd like her to think about. Then he says:]*

What are your thoughts on this?

Tam: It does get hectic this time of year. Are people upset with me?

Jin: This is not about upsetting people. *[Jin helps Tam stay out of negative thinking.]*

This is about making sure you can maximize your days so everyone gets served, including you. *[Jin directs her attention to point B, the ideal picture.]*

How do you go about prioritizing all the work?

Tam: I'm going to be honest. I've recently just been doing the next thing on my desk. I'm realizing now that this may be part of the issue—not spending enough time on the volunteer program. I just get so overwhelmed with it all.

Jin: Well, let's work this out and find a better way for you. What do you need most?

Tam: I just need things to get done. I don't really follow any type of plan.

Jin: Let's get more strategic with planning your work, including this wonderful Volunteer Management Program you're developing. How can we break this down into manageable parts for further conversation?

Tam: Let's lay out all my goals first. I'm good at keeping hold of a million tasks. This would help me see how to manage them better. Also, let's assess who's going to be involved with each project. This is really helpful.

Tam and Jin continue to talk. Jin gives her feedback and stays committed to coaching. He encourages her to really think about how to change, improve, and find new ways to approach the issues they have uncovered. He doesn't make it personal and keeps the focus on the mission at hand.

The framework provides a clear path to results, with the participant being an active part of the process. I use it often in both my professional and personal life. The more I use it, the more automatic it becomes.

—Workshop participant

The framework presented in this chapter shows you the four essential parts of the coaching process. First, your effort is to clarify what is most important in this conversation. Next, you help the person you are coaching identify the end result. You help her identify her current reality (point A), but you won't want to spend much time there. The destination (point B) is more important. Once you have both confirmed what point B looks like, you are ready to move on to the third stage—closing in on the goal. Here the two of you partner in finding the path to get to the destination. Brainstorming for positive options clears away obstacles and identifies opportunities along the way. Once the goal is clear and you have created a path to get there, it is the time to create accountability, so you'll know how to measure success. And speaking of success, congratulations, you know what the coaching framework is and how to use it. Let's not hang around. Forward!

The Coaching Mind-Set

What will it take to integrate coaching into your daily work? Although your efficacy in providing coaching will depend on mastery of the coaching skills, which we addressed in Chapter Two, the foundation for effectiveness rests on your coaching mind-set—how you think about coaching as a tool for supporting others and how you think about yourself and others while coaching. This shift in mind-set is critical, for it undergirds every decision you make in your interactions with the people you manage and work with. Without making this conscious shift, you may find that in the rush of things to do it is simply easier to tell people what to do and miss the opportunity for learning and development.

So what is the coaching mind-set? It is an attitude and outlook you bring to the coaching conversation. It comes from the inside out and goes beyond just the use of skill and paying attention to how you come across when you coach. How you think about yourself and others will have an impact on what you do as a coaching manager. Are you aware of your impact on others? Can you coach from a place of possibility? Can you let go of anything that might get in the way of drawing forth the best in the other person? Can you put aside assumptions and personal agendas? These are all important elements in creating the

121

right coaching space for others' discovery and development during a coaching conversation.

In a single chapter, it is impossible to explore in depth all the elements of mind-set that someone can bring to the coaching conversation, but we have zeroed in on four areas that we find useful to focus on when making the shift to becoming a coaching manager (also see Figure 4.1):

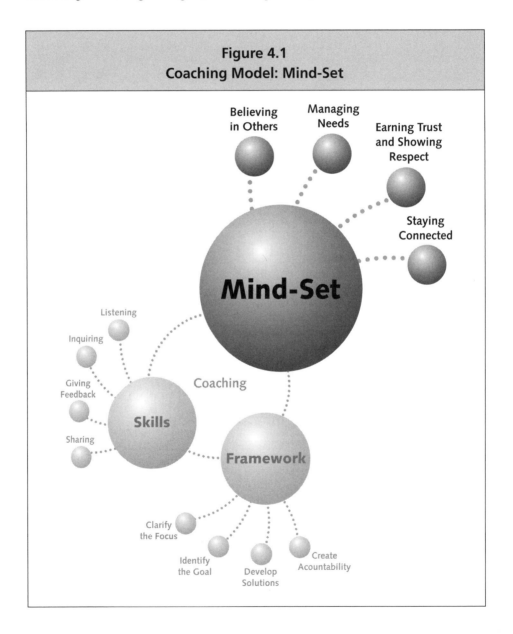

Figure 4.1
Coaching Model: Mind-Set

- Believing in others

- Managing needs

- Earning trust and showing respect

- Staying connected

BELIEVING IN OTHERS

Questions to Ask Yourself Before You Coach

- Do I really believe this person has what it takes?

- Can I suspend any negative beliefs I have about this person?

- Do I stick to the facts as I coach this person?

- Am I able to clear my mind of any history this person and I have had?

Understanding what we believe—knowing the assumptions and expectations that we bring to our interactions with others—is essential to engaging in productive coaching. The International Coach Federation (2008) sets out as its basic premise that everyone is "naturally creative and resourceful" and that our job when coaching isn't to fix people but to support them to "enhance the skills, resources, and creativity they already have."

But what if you think someone is *not* creative and resourceful? This is where your beliefs come in. You may be a frustrated manager dealing with someone who's not performing well. (For information on dealing with non-performers, see Chapter Five.) However, it is important not to let our beliefs about those we coach interfere with our effectiveness. For these beliefs, whether well thought through or spontaneous in response, can lead to a conclusion. These conclusions can then become the expectation. And all too often, such expectations can become self-fulfilling reality. If we want to help people grow and develop, we need learn how to identify our beliefs and put them aside.

How Beliefs Become Reality

In the Oak School experiment, which figures prominently in *Pygmalion in the Classroom: Teacher Expectation and Pupils' Intellectual Development* (1968/1992), Robert Rosenthal and Lenore Jacobson showed that if teachers were led to expect enhanced performance from some children, then the children did indeed show that enhancement. This became known as the *Pygmalion effect*. In this experiment, Rosenthal predicted that when given the information that certain students are brighter than others, elementary school teachers may unconsciously behave in ways that facilitate and encourage the students' success. Later experiments were conducted with graduate students and showed the same effect.

The purpose of the experiment was to support the hypothesis that reality can be influenced by the expectations of others. This influence can be beneficial as well as detrimental, depending on which label an individual is assigned. The observer-expectancy effect, which involves an experimenter's unconsciously biased expectations, is tested in real-life situations. Rosenthal posited that biased expectancies can essentially affect reality and create self-fulfilling prophecies as a result.

Understanding What We Believe

Chris Argyris, who has spent his career researching what it takes to manage effectively, says we all live in a world of self-generating beliefs that remain largely untested. We adopt beliefs from conclusions inferred from observations added to past experience. Argyris (1992) calls this the *ladder of inference* (pp. 88–89) (see Figure 4.2). As we mount this ladder of inference, our ability to achieve the results we desire can be eroded by feelings that go something like this: "Our beliefs are the truth, the truth is obvious, and our beliefs are based on real facts." The data we select are the real data (not just data that we felt like selecting or that were convenient). In other words, the belief I have about you or the assumptions I make about you form my attitude toward you. My attitude will

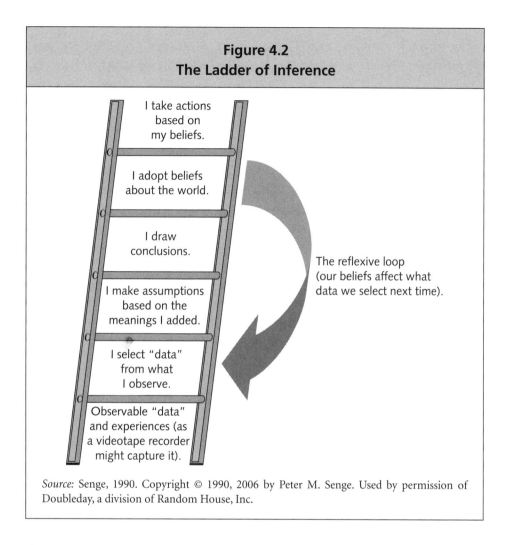

Figure 4.2
The Ladder of Inference

I take actions based on my beliefs.

I adopt beliefs about the world.

I draw conclusions.

I make assumptions based on the meanings I added.

I select "data" from what I observe.

Observable "data" and experiences (as a videotape recorder might capture it).

The reflexive loop (our beliefs affect what data we select next time).

Source: Senge, 1990. Copyright © 1990, 2006 by Peter M. Senge. Used by permission of Doubleday, a division of Random House, Inc.

determine the choice of language I use with you and influence actions I take that will affect how I coach you.

Figure 4.3 shows how the ladder of inference might play out in a situation with a staff person (whom we call Karyn) if the coaching manager is not clear on his or her own attitude. You need to stay *completely objective* (see the discussion in Chapter Two of objective observation) so that you coach from a place that is not removed from the real data. If you move away from the real data that you are hearing or seeing, you will coach based on your *interpretation* of the situation, and your coaching will become less effective. If you go up the ladder of inference, you may limit your beliefs about what is possible for Karyn. By not going

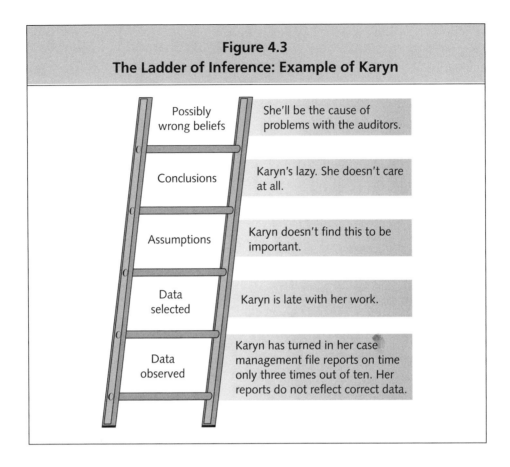

Figure 4.3
The Ladder of Inference: Example of Karyn

Possibly wrong beliefs — She'll be the cause of problems with the auditors.

Conclusions — Karyn's lazy. She doesn't care at all.

Assumptions — Karyn doesn't find this to be important.

Data selected — Karyn is late with her work.

Data observed — Karyn has turned in her case management file reports on time only three times out of ten. Her reports do not reflect correct data.

up the ladder of inference, you stay neutral when you coach, and Karyn gets to identify what is causing her not to get her files in on time.

Identifying Limiting Beliefs

The term *limiting belief* is used in the field of human behavior and psychology to describe a belief that inhibits exploration. As the name suggests, these beliefs set boundaries around our thinking and prevent us from seeing possibilities. Often limiting beliefs are influenced by society, family, or culture. We bring these beliefs—beliefs about ourselves and others—to everything we do. It is important to keep in mind that those we coach have plenty of their own limiting beliefs about themselves without our adding any more. Limiting beliefs that people may have about themselves or others include the following:

There's never going to be enough . . .

It will take too much . . .

I cannot/they cannot

This is too big for someone like me/them

I'm not sure I am ready/they are ready

I will fall apart/they will fall apart if I have to/if they have to stand up in front of people

It's important to help others break out of their limiting beliefs by helping them see what is possible and what they *can* do. It is all too easy for people to focus solely on what they *cannot* do. This is natural because when we do try and then find ourselves bumping up against obstacles, what we experience is the limit, not the possibility. But this is a place where the people we coach can get stuck, and it is your job as a coach to draw on your own experience to help them see another way of looking at themselves and their efforts. This means that if you have a limiting belief about the person you are coaching, it will be very difficult to help that person. Consider these questions:

What limiting beliefs do you have about providing coaching?

What limiting beliefs do you have about others?

What limiting beliefs may those you coach already have about themselves?

What is the real story, and what story have you made up or imposed on the situation?

We have found it helpful for managers who are engaging in coaching to do the following: Write the question "Are you sure?" on a piece of paper and place it somewhere you can see it. This is a suggestion made by Thich Nhat Hanh to remind ourselves that we may not always be right about something and to keep an open mind. And while you are writing down things to keep in mind, we also suggest that you write the following:

What am I grateful for about this person, project, or situation?

What do I know to be true and good about this person, project, or situation?

The people you are coaching, like everyone, are full of possibility. Your goal is to stay connected to that possibility. If they are truly not capable and you've tried everything you can (*and* you have data to back up your assessment), then go ahead, believe differently. (See the discussion in Chapter Five about what to do when coaching is not working.) But while you are actively engaged in the coaching process, you need to know that what you believe in is what you are most likely to get.

Changing Your Attitude: Beliefs in Action

Although it's important to examine and understand our beliefs and how they drive our responses to those we are coaching, it isn't easy to change them. If our belief in someone doesn't serve him or her we may need to shift our perspective. And we *can* decide to change how we respond. We *can* change our attitudes. Even though the attitudes we express do spring from our beliefs, they are also shaped as positive or negative attitudes in response to the story we tell ourselves about someone or something. You can change that story at any time if you are willing to look at new information. If you find yourself thinking things like the following, then it is likely that you are letting your assumptions and beliefs take over and create a negative story:

How can he not know that?

I can't believe she said that.

What are they thinking?

Why do those people act that way?

Who does she think she is, anyhow?

Let's look at how attitude might play out in a coaching conversation.

MYESHA'S STORY: LEARNING TO MANAGE ONE'S ATTITUDE

Myesha and Julie work at a center to advance the work on reproductive rights. Myesha is Julie's manager. Julie is in Myesha's office describing a problem she is facing. Julie recently announced to parents big changes in the application and criteria for scholarships. Her messaging offended some people. She must find a way to address the backlash from a religious group in response to the changes and how she delivered the message.

Myesha, as she listens, is not happy about the situation. It is clear to her that Julie exercised poor judgment in developing her outreach strategy.

Myesha firmly believes that employees need to keep all community members and potential customers in mind when they make decisions. She feels very strongly that employees can't let their personal beliefs interfere with recognizing the needs and concerns of everyone. She suspects that Julie's own assumptions about the religious group led her to write them off and not fully consider their concerns. This makes her even less sympathetic to Julie. On top of this, Myesha feels that she has enough on her own plate, and she is disappointed that Julie doesn't seem to be able to handle this situation on her own.

Here are two possible ways that Myesha can respond to Julie.

Response 1: Myesha Doesn't Manage Her Attitude

As Julie tells Myesha about the backlash from the religious group, Myesha's first thoughts are that the project was too big and that Julie, typical of many urban women of her age, may feel it's OK not to pay attention to certain religious groups. Myesha can feel her anger rise as she tells herself this story about Julie. Myesha can't help wondering whether Julie has what it takes to clean the problem up. Myesha thinks about the loss and damage to the center's reputation and how that will affect future donations. She continues to ask Julie why this happened. She doesn't trust that it was a simple mistake and instead lets on to Julie that she suspects Julie's attitude about the religious group got in the way. There are even moments when she shows her displeasure by rolling her eyes. This is certainly not encouraging to Julie. Myesha is waiting for some sign that Julie can handle this, but Julie's confidence is shaken by Myesha's obvious displeasure. Julie herself begins to feel she isn't up to the task and begins to get flustered by Myesha's questions. They end the meeting with Myesha saying she'll roll up her own sleeves to deal with this one. Myesha leaves the conversation owning the problem.

Response 2: Myesha Manages Her Attitude

As Julie tells Myesha about the backlash from the religious group, Myesha's first thoughts are that the project was too big and that Julie, typical of many urban women of her age, may feel it's OK not to pay attention to certain religious groups. Myesha can feel her anger rise as she tells herself this story about Julie. *But then she does something important.* She stops the voice in her head that's spinning this story. She forces herself to look clearly at Julie and to remember where she has been successful in the past. She reminds herself that she has no idea what Julie's attitude is toward this religious group. And most important, she remembers how important it is that she use this moment to let Julie learn.

Even though she is very busy and very worried about potential loss if this isn't handled correctly, Myesha decides to begin her discussion with Julie with the expectation that Julie can deal with the backlash from this religious group, even though damage control will be required. Instead of focusing on what Julie did wrong, Myesha starts coaching Julie about next steps. She makes it clear that Julie will need to handle this and that as her manager, she will be as helpful as she can but it's Julie's responsibility. Myesha's words are constructive, optimistic, and encouraging. As Julie listens, she begins to see clearly what she can do and her confidence grows. Julie begins to express some of her own ideas about how to proceed. Myesha finds that she is pleasantly surprised. She shares her thoughts and allows Julie to choose what to do next. The result of Myesha's coaching allows Julie to find a plan that she will own and execute.

Because Myesha is willing to challenge the story that is unfolding in her head she is able to influence her attitude toward Julie and Julie's mistake. She is able to examine her beliefs and assumptions and, if not change them, at least put them aside and not let them influence how she responds to Julie. It is important to remember that your attitude is your choice.

MANAGING NEEDS

As a manager, you have an agenda that grows out of the needs of the organization as well as your personal needs. What these needs are, of course, depends on how you feel about your work and what you want to get out of it. You are used to thinking of your organization's needs. You may also be used to considering your own needs. What may be a shift for you as you develop a coaching mind-set is learning how to balance these needs with those of the people you are coaching. At any one moment when you may be feeling the pressure of attending to someone else's needs, it may feel as if you are serving too many masters, as if you are being pulled in too many directions. It is useful, then, to stand back and appreciate how the needs of the organization, you, and the people you are coaching can be aligned. As with any group, you are interdependent. When the people who report to you are thriving and can operate independently, everyone benefits.

I think it is a very compassionate and respectful way of managing. I have become more patient with people and am able to better attend to individual needs as well as my own needs.

—Josephine Pritchard, program director,
Coastside Children's Programs

Although it is useful to keep this network of needs in mind, a coaching mind-set requires that you be able to understand when to let others' needs drive your interactions, when to let your needs as a supervisor take over, and how to do this while taking your own and others' personal and emotional needs into account. It sounds like a tall order. But what's important is awareness, not perfection.

Aligning Needs of Others with the Organization

Although as a supervisor you are always a supervisor, you need to learn how to, at times, take a break from the role, tuck your supervisor's hat in your back pocket, and let the people you supervise take the lead. In these conversations their needs come first. Even though you may feel that it is your job to direct and advise, they may not need that kind of interaction. They often don't need to be told what to do—no matter how helpful your direct advice; instead, what they really need is a partner with whom they can brainstorm and think through how to address problems and find solutions. When you are involved in a coaching conversation, your first job is to be the ally of the person you are coaching.

When you wear the coaching manager's hat, tuck your supervisor hat in your back pocket for a moment.

Not only do you need to stay focused on the needs of the other person, you also need to be flexible enough to let the other person drive the agenda. The people you are coaching may need to take the lead, and you will then let yourself follow. Staff may bring to you a desire to take more of a lead, or an issue they are having with someone or with a task, or an opportunity or idea they have identified that needs more thought. Those you manage have desires, ideas, thoughts, issues, and challenges they want to discuss as they go about their work. This is the other person's agenda, and, for the moment at least, you let it be yours.

There will also be times when you will set the focus of the coaching conversation. In service to the organizational mission and the goals, strategies, and actions that need to be taken, you may call a staff person to your office to bring organizational needs into focus. Perhaps there is an opportunity for that person to lead or a program needs attention or there is a task issue or there is a need to do things a little faster. (See the section "Coaching When the Manager Sets the Focus" in Chapter Five.)

Both agendas are prevalent and important. The goal is to address the needs of the person you're coaching while continuing to serve the larger organizational mission. We call this "standing in the mission" while coaching others (see Figure 4.4). We're all here to do the work. The question is, how can you support someone else's needs so they can do their work smarter, better, or faster? Or with greater satisfaction? By paying attention to the needs of others in this way, you are taking on the role of servant leader. As the authors of *The Art and Practice of Leadership Coaching* write, "The leader or coach shifts from directing to serving people by guiding, supporting, and cheerleading them as their needs require. The coaches now become servant leaders" (Morgan, Harkins, and Goldsmith, 2004, p. 128). By allowing yourself to make this shift to serve the needs of those you supervise and by allowing their agenda to take front and center for the moment, you are essentially serving the agenda of your organization.

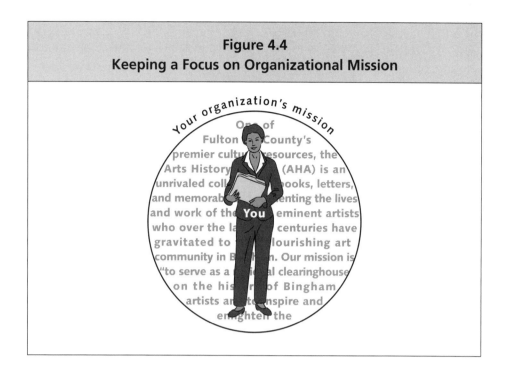

Figure 4.4
Keeping a Focus on Organizational Mission

Your organization's mission

One of Fulton County's premier cultural resources, the Arts History (AHA) is an unrivaled coll books, letters, and memorab enting the lives and work of th **You** eminent artists who over the l centuries have gravitated to lourishing art community in B n. Our mission is "to serve as a al clearinghouse on the his r of Bingham artists a to nspire and enlighten the

Handling Personal Needs

What happens when you as a manager start having conversations with your employees about their own struggles on the job? Even if you keep the conversations on work-related matters, good coaching conversations can't help but get somewhat personal. People reveal their concerns and struggles. They often talk about what aspects of their personalities or personal lives might interfere with their work. You may be drawn into revealing things about yourself in order to help. Or you may feel a strong need to keep those things to yourself, even though you suspect it might help those you coach if you could expose yourself more. There is no simple answer here. But we do know that being caring and empathetic is essential to being a good coaching manager, indeed, to being a good manager, period. Discover the right balance for the person in front of you.

According to leadership research by Jim Kouzes and Barry Posner (2007), most people rate having a caring boss even higher than they value money or fringe benefits. In fact, the same research shows a correlation between, on the one hand, how long employees stay at an organization and how productive they are and, on the other hand, the relationship they have with their immediate supervisor. "The best managers in the world are not only experts in systems, processes, and technical competencies—they are committed to knowing their people. And, because of this, they increase your engagement and productivity at work" (Rath, 2006, p. 2).

Coaching When It Gets Emotional

It's also OK for a staff member to show emotion about something at work. Susan Scott, the author of one of our favorite books, *Fierce Conversations* (2004) says: "When we get squeezed—when things aren't going well for us—what comes out of us? Whatever's inside us. To pretend that what's going on in our personal lives can be boxed, taped shut, and left in the garage while we are at work is hogwash. It seeps in everywhere. Who we are is who we are, all over the place" (p. 5). Dealing with emotional situations calls for the coaching manager to balance his or her own feelings and reactions.

The coaching conversation will occasionally reveal something distressing or poignant for the person you are coaching. Maybe she is talking about an amazing opportunity to engage in a new program but is afraid she will get in over her head. Maybe she is going through a very difficult situation. You may even find yourself identifying with her. Remember to keep your attention on how she is dealing with the situation, not your reaction to it.

Sometimes a supervisor tells us, "I'm not a therapist. Why would I encourage people to sit in my office and talk about their feelings?" We do suggest that people are simply human and will have emotions. We don't suggest you provide therapy whether you are a therapist or not (see "What Coaching Is Not" in Chapter One). Your colleague or staff person may just need an ear. Listen, pay attention, provide support, and talk about how to move things forward. You may feel like a counselor for a brief moment. Yet if you master the coaching approach, it will be just a moment, and you will always help the other person move quickly and efficiently toward performing her best. If, however, this person is exhibiting behaviors that may call for support beyond what you can provide, be sure to speak with your human resource manager or an HR expert (as discussed further in Chapter Six). Here is where you need to pay attention to your own needs. If you feel strongly that you are in over your head or that someone's behavior is inappropriate or even threatening, it is essential that you act on those feelings and get help.

Showing Empathy

We express empathy to show we understand and care. It's a part of healthy emotional intelligence. Empathy is useful when used appropriately while coaching. Go ahead. Say you understand. Express your support, and be careful not to over-empathize. Too much empathy may validate a person's feelings of helplessness. Show you care, and then help the person move forward. You might say something like this:

I can see why you would be rather upset, given the situation. Where do you need to go with this?

It is not easy to accept difficulty of this magnitude. What help will you need?

I can hear what you are saying. I'd like to help you get through this. How can I help?

Overempathizing, in contrast, sounds like this:

Oh, I totally understand your situation. I know exactly what you are saying. This happened to me. Blah, blah, blah.

No two stories are alike, though they may be similar, so be careful you are not intruding into the person's experience. Instead, use one of the empathizing statements that we have supplied here.

You want to express shock, so you say, "That's just vile and horrible!!!" But be aware of how you express yourself. You may intend to show you care and end up inducing more fear in a person who is already afraid.

Think of it this way. Is your expression of empathy, whether verbal or through your body language, supporting the coaching conversation toward a better outcome? Are you supporting the person in a way that helps her move forward, or are you causing even more anxiety, sadness, distress, or contempt? Balance will be the key. *Think before you act* is a safe way to go when dealing with emotions.

EARNING TRUST AND SHOWING RESPECT

Earning Trust

Trust is the basis of a good coaching relationship. As a coaching manager, you offer yourself as an agent of support, asking people to share their best thinking out loud, to work out new ideas, and to forward their action to best serve the organization. In *Foundations of Social Theory*, James Coleman (1990) offers this precept: "The placement of trust allows actions that otherwise are not possible" (p. 97). If we expect our colleagues and staff to respond to our coaching, there will need to be a good dose of trust present. Trust is earned, not necessarily given. It is essential that those you coach trust you. And it is essential that you respect them. These go hand in hand and help reinforce one another. The more you show that you can respect the people you manage, the more they will trust that you understand them. The result is a level of comfort that will allow for honest and straightforward communication. Beyond showing respect, you can build trust by a series of actions and behaviors that show you are credible. Look for opportunities to make sure people feel included, considered, and informed and are made to feel safe at work and while you coach.

 Listen with respect. Encourage and respect different points of view. Be aware of and respect different ways of communicating.

Credibility is gained "when one is perceived by others to be ethical, moral, fair, and just honest," says Sebastian Rupert Mampilly of the School of Management Studies, Cochin University of Science and Technology. The qualities of being honest, inspiring, and competent constitute what researchers refer to as credibility. Indeed, research by Kouzes and Posner (2007) has discovered that honesty is the number one quality that people admire in their superiors at work. According to Kouzes and Posner, more than anything else, people want leaders who are honest, who walk their talk, whose actions are consistent with their words, and who follow through on their promises. All of these qualities make for credible leaders.

Kouzes and Posner discovered that people who perceive their manager to have *high* credibility are significantly more likely to

Be proud to tell others they're part of the organization

Feel a strong sense of team spirit

See their own personal values as consistent with those of the organization

Feel attached and committed to the organization

Have a sense of ownership of the organization [2007, p. 37]

People who perceive their manager to have *low* credibility are significantly more likely to

> Produce only if they're watched carefully
>
> Be motivated primarily by money
>
> Say good things about the organization publicly, but criticize it privately
>
> Consider looking for another job in tough times
>
> Feel unsupported and unappreciated [2007, p. 37]

What does it look like to walk the talk? It means being consistent and reliable. A credible manager is one who sets forth clear expectations and applies them fairly to everyone. Should it be necessary to make an exception for one person, it is important to explain carefully to all the others so they understand your thinking and see that consistency and reliability are things you value. Of course, you can't be perfect. You are human. But the more you can value and work toward credibility, the more you can build trust. And with trust will come better relationships and responses from the people you coach.

Showing Respect

Respect grows out of understanding. When you can honestly see, appreciate, and understand those around you, you can build a genuine respect. You do not need to agree, but it is critical to work to respect and honor differences. This can often be harder than we think because often differences and how they manifest themselves can take us by surprise. As a result, cultivating respect demands we discipline ourselves to constantly stretch our thinking, remain open to different perspectives, and challenge our assumptions.

Given the wonderfully diverse nature of the nonprofit sector, it is extremely likely you will find yourself coaching someone of a different age, gender, race, ethnicity, or sexual orientation (among other things). In light of this fact, there are a few things about culture we'd like you to consider. Everything you have ever learned, experienced, endured, or responded to, and the influence of the societies you have lived in, up until this very moment, has shaped how you see the world and those in front of you. Now, imagine that the same is true for the people you manage. When you or anyone else looks at the world, you don't just see the world; you see it from your own perspective, and many different things go into shaping your perspective. This perspective is often referred to as a *cultural lens*.

This lens can affect the way people communicate with and understand one another. Therefore, "[i]t is essential that the coach, and if possible, the coachee, be vigilant regarding the potential impact of diversity of experience, background, outlook, and even personal style" (Hunt and Weintraub, 2002, p. 67).

People may also sometimes see situations differently, depending on their individual cultural lens. Consider the following examples:

- A Vietnamese housing manager takes time to achieve consensus from a group. This may be interpreted as an inability to take personal responsibility to make a decision. *Or* it may be seen as valuing the importance of inclusion.

- A twenty-two-year-old youth advocate arrives to work at 10 **A.M.** most mornings and stays at work until 7 **P.M.** or later. This may be seen as unprofessional or as a disregard for "normal" working hours. *Or* it may be that she was raised in a generation that values a different type of work style and schedule.

- A female program coordinator doesn't apply for a management position that is posted internally at your organization, even though she is qualified for it. It may be seen by some as lack of ambition. *Or* it may be seen as valuing coworkers and disliking competition with them for personal advancement.

- A Latino team member withholds news that might be considered bad or negative. This may be seen as being indirect or avoiding conflict. *Or* it may be seen as refraining from being tactless or humiliating.

We're not usually aware of our lens. We tend to think that we just see the world. But we all have filters, and it's important to be aware of them. As you work with your staff, how aware are you of your own cultural lens? What are some of the things that might affect the way you see the world? Take a moment and think about all the things that influence how you see the world and your workplace. You may even want to jot them down.

If you want to go further, here's an exercise to consider: draw a long, narrow circle in the middle of a sheet of paper. This represents your cultural lens. Next, write or draw all of the things that contributed to your cultural lens. They might include race or ethnicity, family background, educational background, community you were raised in, and so on. Ask your staff to do the same exercise to represent their own cultural lenses. Finally, you and your staff can share cultural lens stories with one another. (Laurin Mayeno and Jacqueline Elena Featherston adapted this exercise by Ben Fraticelli of Community Health Academy.)

As you and your staff work with a culturally aware approach, it helps all involved to better understand their own cultural lens. It helps them see the formally "invisible." It recognizes that perspectives through other cultural lenses carry new wisdom and new ways of working together. How can you seek to understand and respect the different perspectives of those you are coaching? How are you aware of the cultural lenses of others?

All of us are bonded to others in our similarities by birth, by environment, by race or religion, by region, by nature, by talent, by survival, or by diversion. This is the beauty of culture. We define *culture* as the beliefs, values, customs, and behaviors of a particular group of people. This could mean a group of urban gay men, a group of mothers, a group of young organizers, a group of caseworkers, a group of people with disabilities, a group of African American women, a group of those who speak English as a second language, and on and on. Each of us is a member of a number of groups that may be different from each other. And inside each of these groups, each one of us is different. This is something wonderful to regard. And regard this we must as we coach people through learning and development. Respecting others means engaging in culturally aware coaching. For more information on culturally aware coaching, please see Resource C.

STAYING CONNECTED

Staying connected is a part of the solid foundation in a coaching conversation. When people need help, they are most likely to share their needs, issues, and solutions with those they relate to, those they have an alliance or bond with, and those they trust. Staff will do their best thinking when they feel a connection with you. You are in charge of this connection. You must place yourself in a space of full interest in the other person. Watch what you say to be sure it includes the person, not excludes them. Put yourself aside for a moment and focus fully on the other person. This way they will know you are meant to have a real connection.

KARA'S STORY: CONNECTING WITH OTHERS

Kara is a program director at an international agency that promotes resolution to conflict in African countries. She is used to reaching across divides to find balanced solutions. Ellen is a new interpreter who works on Kara's team. Kara is coaching Ellen to help Ellen think about how to adapt to the new culture she finds herself in. While coaching, Ellen reveals that she is already having problems with three other members of the team. She has a greater sense of urgency than some of her teammates, and she is questioning some of the practices of the agency. Ellen has a very strategic mind-set but she feels this agency puts relationships first.

Although this is the time she had agreed to meet with Ellen, Kara feels pressured because her meeting in Chicago needs preparation and it's only hours away. As soon as Kara is aware of the pressure, she makes a conscious choice to place her concentration on the task at hand. She brings her full attention into the room, focusing in on Ellen so she can hear everything Ellen is saying. Kara wishes Ellen would just get along with people, but she opens up in herself a desire to be interested in how Ellen is seeing the situation. Kara's curiosity helps Ellen explain her thoughts. Kara starts to see links between what the agency wants and what Ellen seems to be complaining about and wants too. Kara is making moment-by-moment choices to avoid making assumptions about Ellen, to read the cues in Ellen's voice, and to stay in the moment, dancing with Ellen.

The tone of Ellen's voice is tense. Kara makes no judgment. She knows Ellen wants things to go well. Kara's commitment to sustain a connection to Ellen builds a deeper alliance and avoids any argument about what's good or bad. Instead of unconstructive conflict, they open up points for discussion. Ellen feels she's being understood because her point of view is considered. She feels a bond with Kara, even though the conversation is difficult. The connection Kara provides gives ground to opportunity for learning from both sides.

 ## Questions to Ask Yourself Before You Coach

Am I able to stay present for the other person as we discuss things?

Can I let go of other distractions?

Do I use language that includes and engages the other person?

Do I show that I have time to help the other person?

Being Present and Getting Focused

Yesterday is history, tomorrow a mystery, today is a gift, that's why it's called the "present."

—Alice Morse Earle, 1902

Claire Raines and Lara Ewing, in *The Art of Connecting* (2006), talk about great connections starting with the mental flexibility to see and hear the situation from different points of view, allowing for a holistic, balanced "take" on what's going on. They go on to describe a master of connection, Terry Gross, radio host on National Public Radio since 1987, who says, "I listen as hard as I can, and follow people into places they want to go and then lead them back" (p. 9). In coaching we talk about the ability to dance with people in the moment. The only way to follow people into the places they want to go and then lead them back is to stay focused on them. To do this, we need to be aware of what might draw our focus away.

Engaged listening has helped me see my staff more clearly as human beings, and I think, subsequently, understand and appreciate their unique skill sets. It also makes me be more "in the moment," which is a more enjoyable way to work.

—Coaching workshop participant

There are three spaces our minds can be in when coaching others: the past, the future, or the present. There's nothing wrong with analyzing the past or with thinking about things that haven't happened yet. But can your mind really be in two places at once? We suggest that while coaching, the best place your mind needs to stay is in the present moment. This will help you focus on the person, follow him clearly, and hear what he is really saying or thinking. Your mind may be able to skip very fast from one thing to other. You may be able to listen and be summing up what it all means at the same time. We suggest you listen; *then* you sum it up. One thing at a time.

John Kuypers (2009) of Present Living, Inc., says, "Being present happens when you stop comparing ('judging') the present moment to past experiences or future expectations. Regardless of what other people are doing or what situation you are facing, you are centered and calm." Slow down. Stay here a moment. See what is really possible. You may get more than you think.

Most obstacles to being present are self-imposed. It is possible to build the habit of staying present, which is useful both in coaching and in your other interactions as a manager. Next are three disciplines you may want to experiment with in the course of your day, to cultivate your ability to focus.

Notice   Become fully intentional about your purpose in this moment, whatever it is. If you are at a meeting, for example, it can be tempting to think about everything that is waiting for you on your desk. But, again as an experiment, just try bringing your full attention to what others are saying. Try taking a breath and sending your attention out of yourself and your thoughts of the future and listening carefully. You may find that this changes your experience of the meeting. You may find yourself becoming more engaged and interested. And you may find that you pick up on something important that you might not have fully appreciated if you hadn't been listening carefully. This isn't easy; we recognize that. But it can enhance your ability to coach, and practicing it in other areas of your life as a manager will be useful too. In Chapter Two, we talked about how to practice the art of observation. Your ability to simply see objectively what is happening, like a video recording, takes being in the moment.

Let Go   Again, you can practice this discipline anytime and anywhere. Learn how to take a few minutes to quiet your mind. Notice whatever thoughts might arise. Now let them go. Don't think about them. Allow them to pass on. Have no opinion of your thoughts. Themes may present themselves. Allow these to pass through too. Don't worry if you can't do it perfectly. Practice over time.

Decide Now It's your choice when you are interacting with staff how you will come across. Will it be as the coaching manager or will you be playing some other role? It's important to make a conscious decision. All too often we let old habits decide, and we forget to make our own choices. It's a useful exercise to stop, think, and decide.

One thing that Judith likes to do to be present is sit quietly for two minutes before coaching someone. In those minutes, she asks herself how she can be of greatest service to the person she is meeting with. Then she's quiet. She lets her mind rest. When the phone rings or the person walks in, she feels fully present and in the moment for that interaction.

Being present helps the person you are coaching. There will be more space in your mind for you to retain her thoughts, to be recalled later in the conversation or to use when helping her sort things out. Things may pop into your mind that you might use to prompt her further into the conversation. These practices can help you build the muscle of being present and staying focused when you are coaching.

Using Language That Connects and Includes

Words are the very core of connecting. Think about the feelings generated by the right words at the right time or by the ill-timed phrase or tired cliché. In coaching we use words and gestures that open doors. We must guard against unintentionally using words that disconnect and shut people out. Our words should boost new possibilities, rather than set things in stone.

Let's have a look at the power of two simple words that can make a huge difference. Consider the simple use of *and* instead of *but*.

Exchanges Using *But*

1. You say, "Here's my opinion." The other person, Chris, says, "But you need to think of it this way."

2. You say, "I'm going to concentrate on this today." Chris says, "But I want something else done."

   What is implied after the word *but*?

   Do you feel heard and included?

   Has anything been negated because of the use of *but*?

   Let's try using *and* instead of *but*.

Exchanges Using *And*

1. You say, "Here's my opinion." Chris says, "I hear you, and I have a different opinion to add."

2. You say, "I'm going to concentrate on this today." Chris says, "I hear what you are saying, and I want something else done first."

   How do you feel now?

   Do you feel included and heard?

   Even if Chris disagrees with you, do you at least feel validated?

The different impacts of these two little words have a huge bearing on whether people will stay with you during a conversation or whether they feel negated in some way. Exercise 4.1 shows what a difference a small word can make. Our goal in coaching is to create a space of inclusive thought and ideas. The careful use of language when coaching will help you keep your listener engaged.

EXERCISE 4.1
Using *And* Instead of *But*

Try this exercise with your group. Form groups of up to eight people and ask the members of each group to stand in a circle, shoulder to shoulder, facing each other. The goal of the group conversation will be to create a staff retreat with a budget of $5,000. Go around the circle twice. In the first round each person will get a turn sharing one thought about how to create the staff retreat. Each person will connect to the person before him or her by using the word *but*. Go around the circle as many times as possible in two minutes, with each person always connecting to the last person by saying *but* before adding his or her next thought. In round two, repeat the exercise, this time connecting to the previous person's thought only with the word *and*. Discuss the impact of *but* versus the impact of *and* on the group.

Look at the words in Chart 4.1. Notice which words you use unconsciously and the increased positive impact you might have using other words instead.

CHART 4.1	
Language: Do Use and Don't Use	
Do Use	**Don't Use**
Many times you . . .	You never . . .
You have yet to . . .	You always . . .
It might serve you to consider . . .	You should . . .
It's less than wise/prudent to . . .	It's ludicrous or ridiculous . . .
Possible options . . .	No way . . .
Highly suggest . . .	I insist . . .
Even better than before	Better than before

Always take into consideration the other person's culture; words may have different meanings for different people.

> Both/and thinking means making room for more than one idea and point of view at a time, appreciating and valuing multiple realities—your own and others. Although either/or thinking has its place, it can often be a barrier to human communication.

Become as conscious as possible about the impact of your words. The careful use of language when coaching will help you keep the other person engaged. In certain contexts or situations, some words can be simply reshaped to have a more positive impact.

Keeping the Focus on the Other Person

Because coaching is not about you and it is about the other person, you need to keep the attention on that person and not drive the attention away, back to yourself. The connection can be lost in seconds when we are not aware of our impact. We can pull the attention to ourselves in many ways; we can tell too many stories, we can speak too much, we may try to have the last word, or we can self-reference too often.

While working on a large coaching program in 2007, Linda Miller, a good friend and coauthor of *Coaching in Organizations* (Miller and Holman, 2008), trained coaches and managers to limit the mentioning of self in their statements or their questions.

Here's an example: "Tell me what you are thinking." The reference to self— "tell me"—pulls the energy away from the conversation being about the other, and it becomes about you. At worst, this can create a feeling that the coach has authority on the issue. When you say, "I'm trying to understand," that makes the person receiving coaching have to take care of what you are trying to do rather than focus on what she is trying to do. Sometimes we do it out of habit to fill the gap, if only for a moment. A moment is all it takes to disturb the brilliant thinking of your staff person. At worst, people report that managers who use too much self-reference come across as their parents, therapist, or priest.

See how to shift your self-referencing in the examples here:

Instead of saying: Tell me something.

Say: Say something about . . .

Instead of saying: Let me understand you better.

Say: Are you saying . . . ?

Instead of saying: It sounds to me like . . .

Say: It sounds like . . . ?

Instead of saying: I think I know what you are talking about.

Say: You seem to be talking about . . .

Self-referencing can be kept for times when you are explaining yourself or your point of view, or when you are in a conflict situation:

Where I see this going is . . .

For me, I believe . . .

This is just my thought . . .

Coaching means keeping the focus on the other person. Of course, you can share your thoughts and expressions. We'll cover that later (also see the discussion of sharing in Chapter Two). Simply attempt to catch yourself when you over-use self-referencing. Turn the words around or leave out several words that point to your needing something. Shorten what you are saying. If you lessen your self-referencing, you keep the focus where it should be.

Using Body Language to Connect

When connecting with someone, what you do with your body often speaks louder than your words. Think of a time when you approached a person who was frowning, looking at his computer instead of you, or leaning back with his arms crossed. What impact did it have on you? Now think of a time when you approached someone who was smiling, looking in your direction, and showing that he was ready to listen. What impact did that have? Do you notice any difference? Our body language sends messages to the people who approach us. Dane Archer, a professor at the University of California at Santa Cruz, says there are many different *channels* of nonverbal communication: facial expressions, hand gestures, body movements, touch, and personal space.

You may have gotten advice to keep eye contact, stand up straight, keep your arms open, or lean toward someone. A small word of caution: these are generally acceptable in Western culture but may be inappropriate in other cultures or certain situations. More useful advice is to relax, breathe, notice what the other person is doing, judge how much space to take up with your gestures, and be yourself.

Small changes in body language can often have big effects. An example from our consulting work is Henry, a manager at an affordable housing organization who was very good at the technical side of his work but who was struggling to build good relationships with his staff. We asked Henry to practice smiling at half the people as if he was pleased to see them (even if he wasn't for now) and to also smile before he went on to respond to anything this group asked or said. He was asked to continue as usual with the other half of the group. Within three weeks, those Henry smiled at said something dramatic had occurred. He had softened up to the point that they believed he really cared about them. When they approached him in the morning and during the day, they saw less eye rolling (it's hard to roll your eyes and smile at the same time). Henry had not said anything more or less; his smile simply created an opening. We had encouraged Henry to manage his own expression in order to be more accessible to others. Henry reported that his staff seemed more engaged with him. He also said it made him feel better about them, too. He now reports he's actually been able to coach some of his team, and he's getting more work done through others.

Being Available

If you have said you have a few minutes for someone, those minutes are for that person. It's a time to be completely available to be with her and help her move from point A to point B.

Many managers, when introduced to coaching, worry at first that it may take more time than other management approaches. The reality is that a few minutes now for focused coaching can save a lot of time later. Using this immediate approach may release you in the future from being a firefighter when everything's ablaze, a doctor when a diagnosis is needed, or a teacher of the same curriculum you've taught before. You make time in the present to help another person take charge of her own thinking and solutions now and going forward. She takes the action. The burden is off you. That's worth a little time, don't you think?

You have plenty of different demands on your limited time. Setting a time frame for a coaching conversation is a good way to maintain control of your schedule. If someone comes into your office and asks for a few minutes of your time, it serves you to be specific about how many minutes you really have. Some coaching conversations need only two minutes while you are walking down the corridor. You might call someone in to be coached about a report, which could take five minutes. Another occasion might be a one-on-one meeting that you provide thirty minutes for. Let the person know. You'll be more present to coach if you set limits. This is not rude; quite the contrary. You are being honest with a person who wants your assistance. If you are having a more formal meeting with someone, you might want to break your time into specific chunks to allow the right amount of time for each issue. You might say, "Let's spend fifteen minutes laying out the plan for next week, five minutes on updates, and ten minutes to think about how to deal with that employee problem you're having." This helps maximize your time together and minimize stress caused by poor time management.

Here are some additional suggestions to make the time to coach:

Put time aside; physically schedule the conversation in your calendar.

If you don't have time when someone comes in, ask to reschedule and *then put it in your calendar.*

When it's time to coach, turn off your e-mail and cell phone, and shut your door.

Set aside anything that may distract you.

You will need to clear away all distractions that might prevent you from being fully present in the coaching conversation.

Remember, it is the decision you make to be consciously connected that will help create the bond between you and the person you are coaching. Staying connected is a part of the solid foundation in a coaching conversation. You are in charge of this.

A WORD ABOUT CONFIDENTIALITY

Confidentiality is often defined as "what you say in the room stays in the room." Depending on the content or nature of the coaching conversation, you may want to set expectations up front in a conversation regarding levels of confidentiality. There is another dimension to confidentiality that includes asking permission to share or discuss any statement another person makes of a personal nature. It helps to remember that the story belongs to the teller, not the listener.

As we shared earlier, we do not attempt to explore in depth all the elements of a coaching mind-set. However, we hope we've made a case for paying attention to the four components we've walked you through. When you pay attention to how you come across and stay connected, you create the space for coaching to happen. Simply applying coaching skills and a framework without a coaching mind-set may get you fewer results than you're looking for. At worst, it could ring hollow with the person you are coaching. The attitude and outlook you bring to the coaching conversation can make all the difference.

Now that you're familiar with mind-set, let's take a look at when to coach.

Knowing When to Use a Coaching Approach

Now that you understand the foundational coaching skills, the coaching framework, and the mind-set necessary to be your best while coaching, you probably feel ready to apply what you've learned by grabbing the first person you see and attempting to coach him or her. We applaud the enthusiasm! But before you move forward, it's important to know when to use a coaching approach and when not to. In this chapter, we present how to use a coaching approach to address a range of situations as we explore the following:

- Providing coaching for the different stages of the learning
- Coaching when the manager sets the focus
- Knowing what to do when coaching is not working
- More opportunities to coach

In this book, we've attempted to focus exclusively on the management tool of coaching. We do not attempt to address other skills, such as how to direct, instruct, or teach, but we do know that some amount of coaching will be useful, no matter which management tool you are using. It's just that some situations need more coaching, and some situations need less.

 In each situation you can provide a little or a lot of coaching. What kind of and how much support you provide really depends on what the other person needs in the given situation.

Let's start by looking at a simple case for coaching. Marcus is a program director who has worked in his organization for years. Considered a top performer, he meets all his deadlines, brings in lots of money from funders, and is loved by clients. He does such a great job that his manager, Aretha, is really comfortable letting him do his own thing. She spends all her time focusing on her "problem staff" and those new to tasks. One day, Aretha hears through the grapevine that Marcus is unhappy. Aretha is shocked! When she checks in with him, he says he never gets any feedback and misses thinking things through with her. He wants *some* support, not *no* support, and he has no idea how he is doing. In the absence of coaching and feedback, Marcus has begun to doubt his performance and his contribution to the organization. What's the moral of this story? Some of our top performers are hungry for attention. Make sure they get some nourishment by providing coaching.

This is just one example of when to coach. Next, we're going to share several examples that demonstrate when to coach (in lieu of things like instructing or directing) and when to consider holding back. As you will read, your approach really depends on what stage the other person is on the continuum of learning, competency, and commitment.

PROVIDING COACHING FOR THE DIFFERENT STAGES OF LEARNING

You've probably noticed that people are at different levels of ability and development in relation to each task they do. And as a manager you probably recognize that different staff need different kinds of support to help them move forward or advance their thinking. Some people need more instruction, training, guidance, and advice. Some need help thinking about their process and actions. Others just need to be listened to, confirmed, and mirrored. In each situation you can provide a little or a lot of coaching. What kind of and how much support you provide really depends on what the other person needs in the given situation.

This leadership response is often called *situational leadership*, or a *flexible leadership style*. This school of thinking is influenced by the work of Ken Blanchard. In *The Three Keys to Empowerment*, Blanchard, Carlos, and Randolph (1999) state:

> By matching leadership style to the development level, leaders and team members help ensure that competence and commitment for the task of empowerment continue to move toward high levels. In other words, given the appropriate amounts of directive and supportive behaviors at each stage of the journey, people move from one level of development to another, from being 1) enthusiastic beginners in a task to 2) disillusioned learners about empowerment to 3) capable but cautious performers to 4) self-reliant empowered achievers [p. 28].

For a deeper understanding of the development cycle and appropriate leadership actions, see *Leadership and the One Minute Manager* (Blanchard, Zigarmi, and Zigarmi, 1985).

When you boil this down, the amount of coaching you provide needs to be adjusted depending on (1) the staff person's knowledge and skill level and (2) his interest in the task and his self-assurance. Ken Blanchard calls these two things *competency* and *commitment;* others call them *ability* and *willingness.* Regardless of terminology, the point is that between giving advice and delegating, there is a space for us to coach. The best questions to ask are, "What does this person need right now?" "How can I best help this person right now?" "How much coaching will be useful?" Be sure you use other approaches as the situation calls for them.

Different strokes for different folks. Different strokes for the same folks, depending on the goal or task.

—Ken Blanchard, Patricia Zigarmi, and Drea Zigarmi,
1985, p. 61

When Someone Is Seasoned at a Task

Example. Janice oversees a life skills program. She's very informed and organized, and runs a tight program. She has a solid team that enjoys and respects working with her. They do a great job. You want her to introduce a new process to the program that she used before in another agency. It was very successful.

This is a time to delegate and follow up with coaching support as needed. If you know Janice can do the task, you delegate the task, then you let go. You don't disappear though. Agree on goals, timelines, and boundaries. Let her decide how to get things done. Be available to brainstorm, ask provocative questions, or stimulate thinking, if she needs or wants it. The key is to realize that you no longer need to be directive. Delegate the task.

I am responsible for overseeing two neighborhood planning projects and am working with two outstanding community organizers who lead these projects. There is no way I can know as much as they do about all the important people and neighborhood dynamics involved in their work. The coaching approach really helps me help them make sense of what they are encountering.

— Cathy Craig, Bay Area Local Initiatives Support Corporation (LISC)

So in this situation you might say such things as, "Here's what we need. What's your plan?" "I trust you to succeed. What do you need from me?" "Do you need to discuss anything?" Ask how often Janice would like to discuss things and agree on how much feedback would be useful to her. Give her appreciative feedback.

In our opening story, you met Marcus, who is seasoned at what he does, delivers on his goals, and appears to be doing well. It may seem that he doesn't need any coaching, though as you found out, just because he knows what he's doing and has done those things many times before, that doesn't mean he doesn't want thought-provoking conversation or doesn't need feedback, both appreciative and developmental (see the section in Chapter Two about giving feedback). He does. Coach him as needed. Give him feedback as often as he needs.

When Someone Is Familiar with a Task, Yet Something Is in the Way

Example. Jesse is on the interviewing team in her organization. She's great on a panel. Jesse would like to better facilitate group discussions and team meetings.

This is a time to provide ongoing coaching, with very little need for instruction or direction. Watch out! It's easy to think someone is familiar enough with a task that she doesn't need any coaching when the task changes. Jesse is skilled on a panel and has been holding team meetings for a while. She's familiar with what needs to happen. And Jesse wants to grow. Don't leave Jesse to figure it out alone. Provide ongoing coaching to expand her self-confidence, expand her skill levels, and give her feedback on how she's progressing.

Example. Alek works for a public interest research group and is great at organizing. His manager wants to prepare him to step into the role of director within the year.

In the case of Alek, it's time to leverage his talents and strengths. He's a high-potential candidate worth investing in. Coaching Alek on a regular basis will help him identify what to work on, foster new ways of stepping up, develop his leadership presence, and more. He may need some training along with coaching for things that are new to him. You might even assign a reading list and explore other ways to build on his strengths. Remember, he's got a lot that he already brings to the table, and coaching will help him take it to the next level.

Example. Talia is a very good curriculum writer in an organization that is trying to close the achievement gap in reading in her state. She is losing faith that they are making progress. She feels like giving up.

Let's look at Talia. She does not feel good about what's going on. She knows how to write curricula. She's actually quite talented. She's despondent that there aren't more results. Your coaching can help her realize the bigger picture or what it takes to see results over time. Your coaching may provide her with someone with whom to talk through her fears. She may need only one coaching meeting to do this. She won't need much, and you can be of help. Listen a lot. Help her see her way through.

There are many opportunities to grow people's self-confidence and self-reliance. When people are familiar with a task, yet something is holding them back or they are simply not quite there yet, coach them to think about what they do know and what the next steps might be. In such a situation you might say such things as, "Let's think through this together. What do you think will help in this situation?" "What are your options?" "May I share a thought?" "What do you think? What else would help you here?" "I'm here to support you if you have concerns. Who else can support you?" Remember to affirm the person. Brainstorm to encourage creative solutions. Creativity is rarely a linear process. Recognize the person's courage to step up to the plate. Find out about any questions. Be consistent with coaching, and support the person's learning and growing in ability. You may want to ask how often the person would like to check in during this learning stage. Make sure you're available when needed. Be a thought partner.

When a Person Is Somewhat Familiar with a Task, Yet Hesitant

Example. Jamal is a fairly new special events coordinator for his community center. He is known as an all-around nice guy. He has some hesitation about a cross-cultural event he's managing. He feels alone. He avoids working on this event and busies himself with other work.

This is a time to coach *and* instruct. When someone has just enough experience with a task to understand how much he doesn't know, he can get nervous. Let's look at Jamal's experience. He's still learning the job. Just because he's a nice guy doesn't mean he's a guy who knows how to do everything. This particular event may be more challenging or call for more thought than he had anticipated. If you notice enthusiasm is beginning to wane, support the value and contribution this person is making. He may procrastinate. Step in and suggest you work together to get what's needed to succeed.

Here you might say, "Let's discuss how to do this. Here's a suggestion, what do you think?" "Is there anything that needs further explanation?" "As we think together, I'm confident you will better understand how to approach this. What do you need to help you build your skills?" "Let's keep in touch often and think together about this." Tell him you'll provide extra coaching. You'll need to assess the situation. It might be that Jamal needs a combination of instruction *and* coaching. You might lead the conversations and give him time to think and create. He's growing his competence and his confidence simultaneously. Stay close. Monitor often, yet give him enough space to flourish.

Example. Ophelia is a dynamic caseworker whom clients love to work with. She has been having some difficulty with her team members. She's not interested in what they have to say. She avoids team meetings. People say she doesn't respond to e-mail. You need her to engage her team.

Coaching can help here, too. Provide coaching to give her a place to express what's going on for her and to help her identify reasons she's showing less interest, yet be sure to coach her toward what she can do to reengage. She may have her own interpersonal skill issues, she may need to shift a behavior, or she may need to get help having a hard conversation to solve internal conflicts. The goal of coaching is to help her reengage with her team.

When Someone Is New to a Task

Example. Haley is a managed care advocate for gay men. She continues to work well with the individuals and families she has served over many years. She wants to take on the annual assessment of caregivers and is eager to give it a try, but she's never done this task before.

This is a time to instruct first and provide coaching when you think appropriate. Everyone has to start somewhere. Not being experienced is appropriate for a person new to a task. Let's review Haley's situation. She's experienced and doing well with those she serves. Working on the annual assessment of caregivers is a brand-new task for her. It's easy to forget she is new at this. Those learning a new procedure or even new employees may be enthusiastic about doing it, which goes a long way, but enthusiasm is different from know-how. When a person is learning something new, it's appropriate to be instructive, to give advice, or to simply tell the person what to do. This person may need to see how you demonstrate the task.

In this situation, you might say such things as, "What skills that you already possess can be leveraged here as you learn the task?" "Let me show you how this is done so you can build your skill." "We'll check in regularly to be sure you are progressing. Are you clear about the expectations?" By this, we mean you should understand the person's level of accomplishment and adjust the way you interact accordingly. Give her the tools she needs, and be sure to monitor her more closely in this learning stage. You can coach along the way. Listen well. Ask questions to help her stretch her mind.

Another common situation is when a staff member needs to do a task that he's done before but in a different way. There could be updated procedures or priorities. In this case, don't assume he knows what he's doing. The new information may really throw him. Be explicit about the expectations, quality, and standards he is being asked to grow toward. Check for clarity.

Everyone can do with a little coaching now and then. Some need more than others. This is absolutely appropriate. You will need to assess each situation. The answers to these questions will help you get a clearer picture of the situation:

To what degree does this person already know what to do? What's the evidence?

Is it the first time the person is seeing this, doing this, hearing this?

Does the person have the skill to do the task?

How does the person feel about what she or he is about to do? Is she or he confident?

Does the person take ownership of the task?

Am I making this more urgent than it is and going into *tell* mode?

COACHING WHEN THE MANAGER SETS THE FOCUS

Remember, coaching can be used to help others grow, develop, or improve on small and big things. There are two ways coaching can happen: The first is when someone comes to you and asks to be coached. The second is when you go to somebody to ask him or her to think about a different action or behavior. As we mentioned in Chapter Four, there will be many times when you, as the manager, will need to present the focus for a coaching conversation, for instance, when you have an agenda that is based on the needs of the organization. In Chapters Two and Three, we gave you the skills and framework to apply in both situations. In this section, we offer some guidance on how best to approach this coaching situation.

First, decide if you have a reason to provide coaching and confirm that this is the path you need to take. Write down the answers to these questions:

Is there anything you would like a person to do more of, less of, faster, smarter, or in a different way?

Do you need someone to think more, work on ideas, or plan for new action?

Is there an opportunity for someone to grow, expand, take advantage of, or to take more of the lead?

If you answered yes to any of these questions, it's highly likely that you want or need one or more people to do things because it will help achieve the mission.

In these instances, you will need to lead the way and set the focus in the coaching conversation. But before we show you how, we suggest that you complete Exercise 5.1 to assess the person's readiness for coaching.

EXERCISE 5.1
Is This Person Ready for Coaching?

You may be ready to coach someone, but it's possible that the other person simply *isn't ready* to be coached. Before jumping right in, take a moment to review the following list of questions:

1. Where is the person in relationship to the task? Is this a coaching opportunity, or does the person simply need to be given information or training?

2. Is the person open to new ideas and new ways of doing things to facilitate positive change and growth?

3. Is the person prepared to tackle the tough issues to close the gap between where he or she is now and where he or she wants to be?

4. Is the person open to a thought partner who can share the successes and offer help with the challenges?

5. Does the person see coaching as an investment in his or her leadership and growth or as a punitive measure or a mandate from you?

6. Does the person seek input and feedback from others?

7. Is the person willing to consider input and feedback from others?

8. Is the person willing to take steps to change behavior when appropriate?

9. Is the person willing to try new ideas and new ways of approaching problems?

10. Does the person have the time at this moment to discuss the issue at hand?

Depending on the answers to these questions, you may proceed along the coaching path, or you may need to employ another managing tool, such as instructing or delegating. It's important to find the right tool for the right situation.

Once you have determined that the person is ready to be coached, you can get started on the actual process. To set the agenda based on organizational needs, open the conversation, guide the person to focus on the specific issue or opportunity you are presenting, and then return back to the coaching skills and framework you have previously learned in this book. Even though you will take the lead in setting the focus and agenda for the conversation, be very careful not to dominate the conversation or give a monologue. This is coaching, after all.

Start to prepare for the conversation by asking yourself the following:

What is the real focus of this conversation?

What am I trying to achieve with this person?

Where should I focus?

What am I requesting?

How open am I to helping the person think through change or solve his or her own problem?

What might be the one or two key areas of growth that will most serve this person?

What will I need to take into consideration about this person?

The following guide can help you focus your attention by category. In some cases there will be overlap.

Information and knowledge. Is this person stuck for lack of resources? Does this person need more information or knowledge in order to move forward? If yes, find out how to get what's missing or how to use existing information.

Skills, capacity, and proficiency. Does the person have the ability to do what's required? When it's a question of capacity, ask questions about how skills can be improved. If those skills can't be improved, ask how the person can make the best use of his or her capabilities.

Planning and time. Does this person need to be more organized or to manage time in a different way? Are you seeing this person overwhelmed by demands? Focus your inquiry here to improve planning and the use of time.

Relationships and associations. Does this person get along with others? Would this person be better off relating to other people—at all levels in the organization— in a different way? When there is conflict, when interpersonal skills need improving, when the employee has difficulty discerning nonverbal cues (reading people), ask questions to help the person become more approachable and a better negotiator.

Support structures and tools. Does your staff person have enough support? Are necessary tools available? Focus here if the person needs project support, access to training, or tools such as spreadsheets, charts, and forms.

Leadership. Is this a matter of leading in a different way? Is this person an adequate guide? Should this person be actively developing others? Does the ability to strategize and plan need improvement? Does this person demonstrate vision, fairness, and problem solving? Are more patience and composure needed? Are decisions difficult for this person to make? Is this person innovative when appropriate?

Ownership, investment, motivation, and confidence. Does this employee have enough motivation and confidence to own the situation? You would look here if there was a question of the ownership, confidence, or drive that a person has toward a task, project, program, or needed change.

Behavior and self-management. Does the way this person acts need to be looked at? Pay attention to emotional temperature. What is being communicated by carriage and demeanor? Ask questions to uncover growth opportunities, better communication, interpersonal skills improvement, and expanded self-awareness. Is the person open to change?

As you ready yourself to hold an efficient conversation to help a person grow, remember the coaching framework. The first step is to clarify the focus. This does not change, even if you are bringing the focus of the conversation to the person you are coaching. Here's how to clarify the focus of the conversation when you bring the agenda:

- Stay objective. Facts are facts. You don't need to take what's going on personally. You want to encourage people to do their best.

- Set the context. Point to what the organization needs (what point B looks like).

- Create a space to think together. Invite the person into a circle of possibility.

- Understand what the other person's motivations are, and connect what you need with what's important to that person.

- If necessary, show how the focus of the conversation has an impact on the organization. Who will benefit if this person succeeds further? Gain agreement about the value of the topic under discussion.

- Get specific about your request. Make clear what you are asking.

- Stick to the reason you are making this request. Keep your opinions and judgments out of the way.

- Remember to use all of the coaching skills: listening, inquiring, giving feedback, and sharing.

- Keep your sentences short and to the point. You are coaching now.

If the conversation starts to stray, restate the purpose of the discussion and then revert immediately to using the coaching approach.

The following example can help you understand how to put all of this into action.

EXAMPLE OF COACHING WHEN THE MANAGER SETS THE FOCUS

First, clarify the broader focus. "Sam, today I'd like us to talk about a couple of things that would help you engage your team even more. Could we think together about additional ways for you to really motivate and inspire them to greater participation concerning your aims to win over more new youth leaders for this national youth-in-politics initiative? I realize your goal is to have your team bring about more awareness with the youth on the issues and concerns that are the focus of the current movement." (You're saying what's in it for Sam.)

(Wait for confirmation.)

Next, set the context. "You and I both want your team to succeed with this high-profile youth leadership program. I think we agree that a large portion of our funding rests partly on the success of this program. Is that true?"

(Wait for the answer.)

Next, clarify the narrow focus and make the request. "As we consider how to really engage the team, I'd like us to look for more ways to get their input when planning. You know how important it is to keep communication flowing. Would you be willing to work on these with me?"

(Wait for a response.)

Then use all your coaching skills and the framework:

"What other areas might we focus on to engage the team even more?"

"What are your thoughts about what will help the team?"

"What do you think about what I suggested?"

"How will focusing in on these possibilities help the team?"

Ask questions to keep the conversation focused. Stay as detached as possible. Allow Sam to come up with creative ways to find solutions. Then use the rest of the framework (as described in Chapter Three) to help Sam see what is possible for himself, identify solutions, and change direction between point A, where he is now, and point B, where you or the organization need him to be. Then be sure to coach for accountability and clear agreements.

Now that you have better grounding in how and when to use a coaching approach, let's move on to those instances when coaching just isn't working.

WHAT TO DO WHEN COACHING IS NOT WORKING

When There is Disagreement About Ability

What if *you* think someone is new to a task or not skilled enough to carry it out, but *the other person* thinks she knows what she is doing? We get this question a lot in our workshops. Situations like this can cause a lot of frustration on both sides. The manager may be frustrated because a task isn't getting done correctly. The staff member may be frustrated because she's feeling micromanaged.

There is something called *unconscious incompetence* (Mind Tools, 2008). A person might *think* she's competent at a task, when she's really not. Your goal as a coaching manager is to do three things:

1. Assess whether the person is, in fact, incompetent at the task.

2. Provide feedback about the behavior. (See Chapter Two.)

3. Help move the person from unconscious incompetence to conscious competence.

Figure 5.1 illustrates the movement from unconscious incompetence to conscious competence.

Figure 5.1
From Unconscious Incompetence to Conscious Competence

When a person is in a state of . . .	What to do about it:
Unconscious incompetence (we don't know what we don't know)	This is a time to give very specific and direct feedback (see Chapter Two).
Conscious incompetence (we *know* what we don't know)	This is a time to instruct, tell, direct, and provide coaching support and feedback.
Conscious competence (we know what we know)	This is a time to coach and provide feedback to reinforce what the person is doing well and might want to do more of.
Unconscious competence (we can do it naturally, without even being aware)	This is a time to coach and provide feedback to help remind the person of what he can do naturally and may not even think about. Help hold up a mirror so he can see his talents and claim them.

Source: Adapted with permission from Mind Tools Ltd. © 1995–2009.

When It's a Question of Missing Talent

Of course, we all hope our staff members will prove to be knowledgeable and skillful, and will take ownership of their tasks. Unfortunately, this isn't always the case. Sometimes we find that someone's performance is continually poor, even after a great deal of coaching and instruction. Sometimes it's just a case of missing talent. This is not a bad thing. It may mean things need to be reorganized.

Talent is different from knowledge or skill. Knowledge and skill can be learned; talent cannot. Knowledge consists of facts and lessons that can be learned. Skills are learnable. Talent, however, is a person's "naturally recurring patterns of thought, feeling or behavior. When you put all three (skills, knowledge, and talent) together, you get a strength" (Buckingham and Clifton, 2001, p. 29).

If you're uncertain whether or not someone has natural talent, check out the person's knowledge and skill first. Have him take a workshop or shadow someone. Give him the information and training he needs. Then, let him take on the task.

Give coaching for support. Ask what's working and what's not. Ask what he needs to fully take the task on. If, after all this, the person is still struggling *or* he really dislikes the task, it may be he simply doesn't have a talent for it.

Then you have some decisions to make. There are strategies you can consider to help someone manage when the problem is a lack of talent. Here is a personal example from a CompassPoint staff member:

> As a project director, I am fortunate enough to be able to apply a lot of my talents at work every day. I have a talent for relating to people, for learning quickly, and for accessing, processing, and managing a lot of information. I put these talents to use by coaching, training, and acting as a project manager. However, I do *not* have a talent for managing budgets. Unfortunately, budgets are a part of my job description. I am responsible for several programs with extremely large budgets. I can't *not* manage my budgets.
>
> Here's what I have done to manage for my lack of talent in this area: I took a Budgeting for Proposals workshop. I read a financial management book. I have regular meetings with my organization's finance team. I ask a colleague to double-check all my budgets before I submit them. Finally, I make sure that any project I manage includes a team member who is really good with numbers. I am still responsible for managing budgets. However, I've found strategies to manage for this area so that I can focus the majority of my attention on the things I'm really good at.

As a coaching manager, you can help your staff manage for tasks they aren't naturally talented at. You can also reassign the task to someone who is a better fit for it (if this is an option in your organization). You can read more about dealing with talents in *Now, Discover Your Strengths* (Buckingham and Clifton, 2001, pp. 48, 67).

When a Staff Member Is Not Improving

Although there are strategies for dealing with lack of talent, it may be that you've tried them and they haven't worked. We hear this frustration a lot. Someone on your team is lagging. You started by giving her enough space to figure things out. Yet she didn't respond. You helped her strategize ways to manage for the task. That didn't work either. Or maybe she has done well at a task before, but now she seems to be going backward. Both of you know there's room for improvement. You've tried telling her what to do. You've given her resources. Now this slowdown is having a negative impact on the whole program. What do you do?

First, assess how your own approach has been with this person. We encourage doing this first, because when a staff member isn't improving, we often see managers jump right to what that person did wrong. Instead, start with what role *you* might have played in this situation. Ask yourself these questions:

Were your expectations understood? Were standards clearly laid out from the start?

Was there a contract for action? (See Chapter Three.)

Have you only been telling the person what to do? Or have you helped the person think through the situation?

Have you helped the person break the task into manageable and achievable chunks?

Have you determined whether this is a knowledge, talent, or skill issue?

Have you been monitoring the person's progress? Does the person get timely feedback and coaching?

Is there an underlying issue you don't want to face or the other person doesn't want to face?

Have you been putting off giving the person help because you are too busy?

Have you backed off because you don't want others to think you are micromanaging?

Are you uncomfortable managing the person?

If you haven't adequately addressed what the person needs, you may need to acknowledge this and apologize. We are all human, and a little humility can go a long way.

Next, consider possible underlying reasons why the person isn't making progress:

Is she at a loss as to where to start because of lack of skills?

Is she disorganized and unable to prioritize her work?

Is she feeling overwhelmed?

Is she saying yes just to make you happy but then doesn't follow through?

Is she bored with the task?

Did she used to be proficient and now is not?

Does she want more challenge?

Does she appear to lack confidence?

Is there a talent mismatch?

Is she distracted by personal issues?

Is she just not a good fit for the organization at this time?

Has she not yet received adequate support?

Then assess how important the issue is.

- If it's a minor issue, it may not matter whether she improves or not.
- Even though the issue is small, it may have a big impact.
- You could give this small part of her job to someone else.
- If this is a central part of her job, there must be at least some improvement.
- If this is a central part of her job and it must get done correctly, you might have to give this job to someone else.
- Decide on the length of time your organization is willing to wait for necessary improvement.
- Decide how much time you or others can devote to helping her improve.
- If improvement doesn't happen in a reasonable time, you may decide that this person cannot remain in this position, or even within your organization.

Dealing with a staff member who is not performing can be a difficult process, but it is one that needs to be addressed for the sake of your organizational effectiveness and, really, for the benefit of the individual in question.

MORE OPPORTUNITIES TO COACH

Before we close this chapter, we want to give you some more ideas about how coaching can be used in an organization. Here are just some of the many activities in which a coaching approach may be useful:

Planning—to motivate creative thinking or to move things into manageable chunks

Problem solving—to consider all solutions and to bring about new perspectives

Decision making—to facilitate understanding and bring out the best thinking toward a decision being made or to support a plan for communicating decisions that have been made

Fostering collaborative environments—to bring all voices forward and create an inclusive experience

Developing strengths—to leverage and grow talent, knowledge, or skill

Managing for weaknesses—to develop strategies to make the job doable

Tackling difficult tasks—to break things down, open up possibilities, and create a plan

Fostering accountability—to create clear agreements about commitment to action

Creating awareness and adjustment of behavior—to bring to light new ways of being or to develop new habits

Refining communication and interpersonal skills—to develop expanded capacity

Managing change—to provide support for others to understand and buy into change

Developing leadership—to help a new leader expand how he or she sees and approaches situations and opportunities

Providing post-training—to turn knowledge and awareness into on-the-job action

Balancing work and life—to consider priorities and to create steadiness between both

In this chapter you learned the coaching approaches to use in different scenarios, as well as steps you may need to take when coaching just isn't working. Now you're fully prepared to apply the components we've covered: foundational skills, framework, mind-set, and approach. In Chapter Six, you learn how they can be used in concert, through real-life coaching scenarios drawn from the nonprofit workplace.

Coaching in the Nonprofit Workplace

How does coaching work in the real world? We asked participants from past Coaching Skills for Nonprofit Managers workshops to share their most pressing coaching questions. We include those questions and answers here so you can benefit from them. (Special thanks to Rich Snowdon for his contribution to this chapter.)

This chapter is organized into four broad topical sections about coaching in the nonprofit workplace:

- Coaching up, down, and across the organization
- Coaching and self-management
- Coaching in difficult situations
- Coaching top performers

Within each of these sections, we present the most common coaching questions we encounter in these areas. For each question, we provide you with a detailed explanation or approach to responding. Many of these discussions include a real-life scenario and dialogues drawn from our experience coaching nonprofit sector leaders and managers, as well as a list of questions we have found helpful in responding in each of these coaching situations.

169

For easy reference, we have also provided an index of the questions, with the page number each begins on, so you can quickly turn to the information you need.

Chapter Index

I have a staff member who is completely capable, but he's checked out. I don't think he really wants to be here anymore. How do I bring this up? (page 214)

I think a staff member needs therapy or personal counseling. What should I do? (page 218)

My staff member is not improving. What do I do? (page 219)

Coaching Top Performers

Should I use the coaching approach with my best performers? (page 228)

How can I use coaching to leverage my staff person's strengths and get her ready for a larger leadership role? (page 229)

I want to use coaching to develop the leadership of my staff, but how do I start? (page 233)

COACHING UP, DOWN, AND ACROSS THE ORGANIZATION

Question: When Do I Stay in Questioning Mode, and When Do I Need Simply to Tell People What to Do?

What's your goal in your particular situation? Is it to give people information so they can act on something? Or is it to foster learning and get people to develop themselves? If they need information or if it's their first time doing a task, you can simply tell people what they need to know. If it's time for them to brainstorm or take more initiative, then it's time to use your coaching skills (as discussed in Chapter Five).

Remember, coaching can fluctuate between inquiry (asking questions) and direction (telling someone what to do or instructing). However, a fundamental principle of coaching is that the people you're coaching can find solutions to their own problems. In this view, it's not your job to fix all things but simply to help others find solutions and develop a sense of responsibility. Be willing to set aside your own answers, even if it's difficult. However, there is nothing worse than watching people struggle with something they're new at when you can help them. Ask people what they need, and go from there.

If you answer yes to any of the following questions, go ahead and coach people instead of giving them answers:

Is this person fairly familiar with this task?

Do you know she can do the task or deal with this type of situation?

Is it time for this person to find answers for herself?

Is this person capable of thinking more about this situation?

Could this person learn from this situation if she thinks more about it?

Does this person need to use this situation to develop her thinking?

Have you been telling this person what to do for a while now?

Do you feel that "it's my job to give out answers to everything"?

Does this situation feel like an emergency, though in reality it isn't?

STAYING IN QUESTIONING MODE

Jess is an executive director of a women's health organization. Her associate director, Angela, is continually coming to her for solutions to problems in dealing with staff. Jess is really popular with her staff, in part because she's got an open-door policy and is always available to give people the answers to their problems. She's a fixer. Unfortunately, she's exhausted, behind on her fundraising deadlines, and stressed out because she doesn't have time to do her own work. She knows if she doesn't do something different, she won't be able to keep up.

Angela: Hey, have you got a minute?

Jess: Sure, what's up?

Angela: I'm really struggling with what to do about James. He keeps missing his deadlines, and when he does turn his work in, it's not very good.

Jess: You've come to me several times in the past couple of weeks about James. What do you think is going on here?

Angela: I don't know. I was hoping you could tell me. What am I doing wrong?

Jess: Well, I could give you some suggestions about what I think might be going on, but my guess is you've got some ideas yourself. How about if we think through this together?

Angela: That sounds good.

Jess:	What are your expectations of James?
Angela:	I expect him to turn in his stuff on time!
Jess:	When you say "turn in his stuff on time," what do you mean by that? What, specifically, do you want him to do and by when?
Angela:	Well, I need him to complete his research on potential funders and give me a list by the end of the week.
Jess:	If he did this right, what would the research look like to you?
Angela:	He would have used FC Search to find foundations that fund health care or women's issues, and he would put contact information and grant-giving guidelines in a spreadsheet.
Jess:	What else?
	[*Angela goes on to share her expectations of James.*]
Jess:	Have you shared these expectations with him?
Angela:	Well, not this specifically.
Jess:	So, what do you want to do about it?
Angela:	Well, I think I need to talk to him again to make sure he's clear about what I'm asking.
Jess:	What else do you think he might need to complete this task?
Angela:	I guess I need to ask him that, too. But I'm guessing he may not be very familiar with FC Search. It can be kind of hard to navigate. I should probably spend some time with him on that, since it's his first time.
Jess:	So, what's your plan?
Angela:	I'm going to talk to him today.
Jess:	Great! Let's check in after you've talked to see how it went.

Questions to Use When Determining When to Coach and When to Tell

When have you experienced something similar?

How can you use your abilities to find a solution?

How is this affecting your work?

What are your expectations in this situation?

What would success look like here?

Where are you in the process of making this work?

What have you not yet tried?

What ideas do you have?

What else can you consider?

What might you do differently this time?

Who or what could support you in this?

Here's my thought. What do you think?

Question: How Can I Use Coaching to Help New People Succeed?

What do you need to do, aside from getting people a desk, a phone, and the HR policies and procedures manual? (You have one, right?) First things first. Make sure you take care of the role-contracting piece (see Chapter One):

- Get clear about what the new staff member's role will be, whom he will report to on each program or project, and who will report to him. Make sure you know how to set clear expectations.

- Set clear goals and together gain agreement on expectations for each critical task he needs to complete. Be clear about standards that will be expected in the first thirty, sixty, and ninety days.

- Be clear about how much decision-making authority he has on each goal or responsibility area.

  Then, go into coaching:

- Ask the person what he loves to do, feels good about doing, and wants to learn in the future. This will help you figure out his potential talent. (Or have people take the Strengths Finder assessment found in Tom Rath's book *Strengths Finder 2.0*, 2007).

- Together with the person, assess his level of ability and confidence based on the task. Decide how much ownership and freedom he will have to do each task, and decide on the level of monitoring and feedback you'll provide.

- Talk about culture, how people operate in your organization, specific programs, and even how meetings are run.

- Put together a development plan.
- Make room for his questions and open exploration of possibilities.

When people are new to the organization or to a project, you'll need to strike a balance between how much information to give and how much space to let them think out loud about what they understand.

As you talk about how the organization or program works, be sure to use the coaching approach to access people's thinking. Just because they are new to the organization doesn't mean they are new to all the tasks they are being asked to do. By using the coaching approach, you can find out their skill level, past experience, questions, and concerns about their goals. You might pick up some great new ways to approach a goal or task. You can also follow these guidelines when someone is new to a role but not new to the organization.

HELPING NEW PEOPLE SUCCEED

A manager, Gerard, has just hired a new political organizer on to his team. He's really thrilled because Sebastian, the new guy, has a good reputation as an organizer and has some great contacts who will help the current campaign. Sebastian is fairly experienced, so Gerard wants to find out to what degree Sebastian can take on certain tasks and which tasks he'll need more support and help with.

Gerard: I know that was a lot of information about our staffing structure, the board, and our partners out in the field. Do you have any questions so far?

Sebastian: Yes. How am I going to be interacting with all the field team and our partners?

Gerard: One of your key goals will be to expand on your current relationships in the field. We need to communicate our message to the Office of Governmental Affairs. It's an important part of our fund development. We've heard a lot of good things about what you've been doing. How strong would you say your current relationships are in the field?

Sebastian: I really love working with the community organizers because they are so passionate about what they do. I'm still well

---

connected. A few people do know I was considering a change. They respect what you're doing here. [*Sebastian goes on to talk about his existing relationships and the help he'll need from the executive director.*]

Gerard: Great. Let's talk about how you'll go about getting the message out in a moment. Another of your goals is to bring this internal team together, build their skills, and connect people to your outside partners. Our last leader was a rather solo organizer. Given that, how do you think you can work best with Julio, Helena, and Bob, who will be on your team?

Sebastian: Well, I haven't given that much thought yet. This will be a first for me running a team. I'll be meeting with the team next week when they come into the office. Can you tell me about each one?

Gerard: I would like you to meet each person first. Then you and I can think together about each of the members of your team, what their strengths are, and how to maximize them. What do you think?

Sebastian: That will work. I'd like to also have a team integration meeting where they can ask anything they want about me, and they can let me know how they want to work together.

Gerard: That's really smart. We haven't done that before. Sounds great. Let's talk a bit about the other goals and tasks. As we break out all the pieces, I'd like you to simply say how much experience you have with each element and how comfortable you'd feel taking each part on, or how much direction and support you'd like up front. We really want you to succeed. Will that work for you?

Sebastian: Yes. This is great. I like the fact that we are getting clear up front. If I believe I need help, I'll be straight up about it. [*Gerard and Sebastian talk further about several of Sebastian's goals. Gerard keeps asking Sebastian to talk about how he will go about reaching those goals, to check how skilled and confident he is with each task.*]

> **Gerard:** We've covered quite a bit today. We've discussed where the campaign is currently, and you're clear about the list of critical tasks. How quickly do you want to get the message out to your network?
>
> **Sebastian:** I was thinking the sooner the better. I've composed an e-mail that I wanted your approval on before I send it tonight. [*Sebastian hands Gerard the e-mail composition. Gerard looks it over.*]
>
> **Gerard:** Looks on point. What challenges might we face with any of these relationships as you announce your move to our organization?
>
> **Sebastian:** Nothing I can think of.
>
> **Gerard:** OK. What else can we do to get you quickly working with the new external players?
>
> And so the conversation goes. Gerard is determined to help Sebastian get all the direction and support he'll need by being clear up front about his level of experience and confidence. The conversation culminates with a solid development plan that's set up to help Sebastian succeed in his first thirty days.

This process can also be used to help people succeed when they change roles within the organization or take on new programs or projects.

Questions to Use When Helping a Person New to a Role

What's your experience with . . . ?

What went well the last time you were involved with . . . ?

What would success look like for you in your role?

What will help you get up to speed?

What do you already know you'll need to get going with this task?

What systems are challenging you the most?

How do you feel about jumping in and trying . . . ?

So far, what are you learning about our ways of doing things?

Do you have any insights that we could learn from? What questions do you have about other people's roles or your own role?

What else can we tell you to make sure you're clear about how it all works?

What's the ideal working relationship we could have?

What are your expectations of me? How can I best support you?

Question: I Need to Delegate Something to a Staff Member. Can I Coach the Person While I Do That?

Delegate when all (or most) of these factors are present:

- You know the person is competent.
- The person has done the task or something similar before.
- The person is motivated to get the task done, and you are sure he will keep on it.
- The person is confident he can get it done with minimal monitoring.
- It's time for the person to be challenged because he's ready to take on new tasks.
- You've broken down a goal or task into smaller, manageable pieces. You're confident the person can take on these smaller pieces of the whole.
- It's time to let someone else take the lead, even though you're good at this task.

If you use a coaching approach when delegating, the other person gets to clarify his involvement, gain agreement on his plan, and have someone to brainstorm with.

What is the benefit for you in including a coaching approach while delegating? You know the other person is clear about the goal, the outcome, and your expectations. You also get to gauge his level of self-assurance and impetus toward the task.

Steps to Coaching While Delegating

1. Be clear about what you're asking for. Make sure you've communicated the expected work quality and the due dates.

2. Check for comprehension by asking the person what he understands about the delegated task.

3. Let the person lead the conversation about the *what* and the *how* of the action plan.

4. Ask the person about his thoughts and plans.

5. Be there to help the person think through issues before you leave the conversation.

6. Agree on follow-up procedures.

COACHING WHILE DELEGATING

Gustav is the manager delegating to Javier.

Gustav: We've got to get going now on that filing on the *Children's Trust of San Diego* v. *State of California*. I'd like you to personally handle this all the way through. You did so well on the last two cases. The papers need to be ready, in full, by Friday, the 31st, and taken down to the courthouse by February 2nd. And this time I want us to be sure we're ready with the allocation questionnaire so we can appeal straightaway. Does this seem reasonable? What are your thoughts?

Javier: I feel like we're ready to roll with this one. I'm OK with taking it on. It's just a matter of finding the time to fit it all in. I'll take it down myself once it's done. I know you're concerned about what happened last month. Don't worry.

Gustav: I'd appreciate your making this a priority; now we're up against the deadline. How soon do you think you can get going on this and move it up the priority list?

Javier: The research conclusion has been compiled. We've got most of the statements for the papers. Hmmm. I've still got three other public advocacy cases to present this week and next and a trip to Sacramento next week. Let me think. I suppose I could start it on Tuesday, which would give me at least nine days to submit.

Gustav: What needs to be moved to put this at the top of the list? Who can help here?

Javier: I could get Laura to take on more in the Helman Family Funds case. She's pretty well versed in the details. That would help alleviate some of the pressure.

Gustav: What else needs to move around?

> **Javier:** Let me take a look at the workload and see if there's anything else I can get support on. I know this will need to take precedence now that we're ready to go.
>
> **Gustav:** What else do you need once you've got the time worked out?
>
> **Javier:** Hmm. I'm going to need apportioning of the decree last submitted and the deposition that Julie worked up. I'll get it covered.
>
> *[Javier and Gustav talk over a few other planning ideas before ending their conversation.]*
>
> **Gustav:** Good. I'd like to suggest we check in within the week to see how things are coming along. What would work for you?
>
> **Javier:** Let me get to you by Friday. I'll give you an update and let you know where we are and if we need anything.
>
> **Gustav:** Great. Anything else?
>
> **Javier:** No. Thanks. This is helpful to just think through this now it's here.

Questions to Use When Delegating

How do you feel about getting this done for us?

What support will you need to succeed?

What authority do you need to get this done?

What's your strategy?

What measures do you need to take to ensure you'll get this done on time?

Who will you need to involve in this project/task?

What are your thoughts?

Do you think this is attainable, given the timelines?

What part of this seems simple, and what part of this might get challenging?

How much of a priority do you need to make this, given everything else you've got to do?

How much expertise or experience do you have with this type of thing?

What's the risk you see us needing to take here?

Question: I Was Promoted and Now I Supervise Someone Who Was My Peer. How Can I Use Coaching for This?

Being promoted from within a team is tough. This is true especially if you were close to your team members. And let's face it—this is often the case in informal nonprofit environments. It's understandable that you may be dealing with your own insecurities. Most people do have some level of insecurity, however well hidden. You will have to consider others' egos and opinions and how your position affects your future relationships. You may feel uncomfortable with your new role of delegating tasks to your former peers, giving people guidance and direction, or holding people accountable. This can feel especially challenging when there's a need to be liked and included in the group. Or you may feel completely comfortable with your new role, but your former peers are thinking: "Who is this person? Where did my friend go?" They might resent your promotion.

Fortunately, your transition can be smooth. First, it is important to clarify the following for yourself and with your former peer:

What are your personal feelings about these changes?

How does your new authority affect your former peer?

What are the key boundaries of your new role?

What has worked in this relationship before, and how will you leverage that in your new role?

If you are in possession of information that should not be shared with your former team members, how will you address requests to know what's going on?

How will you demonstrate immediate leadership that helps everyone adjust easily?

How will you manage both your new position and your prior friendships?

How will you deal with conflict? Can you speak openly if you disagree?

Clarification and clear agreements are necessary. Be sure to meet with your staff one on one very early on in the new relationship. Frequent conversations help avoid nasty surprises. You can stay a part of the social group yet learn how to keep the inside scoop inside. Remember, true friends want you to succeed, so be as honest with people as you want people to be with you. If someone doesn't care for your new promotion, allow time for feelings to pass. Focus on the work and what you both can do to serve your organization's mission.

COACHING A FORMER PEER

Hamish: [*A new manager.*] Let's talk about how we'll work together since my move into manager of advisory services for the West Coast. Talking about coasts—how was that vacation?

Angelo: The vacation was excellent. I got to surf a lot. I kind of wish I lived closer to the beach. Anyhow, I'm glad I'm back. Listen, I'm pleased for you getting this position. It's a bit sudden, but you deserve it. You've got some big shoes to wear now.

Hamish: Thanks a lot. I hope we can still carry on as we have before. How could it have been less surprising for you?

Angelo: I don't know. Seems like we kind of knew someone was going to get promoted, and yet it also seemed like no one was really talking about it.

Hamish: I appreciate your thoughts. From your perspective, what might change for you and me?

Angelo: Nothing. It's all fine with me.

Hamish: Is there anything or any situation you can think of that might feel weird with me being your supervisor?

Angelo: I guess it will be weird that you'll be doing my review from now on. You'll score me high, right? [*Laughs.*]

Hamish: That's a good example of the formalities I'll have to take on as your manager. What might I do that would be weird?

Angelo: Maybe if you had to tell me that I'm not doing something really well. Or if you had to tell me to get better at something I do regularly. I guess if you needed to discipline me. That could be really strange.

Hamish: Let's try to make this easy for both of us. So, let's talk about what's being expected of me now from the associate director's point of view. We can also talk about how we might handle things that will be different.

[*Hamish and Angelo discuss the new role. They get clear about the types of duties Hamish will have to carry out and which things he has the authority to oversee.*]

Hamish: You're really my right hand when it comes to the sustainable loans programs and healthy financing for our nonprofit partners, among other things. If I had to ask you to do something quicker, faster, differently, how could I ask that in a way that would work for you and me?

Angelo: I'm really not sure. I guess just like you did before.

Hamish: What if I needed to ask you to change something you're doing or shift the way you approach recipient organizations? How could we discuss these things so you and I both stay open to the conversation?

[*Hamish and Angelo talk about how to approach future conversations.*]

Hamish: I'll need to get used to my role. Let's keep talking about how best to make it work for everyone. As I learn more about my duties and responsibilities, I'll be sure to let you in on as much as I can. Will you do me one favor?

Angelo: Yes. What?

Hamish: If the team needs me to be or do something differently, please be straightforward with me. Let me know about it. I don't want unaddressed issues to become sources of discontent.

Angelo: Yes, I'll tell you what I can.

Hamish: Are there any other questions you have about my role and how we'll work together?

Angelo: No. If I have thoughts, though, you know I'll come to you.

Hamish: Thanks for having this conversation and staying really open.

Questions to Use When Coaching a Prior Peer

How do you feel about the new position?

From your perspective, what might this mean for our relationship?

What has changed for you now that I'm the manager of our group?

How can we best work together, given the new situation?

What's most important to you about our new relationship structure?

How might I best approach you if we need more, better, additional . . . ?

What questions do you have about my role?

What else do you want to know about my new position?

Even though I'm now your manager, will you continue to be open to mutual feedback and making direct requests?

From your perspective, how does the team feel about my promotion?

What are your personal feelings about these changes?

Question: What If I'm Coaching Someone Who Doesn't Report to Me?

Even without formal authority to help people, you can partner in their thinking to bring about all manner of improvement. Help people get out of their heads and into action. First, you can ask permission to use a coaching approach. Simply ask, "Would it be useful if we think about this together?"

COACHING SOMEONE WHO DOESN'T REPORT TO YOU

Cassandra works with Ella at a local agency, helping place children with disabilities in public schools. Cassandra is a fund development staff member, and Ella is a fairly new supervisor in the finance department. They've known each other only a few months. Cassandra has been having lunch with Ella for a few weeks. Cassandra notices that Ella is sounding a bit down. At lunch one day, Cassandra decides to talk with Ella about how she's doing. She realizes Ella might need some coaching. The lunchtime crowd is thinning, and now they have privacy at their table.

Cassandra: Last week, you mentioned you were a bit nervous about the upcoming budgets. In my experience, it feels like a really big deal. And then it's over. You'll see. How are you feeling about it?

Ella: I wish I felt that way. I've got to be honest, I'm feeling a little overwhelmed with this new budgeting software. It's more complicated than the one I'm used to. I know it's me, not the system. I'm still trying to learn how to use it, and now the budgets are coming due.

Cassandra: What else is bothering you?

Ella: Well, I've been asked to analyze why we're running $10,000 over budget. We thought we were on target. It looks like something happened in George's group. It might be that they forgot to collect a grant they said they would have by March. There just seems to be rather a lot of disorganization.

Cassandra: Sounds like it's a lot to deal with all at once. What else is making you feel overwhelmed?

Ella: Just more bickering going on in the department than I'm used to. It's not about me. It just seems people are a bit unhappy.

Cassandra: Yes, it's been that way for a while. I'm sorry you're stepping into the mayhem. They do get frantic around budget time. Then they all celebrate after. What will help you get more settled with all of this?

Ella: I really don't know.

Cassandra: Well, would it help if you and I think together about what you need for each issue?

Ella: Sure.

Cassandra: Who could support you with this?

Ella: Well, I could ask Arturo, who's totally a whiz on the system. Lots of people go to him, though. I don't want to bother him.

Cassandra: You know something? I bet it wouldn't bother him. He's really nice and cares a lot about his teammates. What would you like him to show you?

[Ella goes on to tell Cassandra the five key things that would help her get up to speed on the budgeting software.]

Cassandra: So when's the right time to approach him?

Ella: I guess I'll just go and do that after lunch. Actually, it would be a relief to get some help with the system.

Cassandra: What do you need to clarify the situation with the missing $10,000?

Ella:	I need to investigate if the grant was dropped, went somewhere else, or if we got it and put it in the wrong account. I don't want George to feel like I'm probing so I can make him wrong.
Cassandra:	How could you set the context so he'd feel OK about it?
Ella:	Hmmm. Let me think.
	[*Cassandra and Ella continue talking during lunch. Cassandra fills Ella in on anything she can about the people and the organization. She poses simple questions to help Ella think through the issues.*]
Ella:	Thanks so much for your help. I feel a bit better now. At least I know what to do next. Thanks again.
Cassandra:	You're welcome.

Questions to Use When Coaching Someone Who Doesn't Report to You

What's on your mind?

Would it be useful to think together about this?

What are you trying to achieve here?

What do you know that can help here?

How do you need and want to approach this situation?

How does this all add up for you?

What seems to be the real problem?

What do you need to think about?

Who is really involved?

What's so important about this situation?

How is your involvement helping or hindering the situation?

Whom do you need to talk to in order to move on this?

Question: How Can I Coach People I Report To?

First, let's talk about the difference between *managing up* and *coaching up*. Managing up involves working with your supervisor to ensure expectations are understood and you are able to work with her to achieve results for yourself and the organization. Managing up is primarily about *your* role as it relates to your supervisor. What does your supervisor expect from you? What do you need from her in order to meet the mission?

Coaching up isn't about you at all. It's about your supervisor. It's applying the same principles you've learned in this book to help another person think in order to achieve better results. Only this time, it happens to be your supervisor. Before you try to coach up, ask yourself a few questions:

Did she ask for coaching?

Do you have a relationship with your supervisor that includes trust and mutuality?

Is she willing to listen to your feedback and your ideas?

If you answered yes to these questions, then go ahead and coach. If your manager wants some coaching, it's your duty to help her think.

If you answered no, then pause for a moment. When coaching is not solicited by a manager, you do need to get permission to coach. Your supervisor must be receptive to coaching. She must be willing to listen to your feedback and to your ideas.

If there is a particular topic in which you would like to coach your supervisor, you also need to do some preparation. Before you meet, do the following:

- Lay out your facts.

- Think about what she cares about. What's important to her? What does she value?

- Know what you're requesting. What change in her behavior, focus, or leadership would best benefit the organization?

- Spin any grumblings or complaints you or others have about her from negative "it's not happening" statements into positive statements such as, "Here's what might be better for us or the organization."

- Plot out the link between your reason for bringing this to your supervisor and the needs of the mission. Prepare a conversation that maps back from the mission, the strategy to get there, the needs that have to be met by all of you, to the focus of your conversation.

- Prepare any feedback or examples. Make sure your feedback is tied into team or organizational goals (see the discussion of giving feedback in Chapter Two).

When you meet, do this:

- Tell this person you would not be bringing up the subject if you didn't care about her. Or say you know she cares deeply about the issue, and that's why you would like to talk with her.
- Ask if it would be OK to talk about something that will have the maximum benefit for the staff, the clients, the organization, or the community.
- Decide to be an engaged listener. Try to understand the other person's perspective (see the section on listening in Chapter Two).
- Stay open and curious.
- Use the coaching framework (see Chapter Three).
- Use inviting language.
- Don't accuse or judge.
- Let her talk. Redirect if she gets off track.
- Ask how she would like to look at the situation.

Question: What Does a *Culturally Aware* Coaching Manager Look Like?

In some ways, a culturally aware coaching manager's job is to be a continual student. The coaching manager needs to question assumptions, probing multicultural perspectives. First check your own then others' perceptions. The culturally aware coaching manager recognizes that each person and situation is unique. This offers new opportunities for learning for the person being coached, as well as for the coaching manager. Our discussion and scenario of culturally aware coaching comes from the work of Prism Coaching.

BEING A CULTURALLY AWARE COACHING MANAGER

A young Asian American woman is the associate director at a nonprofit organization that has a hardworking board of mostly white business professionals. The executive director wants to share leadership and is developing the associate director to take on a larger role

---

with the board. The organization's staff is primarily young people with a vision and high commitment to improving their communities. The associate director is seen by her own staff as "boss," "leader," maybe even "mother." The board, on the other hand, views her as a "youth" and unconsciously applies the stereotypical Hollywood image of Asian women in their heads. Although the staff may think of her as powerful, the board sees her as just the opposite. In fact the board often undermines her authority, deferring decisions to the executive director only.

A culturally aware coaching manager could support the associate director to recognize her own cultural perspective as valuable. The cultural dynamics at work are not only issues of race. Age, gender, and socioeconomic differences also play subtle and not-so-subtle roles.

If the executive director is acting in a coach role and engages in culturally aware coaching, what might happen? She might guide the associate director to brainstorm ways in which she could voice her vision and assert her own leadership style. She could address whether she is being seen in a stereotypical role. If there are areas of skills development she needs to acquire, the executive director can help her identify them and map out strategies to meet her goals within this landscape of cultural assumptions.

Here are some examples of questions that might be explored for this particular situation:

What are the values of the board and staff members?

Where are they in synch, and where are they conflicting?

How might their cultural values affect how they see each other's roles?

How might the board president and the associate director work in tandem to bring the two bodies together in determining their jobs for achieving joint goals?

Where can the executive director support this process?

A culturally aware coaching manager is able to identify that cultural norms are affecting interactions and tailor her coaching approach to the particular person and situation she is working with.

COACHING AND SELF-MANAGEMENT

Question: I'm Really Angry with This Person and Need to Have a Conversation. What Do I Do?

Here's the short answer: Don't coach. Remember that coaching is meant to support individuals. If you're in a situation where your emotions start to take over, they will prevent you from staying objective and supportive. We recommend you refrain from coaching until the issue is resolved. Here are some potential steps to consider:

First, step away from the situation and get some perspective. If you become upset with someone when you're in a meeting, it's perfectly OK to ask for time to clear your head. Reschedule the meeting for a later date.

Next, take a couple of minutes to get the anger out of your system. When you're so upset with someone you can't see straight, it's impossible to be objective until you've had the chance to vent a little. Here's an exercise for you. Set your watch or a timer for two minutes. Then spend the next two minutes getting all your frustrations out. Write them down, or say them aloud to yourself. This is two minutes of uncensored venting. As soon as the two minutes are up, *stop*. Take a breath and move on.

Spend some time in reflection. We suggest you write down some of your thoughts. Here are questions to consider:

What's really going on here?

What actions did you observe that are upsetting you?

How did those actions make you feel?

What are your needs in this situation?

What is it that you really want from this person?

What is your request of this person?

Take some time here to understand what you'd like. Is it behavior change? Did he do something you want him to stop doing? Did he *not* do something you would like him to do? Be sure to think about the rules of feedback here. Be specific.

Consider the other person's perspective for a moment. What might his needs be? You may be feeling angry. But he may not have intentionally set out to make you angry. He may not be aware of your anger. Or he may be feeling upset as well. What you need to do is ask.

When you're ready for a conversation, share the concrete actions that you observed and how those actions made you feel. Share your needs. Be specific about what you'd like this person to do. Remember, only have this conversation when you can be objective and unemotional.

Our basic concepts for this topic were adapted from Marshall Rosenberg's *Nonviolent Communication: A Language of Life* (2003, pp. 6–7.) If you are interested in going deeper into this topic, we recommend this book.

Question: I Don't Have Time! How Do I Coach Someone When She's Come to Me with a Problem and I Have Only a Few Minutes?

Informal coaching moments pop up all over the place. Can you still coach when you don't have a lot of time? Yes! When you don't have much time, yet a coaching moment presents itself, be sure you do the following:

- Use the coaching framework (Chapter Three) and the coaching skills (Chapter Two) to make sure people are heard, become focused, and get to solutions a lot quicker.

- Set time boundaries. It is perfectly appropriate to let a person know you have four, five, or ten minutes. It's better to be clear about time than to disconnect five minutes into the conversation because you have to leave.

- Find out if this issue might be resolved in five minutes. If not, ask if you could put the conversation off until later.

- Ask what the person needs from the conversation. Does he just need to vent, discuss an issue, or report some news? Provide engaged attention and prompt him with simple questions. Be clear when you only have one minute left.

- If the issue seems complex, clarify up front what the important point is (as discussed in Chapter Three). Get him to focus. Don't be afraid to gently interject to keep him on track. Don't go backward. Ask what he hasn't yet tried, in order to move the conversation forward.

- Get comfortable with a few back-pocket questions. (See "Judith's Back-Pocket Questions" in Chapter Two.) Just five to ten of these questions can help keep everyone on track.

- We live in a world on the go. You can coach by phone and in person. If people need to do some thinking with you when you're not in the office, feel free to coach by phone. Approximately 95 percent of the coaching we do is by phone.

Remember, you'll need to stay connected by using engaged listening while coaching. Warning: don't coach and drive!

- Remember, you may help the person get clear about the situation and yet may not have time to resolve the issue. It's acceptable to leave him with something to ponder. You might say: "I'd like you to consider this until we meet again." Then ask a question.

COACHING WHEN YOU HAVE ONLY A FEW MINUTES

Emily is a service manager for a refugee organization. She has eight direct reports. Emily finds herself in meetings far more often than she wants. This limits the amount of time she has to help her staff. Ursula is one of Emily's direct reports. Ursula stops Emily in the corridor between their offices.

Ursula: Emily, I'm so pleased to see you. Listen, I'm in conversation with a new local business that has a major plant opening up. I feel I'm not able to move forward until I get to talk to you. There's so much going on, I need to get this done so I can get on with other things.

Emily: I'm sorry I haven't been around. I've got about ten minutes right now if we can find a room to talk.

Ursula: I'd really appreciate any time you can give me on this. I've got to work it out.

Emily: OK, let's step in here. So what's your question? [*Emily quickly focuses herself, knowing there are only ten minutes until her next meeting.*]

Ursula: Hmm. They want us to guarantee transportation and housing for anyone they take on. That's not something we guarantee, though it is something we can handle. I don't want to miss this opportunity because this business's plant is so well situated. I don't know how to respond.

Emily: Let's be clear about what we realistically can or can't do. What do you know?

[*Ursula explains what she does know and understand.*]

Emily: What's your biggest question?

Ursula:	Whether or not we can show them how the transportation and housing support services really work—how they support the worker. I don't want to scare this group off, though.
Emily:	What do you think the company's greatest fear is?
Ursula:	People having problems and not showing up for work.
Emily:	What have you done in the past to calm those fears?
	[*Ursula goes on to think about and share the tricky situations she's dealt with before.*]
Emily:	Given that, what will be needed in this situation?
Ursula:	OK, I think it means more than communicating our message. We need to sit down and help this company see how successful we are at partnering with housing and transportation.
Emily:	Who could help you prepare what you need?
Ursula:	Probably Keith Lawson. He dealt with a situation when the plant manager at Leaf Systems had similar issues.
Emily:	That sounds like a good idea. What else do you need?
	[*Ursula talks about the next steps she can take.*]
Emily:	By when can you get that ready?
Ursula:	Friday morning. I'm going to meet with people again next Tuesday.
Emily:	We've got a couple of minutes. What else do you need in this conversation?
Ursula:	Do you have any feedback for me about the general progress of this new inclusion program?
	[*Emily goes on to give Ursula feedback.*]
Emily:	If you want me to connect you with anyone else, please let me know. I'm sorry I haven't been around much with all that's going on with the elections.
Ursula:	Well, thanks for your time today. If I hear anything new, I'll let you know.

Questions to Use When You Don't Have Much Time

What do you need most in this conversation?

What is most important out of everything you are saying?

What can we address right now?

What has got to be resolved?

What are your options?

What have you not yet tried that might be useful?

Who else can help you on this?

What other resources can you tap?

What can you do?

What must you do next?

What support do you need?

When do you need to get going on this?

COACHING IN DIFFICULT SITUATIONS

Question: How Do I Coach Someone with a Know-It-All Attitude Who Doesn't Think She Needs Help?

This kind of person may be lacking in self-awareness and may not even be aware that others have anything to say. Your task is to help build self-awareness. Here are some things to remember as you coach an overconfident person:

- Acknowledge what she brings to the table. Talk with her about using her capacity to engage and help others.

- Encourage self-awareness. Help her realize the impact she has on people and situations. This will take courage on your part.

- Prepare to give behavioral feedback. Be ready with specific examples.

- Speak to what is required of her and avoid talking about how wrong she is. Keep the conversation focused on what is needed.

- Get her to brainstorm new ways of behaving. You may need to help generate options.

- Help her find ways to adapt to different audiences.

- Discuss how to stay open to other people's input and opinions.

- Don't take it personally when she corrects you, takes charge, or informs you. Express thanks and gently ask her to stay open to guidance.

- Don't argue with her. Come back to the issue at a later date if necessary.
- Manage the amount of time she talks. She may go off on tangents. Keep her focused on your request for growth.
- Ask questions that make her go beyond her current thinking.
- Be ready to address underlying issues that drive the person, such as fear, competition, and the need for respect.

COACHING SOMEONE WITH A KNOW-IT-ALL ATTITUDE

Jim is a medical director at an international organization pioneering health care initiatives in the developing world. His job is to oversee the clinical care of patients and the education and training for physicians, nurses, and caregivers in three third-world countries. He's part of a team that will be submitting a paper to a well-known journal. This is a big deal because it will give the organization more exposure than it's ever had.

Due to missed deadlines, the funding to write the paper is long gone. Team members have complained to their leader, Annette. As they see it, Jim's behavior is insulting. He doesn't listen to anyone and has to have the last word. They believe Jim thinks he should write the paper alone because they have nothing to say and are incapable of writing with him. The team sees Jim as the reason they are behind schedule. Jim is displaying characteristics that lead the team to label him a know-it-all. Annette needs to help him see his impact.

Annette: Jim, thanks for stopping by today. We need to talk about how to continue to best manage the work going on with the "Medical Care in Third-World Countries" paper. I'd like to discuss some feedback about your part in the missed deadlines and your treatment of the team.

Jim: You're right. Everyone seems all over the place. I have to constantly remind people about our focus and what the heck we need to be doing right now. No one listens to me. It's as if they feel they could just do it without me. What nonsense. They know this has been my full focus for nearly a decade now. I'm actually sick of how slowly everyone's progressing on this paper.

Annette: You do have the longest history with the program. You know the subject very well. Now I'd like to get to the feedback I was talking about. May I share it?

Jim: Oh, I'm sure they've got feedback now. But where were they when I asked for their opinions on the article? So what are they saying?

Annette: You have a great deal of knowledge about how to submit a paper because you've done it several times before. In the last four interactions with the team, you have stepped in to lead the meetings. You have also not asked for input from the team on the paper. As a result, team members feel they are unable to participate fully. Several have commented that you come across to them as more of a teacher. And an impatient teacher, at that. Does this sound true for you?

Jim: I'm not here to teach them anything, but I feel like I have to.

Annette: What do you suppose you need to teach them?

Jim: I know what'll make sense to journal reviewers. I've done this before. I know what reviewers want to see.

Annette: How do you see people responding to your approach?

Jim: Who cares at this point? Someone needs to whip them into shape. We've been going around in circles for too long. It's time to move on.

Annette: What contribution do you think others bring to the table?

Jim: Oh, they've plenty of field experience. Everyone just needs to get on with it, though. They always want to talk first. I've made it clear how we need to write this. It's to the point where I'm repeating myself. If they'd just listen to me a bit more, we might have this thing written.

Annette: What other role could you take with them that would help?

Jim: I don't know.

Annette: Well, right now, they say you block every idea. What if you could facilitate their thinking instead of degrading it? What would that look like?

Jim:	Not sure what you mean.
Annette:	Well, what would it look like if you posed intriguing questions to help people with their thinking? Turn your directives into questions to think about.
Jim:	I see where you're coming from. If I know there are questions about the research, I could ask them what they're thinking so I don't sound like I'm the only one with answers.
Annette:	How else could you shift the way you guide people? What other questions might elicit focused thinking? [Jim and Annette look at several different approaches until Jim is clear he could take another approach.]
Annette:	Your membership in this team is important. The changes you make will serve those patients you've worked with over the last decade. All of you deserve to be heard and recognized. Now how will you control your patience? [Jim goes on to talk about his fear related to being the only person on the team with experience getting a paper published. He's worried about the deadline. Annette helps him see they will survive and that getting the paper completed is a first priority. She coaches Jim to see how his fear is driving his behavior with others.]
Jim:	I've got to say that I really didn't know what was going on. I know that it's hard for me to work with so many young people. You know how that is. There's so much catching up for them.

Annette sees Jim's last comment as a potential opening to explore his assumptions about working with younger people. They go there next.

Questions to Use When Coaching an Overconfident Individual

What do you think others contribute?

Where's your trust on this issue?

How can you include others more often?

How do you think you're helping this group?

If you allow others to talk as much as you do, what might they say?

What's your greatest fear?

What's your perspective, and how does it match those of others?

What is going well, and what are the facts about any real problems?

What are you really trying to say?

What other ways can you stay in charge yet let go of command?

What tone do you think would work better with this group?

What if you can learn something, too? Can you stay open to that?

Question: What Can I Do About Someone I Supervise Who Is Constantly Complaining?

It's OK for someone to share an opinion. It's OK to take a stand on something we believe in. It's OK to have expectations. It's OK to express disappointment. It's *not* OK to complain in a way that has a negative impact on others. While it's true that a few people appear to love complaining, most complaints come from unmet needs. Instead of looking for positive solutions, people fall back on voicing dissatisfaction. The goal of coaching someone who complains is to help the person make a choice about how to proceed.

Coaching skills have helped me improve how I approach problematic employees. It has given me the tools to better handle the issues at hand.

—Andrea M. Finley, director,
program development, Child Care Links

Look at complaining as the vocalization of unmet needs or unspoken requests. It's an opportunity to help the person think more about what she can do. What choices does she have? What decisions can she make about how to respond from this moment forward?

- Remember: the goal of your coaching is to take a person out of spinning negative energy and into a place of choice and action. If she needs time to vent, let her. Allow her two minutes to get all her frustration out, and then focus on solutions.

- Acknowledge the complaint, even if you don't agree with its context or content. Simply acknowledge that the person is having an issue with something.

- Use neutral language. Try not to assume how someone feels.

- Stay objective as you acknowledge the person's situation. You can say things like, "You sound like you see things differently," "You appear to think it could be done another way," or, "This seems to be having an effect on you right now."

- Focus on expanding the other person's thinking. Keep your opinions to yourself.

- Believe the person can find another path. Help her see the old problem in a new way.

- Help the person understand what she can influence. This avoids feelings of hopelessness.

- Don't tolerate negative thinking. Do point out that it would help the person to think about what she can do, not what she cannot do. Keep advocating toward choice and decision.

- Hold the person accountable for doing something different, soon.

COACHING THE CONSTANT COMPLAINER

Alfonso and Jamie are both property managers in an affordable housing agency. Jamie has been pulling Alfonso aside to complain about her colleagues. There have been delays affecting Jamie's ability to process new tenants. Jamie blames the delays on her colleagues' ineffectiveness. Alfonso has had it with Jamie talking behind people's backs. He knows she's upset with delays on two recently finished buildings. He also knows how deeply Jamie cares about early tenancy, with so many people on the waiting list. Alfonso has started to avoid meeting with Jamie because she won't stop whining about her other colleagues. This has been going on for two weeks now. However,

Jamie corners Alfonso again, and this time Alfonso uses a coaching approach.

Jamie: I've had it up to here with Bettina and April. They know how serious filing their plans is. They couldn't go any slower if they tried. It's the last time I'm going to be bothered to help people out if they don't start moving faster.

Alfonso: You sound like you've had enough.

Jamie: Yes, I have. I'm really angry that Samuel can't get his act together. What's up with that guy! I'm just sick of his antics.

Alfonso: Well, you've been talking like this for over two weeks. Do you want to figure out a way to deal with people differently?

Jamie: There is no dealing with people. I'm not their manager. In fact, if their manager would actually be here a bit more, something might change!

Alfonso: Desmond is out doing a lot of collaborative work with JCS right now. He's aware that you are working with people. What do you want from Bettina, April, and Samuel? What needs to happen? And, look, instead of just coming from that heated place, think about what you could actually do to influence the situation.

Jamie: Oh, that's hopeless! They'd shut me down in minutes.

Alfonso: How could you have a conversation they could benefit from?

Jamie: I don't know what you mean.

Alfonso: May I offer some thoughts here?

Jamie: Yes.

Alfonso: What if you could help people understand the impact that time has on the tenants? If you look at the situation without all the emotion, what is the real reason you want this to change? What's so important that you feel compelled to have people go faster? What's your rationale?

Jamie: [*Whining.*] You know as well as I do that . . .

Alfonso: Hold on a moment. You are so good at finding solutions with other issues. Are you willing to let me help you think about it?

Jamie: I suppose so. You make it sound like I'm being negative. Do I sound that negative?

> *Alfonso:* On this issue, yes. You have come to me the past two weeks with complaints about your colleagues. And I know you could do something here, so let's see what else you can do. What's the most useful thing you can help people think about without accusing them of being a problem?
>
> *Jamie:* Hmm. Good question.
>
> Alfonso spends a little time to help his coworker think things through. Finally, Jamie agrees to approach the building development managers from a different perspective and make some new requests.

Questions to Use When Coaching Someone Who Complains

How is what you are saying helping the situation?

How does the way you think about this situation affect you and others?

What have you not yet asked for?

What do you want here more than anything?

What must you request?

If this moment could be different, how would you design it?

What will help the situation right now?

What is really going on between you and others in this conversation?

What other perspective could you take right now?

What other alternatives can you see working?

Where else might others be coming from?

What action must you take if things don't go your way?

Question: How Do I Coach Someone Who Keeps Everything in and Then Explodes?

Our discussion and scenario of dealing with a person who keeps things that annoy her to herself for a time but then explodes and gets angry with staff comes from the work of Rich Snowdon.

COACHING SOMEONE WHO EXPLODES

You could discipline this person for being so explosive, yet there's a big advantage to trying the coaching approach before taking corrective action. If you can make a positive connection with the person to motivate her to stop this behavior, there is a far greater chance for long-term success. You can always fall back on enforcement if you need to.

First thing is to make sure you take care of yourself. Get clear before confronting staff. Be ready to look at the person's behavior without judgment. This often breaks the spell and allows the person to connect with the part of herself that doesn't really want to be acting this way. Once you've got that connection, you suddenly have a very different conversation. Try to get the person to talk about what she's hoping to achieve or what she needs that's driving the sudden outbursts. Help her see the cause. Be ready to talk about feelings as necessary. She cares about something, deeply. Don't make her wrong. The explosive behavior is unacceptable, yet the person has needs that are not being met. Coach to find out what these feelings or needs are and what can be done about them. Coach the person to find a way to manage herself.

In the following example, you'll see the manager take the pressure off the person who had the outburst. The manager uses a strategy of "being with" that person. The first thing she does is to connect; she puts the staff person first and the problem second. Pressure is not applied. Understanding and forward thinking is.

Scenario

Carol: You know, Chris, right now I'm thinking about Monday when you yelled at Jessica, and then yesterday when you yelled at Judy and pounded your fist on the table. Most of the time you cruise along just fine, but then out of the blue, you explode. What's going on for you?

Chris: Sometimes I have to do that to get my point across.

Carol: Well, that's what I want to talk with you about during this supervision meeting. But I want to do the opposite of supervision.

Chris: That sounds scary.

Carol: It might be. What I want to do is just understand. During this meeting I promise I won't ask you to do anything different from what you're doing. I just want to ask you what it's like when you are in the middle of an explosion and what it's like in the aftermath. Would you be willing to have that conversation with me?

Chris: That's really weird. No one has ever asked me that before.

Carol: And?

Chris: Let me think about it for a minute. Why do you want to understand?

Carol: Because when you have an explosion, it upsets the rest of us. It makes us distance ourselves from you, and we don't want to do that. It creates a tense, unhappy atmosphere. And that's contrary to our organizational guidelines.

Chris: OK, so what do you want to know?

Carol: What's really going on for you before, during, and after an outburst?

Chris: I don't know. People are annoying.

Carol: People sometimes are annoying. What do you know about yourself when you respond like that?

Chris: I guess what sets me off is when the work my staff does doesn't meet my standards. I guess being a manager means your staff won't like you.

Carol: Wait a minute! The most important thing is that the people here really want to like you. They feel intimidated by you when you explode with no warning. But everyone knows how dedicated you are. Not one person has trashed you.

Chris: Wow! That kind of pulls the rug out from under me. I didn't realize I was having that kind of impact on them.

Carol: I kind of thought maybe you didn't.

Chris: I really didn't. What should I do to fix this?

Carol: You know I could just tell you to stop it. And you could tell yourself to stop it. But I don't want to handle it that way. I'm not sure that it would change anything. When you yelled at Judy, do you know what got you started?

Chris: Hmm. When I got the report on diabetes prevention, I realized she was so far off the mark. It wasn't what I asked for. So I blasted her.

Carol: What could you do to make sure work gets done right the first time? What questions needed to be asked before you blasted her?

Chris: Well, I'm always moving so fast, maybe too fast. Maybe I should slow down and take more time explaining what I want and what the standards are. And then maybe I could ask the person to repeat back to me what I've said so I know I've been clear. And maybe I need to do check-ins along the way. Hmm. All of a sudden it doesn't sound so hard. Maybe I've been too frustrated to stop and think things through.

Carol: I know how much pressure your department is under. You take on the biggest projects here.

Chris: Yes, but that's no excuse for blasting someone.

Carol: So what's the next step?

Chris: I'm going to make a promise, to you and to myself, that from now on I'll take the time at the front end of a project so I don't explode at the back end. And I need to apologize to Jessica and Judy, which I want to go do right now. And next time I want to talk with you about this some more. I really don't want to be somebody who intimidates people . [*Chris goes on to talk about what she cares most about, what her value system is, and what she expects in herself and others.*]

Carol: What does this self-knowledge mean?

Chris: It probably means I have high standards. But it doesn't mean everyone has the same standards.

Carol: What else?

Chris: Maybe I need to clarify more what I need up front. Perhaps I need to check on things along the way so I don't become so disappointed all the time.

Carol: And if you did that, then what would change?

Chris: I'd feel like I was more in charge along the way and not have to explode when I get disappointed at the end.

Carol: So, is this about how to stay in charge of the work, the people, and yourself?

Chris: Good point. I think it is. And I don't want to be nasty, making sure things get done. It's not me.

Carol: How would you like to handle taking charge and also manage disappointing situations in the future?

Chris: I'd like to be much more balanced and more patient; more understanding. But also clear about what must be done. I really do believe I have a lot of smarts. What if I could use my smarts to help manage the situation better? Now there's a thought.

Carol: What if you can?

Chris: I want that! But right now, I want to go find Judy and apologize. I want to tell her what went wrong and make a deal with her on this new report that's due next month. This time we'll set aside enough time to have a conversation about partnering appropriately on the reports.

Carol: Cool. I know you can be a great partner in everything you do. People want partnership. Would you be OK if I continue to monitor the situation with you and give you feedback over the next few weeks?

Chris: Yes, that would be great. I'll be more aware of my emotions and look to what I can do to keep up a good relationship. I'll see you next week then.

Source: Copyright © 2008 by Rich Snowdon. Reprinted by permission.

Questions to Use When Coaching Someone Who Explodes

What's really going on for you?

What's driving your feelings?

Where did this come from?

What makes you come across the way you do?

What's causing you to say that?

How can you better manage your emotions?

How does this relate to your other concerns?

What's true, and what assumptions might you be making?

What causes you to have such a hard time with this?

What impact are you having on other people?

How can you better manage your response to disappointment?

How open can you be to another person's different point of view?

Question: How Do I Coach Someone Who Is Resistant?

Resistance is like a momentary refusal to accept change. Have you noticed how easy it is to get someone to buy into a goal, yet it's so much harder to get agreement on what it will take to get to it? This is because we all have different responses based on our needs and fears. Resistance is reluctance to face necessary change. Unchecked, the refusal to accept change causes problems. The longer you tell yourself a story about "why not," the greater the chance temporary resistance turns into digging your heels in. Defiance is self-perpetuating. It can be fueled by your own thinking or by negative group chatter. It's hard—if not impossible—to coach someone who feels contempt. It's smarter to coach resistance early on before it becomes toxic.

Behind most resistance lies a lack of trust. The employees' question "why?" hasn't been answered. And there is nothing like lack of inclusion and secretiveness to destroy trust. There are five main reasons people resist:

1. *Unmet needs.* Management doesn't ask staff what they need before making decisions. Responses sound like this: "I'm not that interested in what's being asked of me." "I don't understand how this change will really affect me." "I agreed to use the new computer system, but it doesn't work well enough for me, so I'm not going to."

2. *Lack of safety.* People need to feel secure. When security is threatened it sounds like this: "I like the way I always do this. It's comfortable now. I don't want to give up doing it this way". "Someone is causing problems, and I'll have nothing to do with them." "I'm going to get a new leader." "I like my old leader." "Why try hard when we don't know if there will be layoffs."

3. *Lack of investment in time or financial resources.* This lack of support might be reflected in attitudes like this: "I don't really want to do more without a promotion." "I don't want to make more effort with less support." "My program has been expanded, and I was hoping to be finished by now."

4. *Threatened identity.* Perceived threats to identity might come across in this way: "I've been passed over for a promotion again so why try so hard?"

"I received development feedback from several people to improve performance, but I think I am fine the way I am." "I have to present to the board tomorrow, and I don't like speaking in front of people."

5. *Change in control.* More or less control upsets the previous balance of responsibility. The response might take this form: "I've been asked to step up into a new role, which I don't want. I'm going to do the least possible." "Our director took back several of my program oversight responsibilities, and I don't like it. Why should I bother?"

Be prepared before you coach. Here are some ways to prepare:

- Accurately identify the change you are dealing with. You may think it is one thing, but the other person may see it as something else.

- Don't take it personally. Although a manager does have a certain amount of impact on how well their people perform, most of the time it's not about you.

- Don't make it personal. This is about the needs of the organization, your team, and your clients. There is no need to criticize the person who is resistant. There's a need to be specific about the type of change needed. Stay objective and don't add your opinion or assumptions. Be clear about your requests. (See "Make Requests" in Chapter Three.)

- Do diagnose the person's resistance. Is it related to needs, security, identity, investment, or control? Does it call for more information, skills, motivation, confidence, time, or support?

- Stay respectful and curious.

- Check to see if the resistance is due to anything you, as manager, are contributing to.

- Don't lose sight of the desired outcome.

- Stick with the facts.

To further prepare for this type of conversation, see "Coaching When the Manager Sets the Focus" in Chapter Five. Your coaching should help the person (1) be as well informed as possible, (2) reveal his or her true thoughts, needs, and disagreements, (3) understand thoroughly what the context and consequences of the required change are, (4) find acceptance to change through new levels of belief and trust, and (5) discover ways of making this change happen.

COACHING SOMEONE WHO IS RESISTANT

Alicia is a senior staff person at Rights for All (RFA)—an advocacy agency working to achieve equality for lesbian, gay, bisexual, and transgender individuals in a large county. Lately, her manager, Eleanor, has asked her to do more computer-related tasks and has taken back for herself the media relations and local partnership tasks. Alicia is getting fed up with not being able to do the job she loves: relationship building. Eleanor noticed that Alicia is very behind on creating a new online system, even though Alicia knows the system will help the cause. They are meeting for their regular one-on-one check-in.

Eleanor: Thanks for meeting today. I want to talk together about your progress with the new online system. What's happening?

Alicia: No problems.

Eleanor: What's important for us to address concerning your progress?

Alicia: Nothing. It's fine.

Eleanor: What's going well?

Alicia: Like I said. It's all OK.

Eleanor: Well, can you update me on where we are now?

[*Alicia reluctantly gives Eleanor some minor updates, then stops abruptly.*]

Eleanor: I think we agreed this had to be a priority. What will you need to get it finished by next Friday?

Alicia: I'll get to it when I can. I've got other things going, you know.

Eleanor: Is there something else going on here?

Alicia: Does it matter?

Eleanor: What do you mean by that?

Alicia: I mean, you decide what I'm going to do and that's that, I guess.

Eleanor: Can you be more specific?

Alicia: This whole online system may have been my idea, but it's not like I'm a computer genius or something.

Eleanor: How has this project impacted you?

[*Alicia rolls her eyes, as if Eleanor should know how it has impacted her.*]

Eleanor:	You just rolled your eyes. What's that remark about?
Alicia:	What do you want? I'm doing my best.
Eleanor:	We are all grateful for the work you have been doing. This system was needed a long time ago, and you are making it happen. I appreciate how you have used your computer skills along with your knowledge of these systems. Do you feel I expect too much from you?
Alicia:	No.
Eleanor:	Then what's going on here?
Alicia:	It doesn't matter.
Eleanor:	It does. How can I help you?
Alicia:	I want to ask you something. Why am I suddenly not involved with the external partners? Why is it that after all this time, I'm being cut off from my relationships? The other day Jenna from WIT called. If you remember, you directly ordered me to put her through to you. What have I done wrong?
Eleanor:	Alicia, I'm sorry if you have been hurt by these actions. I took the external work on because I thought this might help you pay more attention to the online project.
Alicia:	But it's my job! It's my job to maintain professional relationships with statewide media.
Eleanor:	I didn't mean to cut you off. I saw that you were having a hard time getting back to everyone on time. So I decided to take on some of the contacts. I want to provide more space for you to get on with your priorities. I realize now I should have discussed this more with you.
Alicia:	These people are my priorities. What's the point of doing the job if I have no contact with them directly?
Eleanor:	Do you feel I've asked you to disproportionately change your focus?
Alicia:	Yes. And quite honestly, I want the system to work and I really don't enjoy creating it alone.
Eleanor:	We should talk more about this. We must get the online project completed. Given your skills, you're the only person who can take charge. And I hear that you need more balance in what you do. What would make more sense to you?

> *Alicia:* I just don't want to be stuck with logistical details, computer stuff, databases, and writing articles. I thrive on working directly with people.
>
> *Eleanor:* I apologize for not seeing that earlier. So let's keep the "people" aspect of your job central and talk about how to do all the other tasks. Where do we need to start to map out how to get the online project finished and make sure you stay connected to the other work you do? Would this work for you?
>
> *Alicia:* Yes. I want the online system as much as anyone. I just want to be sure I don't end up only writing and doing computer stuff.
>
> *Eleanor:* OK. We'll be sure to make it right. Let's get this plan going.
>
> Alicia and Eleanor go on to talk about keeping focused and making time for the relationships and contacts. Eleanor realizes that even though Alicia has strong computer skills, this is not where she thrives. She must manage the work that she gives Alicia. Alicia comes away feeling that Eleanor really gets her. She cares about her having the work she likes. Alicia works with Eleanor to make a plan to finish the online system by Friday. She feels more enthusiastic, knowing that Eleanor will be sure to allow her relationships to continue.

Questions to Use When Coaching Someone Who Is Resistant

Where are you coming from as you look at this situation?

Do you have enough information, support, capacity, and time?

What has led you to think and feel this way?

What will help the situation right now?

What's preventing you from saying what you really think?

What are the costs of operating this way? What are the payoffs?

What do you require in order to see you act differently?

What other perspective could you take on right now?

What other way is there?

What is your intention? What are you willing to try?

What else should we be addressing right now?

How might your resistance be contributing to the difficulties?

Question: Staff Members Who Report to the Person I Supervise Are Going Around Her and Coming to Me with Their Issues. How Do I Stop Getting Involved and Help Her Be a Better Coach Herself?

Erica reports to you. But Erica's staff come to you instead of her for support and answers. You don't want Erica to fix the problem by criticizing her direct reports. You don't want to just solve this problem yourself either. You do want to help Erica become a better leader and a better coach, so her staff will learn to work with her. Sometimes it doesn't take much. Sometimes a person only needs a slight shift in perspective. When frustration has shut someone down, a little bit of coaching reconnects the person to his or her strengths.

COACHING SOMEONE TO BE A BETTER COACH

Here is an example where Erica sees a problem as being bigger than she is. She doesn't know what to do about it. Her manager, Ricky, helps her overcome her distress. Ricky helps remind Erica of her strengths by acknowledging her. Notice Ricky's use of questions. Those questions say: I'm with you in this. You're not alone. We're figuring it out together. The result is that Erica suddenly gets smarter, calling on her intuition and capabilities, and the problem shrinks.

Erica: I'm so frustrated.

Ricky: About?

Erica: About how my staff keep coming to you to get their questions answered. I want you to just quit talking to them. Send people back to me. How do you expect me to be their supervisor if they're always going over my head?

Ricky: I could do that, and it would just make things worse for you.

Erica: Urrgh! Now I'm really frustrated. Why would that make it worse for me?

Ricky: Because I want you to win.

Erica:	You sure don't act like it.
Ricky:	I'm going to act like it right now. Let's talk about what it will take for people to go to you instead of coming to me. What do you think is going on?
Erica:	I don't know. I know you want me to be a success. And I appreciate your giving me this promotion. But I really don't get what I need to do to get people to come to me.
Ricky:	Let's just take a deep breath and relax. I know that together we can figure this out.
Erica:	OK.
Ricky:	How are you developing your new relationship with your team?
Erica:	Well, I'm trying to just let things take their course.
Ricky:	Which means?
Erica:	I don't want to pressure people. After their negative experience with Ralph, I don't want to be bossy. I don't want to step into his shoes.
Ricky:	I appreciate that because we don't need another Ralph. What else?
Erica:	Well, that's it really. I just figured I'd let people take whatever time they need to get used to me as their new supervisor. I try my best not to bother them. They're good people.
Ricky:	Not bothering them means what?
Erica:	I stay in my office a lot, and sometimes I cheer people on when I have the chance.
Ricky:	Do you know what they say when they come to me? They don't want to bother you! They never have one bad thing to say about you. They just don't want to bother you. But they don't mind bothering me.
Erica:	Well, you're just like that. Everyone knows they can always talk to you.
Ricky:	That's something I've done on purpose—created that sense of welcome.
Erica:	Oh. And I'm sitting in my office. Uh-oh. [*She nods her head as she realizes what's going on.*]
Ricky:	Uh-oh?

Erica: I think I'm screwing up.

Ricky: What I'm seeing is someone who is simply in the process of learning what it is to be a leader. You know, all of a sudden I'm thinking about how much you love salsa dancing.

Erica: I do, but what's that got to do with it?

Ricky: What do you want in a leader when you're on the dance floor?

Erica: Oh. I see where you're going with this. I want someone who is clear, definitive, and direct when it's necessary and yet is very attentive to me. So are you saying that's what my staff wants from me?

Ricky: That's my best guess. I think it would be worth checking out. What do you think they need from you that they still come to me for?

Erica: They need to be able to bother me. And maybe they want me to bother them more.

Ricky: What does that mean?

Erica: Instead of holding back, I'm going to start checking in with them, each of them, at the beginning of the day and at the end of the day. Make sure they're getting what they need. There are only five of them, so I can do that easily. In the meantime, you have my permission to keep talking with them if they come to you.

Ricky: Really?

Erica: Yes, because in three weeks no one's going to be coming to you anymore. I'm going to win people over. I'm going to figure out how to lead people with just the right touch. I'm going to make sure they know I'm interested in every one of their questions. Then they'll start coming to me—because they want to. That's how I'm going to solve this.

Ricky: What are you noticing about yourself right now?

Erica: For the first time I feel like I'm actually taking the reins of this department.

Ricky: Yes. I'm looking at you and seeing a leader. That department has been through a very hard time. They need someone to take them to greatness. They really can be great.

Erica: Thank you. I came in here ready to prove you wrong; now I'm going to go prove you right.

Questions to Use When Coaching a Supervisor Whose Team Avoids Him or Her

What is important about being a leader versus a follower?

What do you want most from yourself as the leader of this team?

What do you want most from others as you lead this team?

What have you spoken to your team about and what's missing?

How clear are you about what each person needs from you?

What is it that people get from someone else that they could get from you?

What might be lacking with respect to your cultural awareness?

What questions would help you know your team better?

What agreements do you need? What's missing?

How can you balance your needs with those of the other person?

What will make for a better relationship?

How can you take charge and still leave room for input?

Question: I Have a Staff Member Who Is Completely Capable, But He's Checked Out. I Don't Think He Really Wants to Be Here Anymore. How Do I Bring This Up?

It's common for people to be hired into a position and over time become bored, dissatisfied, or less interested in their job. This happens when their duties become rote. The question is this: Is this person bored, or is there something else going on?

Here are some of the reasons people regress from doing good work:

- A personal conflict at work
- Lack of interest in the original job
- No way to use strengths
- No growth and no challenge
- Not receiving good feedback when good work has been done
- Lack of clarity about their contribution to the work
- Relationship issues with the manager
- Discontent with salary or benefits

- Being overwhelmed or overloaded

- Passing time until they can find another job

- Being passed over for a promotion

Check in with the person. Stay compassionate and curious. Remember, this is not personal. Don't judge or share your opinions. Don't interpret the situation before asking for the person's interpretation of why things are regressing. Be ready with feedback that's specific and current. Approach with the mind-set of finding out what's going on and what can happen next.

COACHING THE PERSON WHO'S LOST INTEREST (PART 1)

A conversation to check out a person's mind-set about work might look something like this:

Rycha: Hey, Chris, I'm glad we have a moment to talk. I wanted to ask about the employment work group meeting.

Chris: Sure, what's up?

Rycha: Well, the deadline to get the materials out to members was two weeks ago, and you still don't have things ready to go. I also got a call from the facility saying that the rental agreement hadn't been received. At the same time, I noticed the last few times I walked by your desk you were looking at online photos or were on Facebook.

Chris: Geez, I'm sorry about that. I'll get the materials out this week, and I'll call the facility right away.

Rycha: OK, thanks. But let's not worry about that just now. I'm more curious about how you're doing. You've never missed deadlines in the past, but you've missed the last two out of three deadlines that were set for these programs. How are things going for you right now?

Chris: Honestly, I don't know. I've just been finding it hard to focus since we finished putting on the forum.

Rycha: What do you think is preventing you from focusing?

> *Chris:* I guess I'm not as challenged as I was in the past.
>
> *Rycha:* Can you say more about what you mean by "not challenged"?
>
> *Chris:* Yeah, I've done the forums and meetings for the past two and a half years. I was happy doing them because I was learning. But now it feels like more of the same.
>
> *Rycha:* And what impact is that having on you?
>
> *Chris:* I guess I'm checking out. It's kind of hard for me to get excited about these events.
>
> *Rycha:* What would it take for you to get excited about them?
>
> *Chris:* Honestly, I don't know. I mean, it was easier to do when they were new. Also, I was in school part-time, so I had something to look forward to after work. Now that I'm done with school, the work doesn't seem as appealing. I mean, if I have to organize one more forum, I think I'm going to tear my hair out!

Stop! Now that you have some information, you have to make choices. The conversation could go in a number of directions, so consider these questions:

Could you provide Chris with an opportunity to reflect on and discuss what growth or challenge might look like for him at work?

Could you help him think about his strengths and how he can use them in different ways?

Are there other tasks or committees he can participate in that might challenge him?

Can Chris find a way to take what he does to a new level of excellence?

Can Chris develop others who do similar tasks?

Is there professional development he can take to help him grow into another role?

Can Chris move into a more challenging role in the organization?

Although these are great options, many organizations are small and don't have professional development opportunities for staff. If that's the case, the question becomes how can this person find more satisfaction doing the job he has, or is it time for him to move on? (See the section later in this chapter about using coaching to let someone go.)

COACHING THE PERSON
WHO'S LOST INTEREST (PART 2)

Now, let's go back to the conversation.

Rycha: Chris, I really appreciate that you shared what was going on for you.

Chris: Yeah, I'm glad we talked, too.

Rycha: I'm glad we're finding another way to help you expand what you do. *And* I want to be clear that if you're going to be here, you have to be here. These events are critical to our mission. If they don't happen, our clients don't get support. So, now that we've identified next steps, how is it going to be for you to continue working on the forum and work group?

Chris: Well, now that I know they aren't the only things I'll be working on, and I'll have a chance to use my skill for managing data, it will be easier to get excited.

Rycha: What will help ensure they are pulled off successfully?

Chris: I need to think about how I'm archiving all the information so other people can access it. I have a lot of things in my head that no one else has.

Rycha: What do you need to do to make that happen?

Chris: I should calendar in some time to reorganize all the folders and documents on the network.

Rycha: What else?

Chris: I should ask Sadie to take a look to see if it's easy for her to access information. Come to think of it, I also need to spend more time training Sadie so she can take a larger role. She actually really loves the events, and I don't think I've tapped her to do a whole lot.

The conversation continues.

If you can find agreement about what the person will do to reengage or stay on top of his work, be sure to agree on how you will both monitor the situation. Be sure to give more useful feedback along the way. Use your coaching approach when you meet. Meet as often as you can until things get better. If things improve, that's great. If things don't improve, see the discussion later in this chapter of coaching someone who's not improving.

Questions to Use When Coaching People About Their Work Mind-Set

How do you feel about what you do right now?

What has happened recently that has caused you to . . . ?

What changed for you in the last months?

What stands in your way of fully achieving your targets?

What are your goals for yourself? What are your aspirations?

What should we do with the situation?

What do you want to stretch within yourself as you do your work?

What's this adding up to?

What commitment do you need to motivate yourself?

How do you get to fulfill your ambitions working here?

How much do you think you get to use your real talent here?

How does this work satisfy you, and how can we make what you do even more interesting?

Question: I Think a Staff Member Needs Therapy or Personal Counseling. What Should I Do?

First, let's be clear: If people cry in your office or get upset in a meeting, it does not necessarily mean they need therapy. It probably just means they're human! Who hasn't had a bad day or felt overwhelmed at work? Or it may be that they have something personal going on that is affecting their work.

However, many managers are uncomfortable talking about feelings at work because it seems messy. Coaching can open the door to feelings because you're spending time focusing on the other person's experience on the way to getting new results. That said, the type of coaching we discuss in this book focuses on workplace, organizational, and staff matters and is not intended to help you delve deeply into family struggles or mental health issues (see "What Coaching Is Not" in Chapter One).

You may find that coaching is not helping a person move forward. You may sense there is something amiss because of how the person responds. You feel she may need to talk to someone about deeper issues.

Here are signs a person may need personal counseling:

- Frequent absenteeism
- Social withdrawal (from meetings, from lunchtime discussions, and so on)
- Growing interpersonal conflict
- Physical aggression or violence
- Ongoing sadness or fatigue
- Ongoing irritability or anxiety
- Marked changes in weight or grooming
- Too-frequent mention of personal, family, or marital issues
- Mention of depression, acute anxiety, or other type of mood or anxiety disorder
- Mention of physical or emotional abuse
- A substance abuse problem that, possibly, you witness
- Indication of thoughts of suicide
- Expressions of concern from coworkers
- Marked decrease in productivity

As we've stated throughout this book, don't jump to conclusions. First, pay attention to the person and note any observable behavior change. Next, we strongly recommend you do your own research on the topics that may apply to the situation. Finally, talk to your human resource manager or executive director for additional resources and support. Determine what type of employee assistance programs you have available for staff, and offer the employee a referral.

Question: My Staff Member Is Not Improving. What Do I Do?

In Chapter Five, we discuss strategies for addressing a lack of performance or talent in a staff person. If you've tried these first and they're not working *and* you find the situation is taking up too much time and energy, there are two possible paths: (1) the turnaround or (2) the exit (letting someone go or moving him into another position because the current one is simply not a fit). We'll address how to let someone go a little later. Of course, if it has arrived at that place, you must involve someone from human resources or your management. First, let's share what a turnaround conversation might look like:

Path 1: The Turnaround A turnaround occurs when you make one more attempt to work with a person concerning a particular goal or task. In this situation, you put on your supervisor hat alongside your coach hat. As the supervisor, you must be clear that expectations have not been met and be clear about what must change. This goes beyond a request because there is no room for negotiation now. Gain the person's agreement to work on change or agree to come back to the conversation in the near future to discuss alternatives that may include reassignment or separation. You must require improvement within a specific amount of time. You need to set forth a process to monitor agreed-upon action with a certain level of supervisory involvement.

As a coaching manager, you have to provide specific feedback related to the unmet goal or expectation. You coach with an agenda and goal in mind. You let the person know you will work with him to find ways to meet the goal while wearing your supervisor hat, staying insistent about what the expectations are. You may need to offer more suggestions, yet remember to ask plenty of questions so he can think through those suggestions. You remain his ally, holding out hope that he can and will make change happen.

GIVING A LAST CHANCE TO SOMEONE WHO'S NOT IMPROVING

In this scenario, Veronika is supervising Edgardo on a local fatherhood initiative. Although Veronika and Edgardo have met multiple times, Edgardo is still not improving. Veronika wonders if the new position is a fit but is willing to give it one last chance.

Veronika: Since we met at the end of last month, I haven't had any e-mail from you. I want us to talk today about how we'll actually meet that June 25th deadline. You know we need

---

sixty men enrolled into the local fatherhood initiative. It's critical. How are you doing with the deadline?

Edgardo: I'm OK. It's been a little busy of course. The audit's been getting in our way again.

Veronika: It's been busy all around. I believe the last time we spoke, you had set a goal of enrolling twenty new fathers into the program. How much progress have you made?

Edgardo: Well, I haven't got any new guys involved yet. We still only have fifteen.

Veronika: How many men did you speak to in the past two weeks?

Edgardo: Actually, I got sidetracked with the holiday event committee, but I'll get back on this now.

Veronika: Edgardo, I think we both agree that this enrollment process must be filled by June 25th or we won't qualify for the funding and we'll not participate this year.

[*Edgardo nods in agreement.*]

Veronika: You've done a lot of good work on the resource center. You greatly contributed to the "Building Parents, Building Dads" workbook. You asked to be placed as the leader of this program. I want you to succeed. We are four months into a six-month enrollment process, and we've only got fifteen dads. Aside from what we talked about last time, what is getting in your way?

Edgardo: I don't know. I get sidetracked.

Veronika: Are we talking about time management or is it something else?

Edgardo: Well, I don't know. I'm not real good at making those calls.

Veronika: What is it about making calls that gets in your way?

Edgardo: Actually, I feel bad calling people I don't really know.

Veronika: What do you mean?

Edgardo: I just feel awkward.

Veronika: You were able to enroll fifteen people. What dads have you felt OK calling?

Edgardo: I don't know really. It just seems like the first few were easy. Now I'm not sure who to call.

Veronika:	We did give you the lists of dads who've attended other programs. Jeremy gave you a long list of men who are dads returning from the military and dads who've just gotten out of prison. What have you been able to do with the list?
Edgardo:	To be honest, I haven't done anything. I get really stuck not knowing what to do.
Veronika:	When you say stuck, what do you mean?
Edgardo:	I just don't feel right.
Veronika:	What would make you feel right?
Edgardo:	Honestly, I'm not comfortable calling people I don't know. I'm just not.
Veronika:	Hmm. This is the main way to reach fathers. What else is getting in your way of enrolling dads?
Edgardo:	Sometimes I'm not sure I know how to explain the health care program piece and a couple other parts that make me feel uncomfortable.
Veronika:	So you've mentioned that you feel uncomfortable a couple of times today. I appreciate how honest you are being. What would you need to have or need to do to feel more comfortable?
Edgardo:	I really don't know.
Veronika:	Well, let's think about this together. Imagine if this were very comfortable. What would be going on?
Edgardo:	I would be really clear about what we are offering. I would be surrounded by all the information in case they ask me questions. I might even be better because I watched others do the calls successfully. I might feel better if I had some background on the people I'm calling. I am excited about the initiative. It helped me so much.
Veronika:	What if you were only calling dads up to share your past experience with the initiative? How would that make you feel?
Edgardo:	Honestly, if I was just sharing my own experience, I'd feel less like I'm trying to sell people something. I know it's free. It's just a feeling like I'm begging people to be in the program.

Veronika:	What if we spend some time role-playing how you might simply share your experience and then how to ask the potential dads some specific questions about what they might need. Would that help?
Edgardo:	Yes, it would. I feel like I've been trying to figure it out on my own.
Veronika:	I'm sorry I've not paid more attention to you. You must come to me when you feel stuck. Otherwise I don't know what's going on. Now, how might we work together when it comes to further understanding the information available to the enrollees?
Edgardo:	Actually, I don't feel that bad about the information. I think it's mostly about this awkward feeling about calling people.
Veronika:	So what else would help you feel less awkward, apart from us role playing?
Edgardo:	I don't know if you'd have time, but I'd like to hear you do some sample calls and I could listen in. You know I've never done this type of thing before.
Veronika:	[*She sets limits.*] I may not have the time but I will ask Angus to help. Let's spend one week with you shadowing Angus and one week giving you another opportunity to make the calls yourself. Can we agree to come back to this in two weeks, see how you are doing, and how many dads are signed up?
Edgardo:	Yes. OK.
Veronika:	We want the best for you. If you can't get comfortable with sharing your story and cold calling over the next two weeks, we will need to revisit what role makes sense for you. We'll need to talk about alternatives. Are you OK with that?
Edgardo:	Yes. I wish I could be better. I'll do my best. But I do understand where you are coming from. Thank you for giving me another chance.

What Just Happened?

Veronika took the time to better understand what was getting in the way of Edgardo being successful in his role. She acknowledged where she might have played a part and was also clear about what was expected from him in order to succeed. They worked together to come up with a plan to help him become more comfortable with making calls. Yet notice that Veronika was also clear that if something didn't change, they would have to revisit the role he was in.

This is a good example of going back to role contracting and making sure everyone is on the same page. While Veronika should absolutely do everything she can to help Edgardo feel more confident with making calls, it may be that after spending time with him, it's still not a fit. If that's the case, she's been clear from the beginning. This way, there are no surprises.

Path 2: What if I need to let someone go?   Sometimes, no matter what you do, an employee is not a good fit. It might be that an employee is not able to perform to organizational standards. Or it may be that the individual's personal preferences are not a match for the organization's culture. Although you need to have your supervisor hat squarely on for these types of conversations, it is possible to use some coaching for an exit. Here is a scenario with two possible endings: the first is a friendly exit, where the staff member makes the decision. The second is an involuntary firing, where the manager makes the decision.

TWO SCENARIOS: COACHING FOR LETTING SOMEONE GO

Sara is the executive director of Community Consensus Project, and Will is an organizer for the organization. The first part of this example reveals the situation that is the starting point for both scenarios.

Sara: Will, we need to talk.
Will: What do you mean?
Sara: We've got a problem, and it's really serious.
Will: What's that?
Sara: I've gotten three calls from very upset executive directors of three of our sister agencies about the testimony you gave at City Hall yesterday.

Will: Oh, that. Yes, I defended our position. Those developers are jerks, and the supervisors who support them are jerks.

Sara: And did you tell people that?

Will: Pretty much, but I didn't use the word "jerks."

Sara: Can you share your thinking with me about this?

Will: Well, this development proposal is really serious. It would be devastating for the community. We can't mess around here. We're under attack and we have to counterattack.

Sara: What about the work our Message Team did? They put a lot of hours into our strategy for this issue. And they consulted in depth with our allies.

Will: Yes, they gave me my talking points and rehearsed with me. But in the moment, I decided I had to make an executive decision.

Scenario 1: Friendly Exit

Will: . . . I had to make an executive decision.

Sara: Will, I really appreciate your honesty. I appreciate how forthright you are in answering these questions. You're not hedging or covering anything up.

Will: Oh, well. Thanks. Yes, directness is a big value of mine.

Sara: That's something I admire about you, *and* we can't ever have an incident like this again. And we can't ever get calls like this again from our allies. Not ever. Really, not ever.

Will: So what does that mean?

Sara: That means we need to talk this through. Are you willing to do that? Take a breath, get behind the scenes, really dig into this?

Will: Sure. I'm always willing to do that.

Sara: That's another thing I appreciate about you. So what does it mean to you that our organization is called the Community Consensus Project?

Will: Actually, it rubs me the wrong way.

Sara: Because?

Will: Because I'm a fighter, and consensus sounds so wimpy.

Sara: Hmmm, have you ever thought about going over and getting a job at Fight Back? Think about it for a moment. Fight Back and we are like the odd couple. They do great demonstrations. Then when the supervisors see us coming, they're so glad it's not Fight Back that they welcome us in. Would Fight Back be more of a match for your temperament?

Will: It might be. I've known those guys from kindergarten on up. I do like the spirit there, the camaraderie, their kind of street gutsiness.

Sara: I want you to be in a place that's really a match for you. You have so much to contribute to this community, it doesn't matter what organization you're working for. What do you want to do about this?

Will: How about if I go over there this afternoon to talk with one of my contacts about this? Start feeling it out. Is that OK?

Sara: Yes, and there's no rush. Take the time you need. I want this to work for you.

Will: OK. Hmmm.

Sara: What?

Will: Just had a couple of ideas.

Sara: That's another thing I appreciate about you: How you're always thinking and how quick you are.

Will: Well, I'm thinking if I joined up with Fight Back, I might start doing community trainings on how to take a stand. Too many groups around here really are pretty wimpy. They could be doing a lot better.

Sara: Cool. I think the community needs exactly that. And it would make our allies stronger, which would be great for our mission.

Will: And I think, having worked here and appreciating what you do, I could help turn Fight Back into a much better, much more sophisticated ally.

Sara: That would be a blessing. So we've got a deal?

Will: Deal.

Scenario 2: Involuntary Firing

Will: . . . I had to make an executive decision.

Sara: So you were taking the action that in your heart you believed would make the necessary difference?

Will: Yes, that's really true.

Sara: I get that, and it's not a match for us. Remember, we are the Community Consensus Project. Your game plan is totally the opposite of who we are and what we're about. And here's the dilemma. You're a fighter. You have a particular way of fighting that's really you, and you're not interested in changing. True?

Will: Hmmm. Yeh. I hadn't thought about it quite like that. But yes, this is really me. What you see is what you get. And what you're seeing is what you're going to get, today, tomorrow, and the day after.

Sara: So all I can see is that this is a mismatch. You're not a match for the Consensus Project, and we're not a match for you.

Will: Here's what I'm about. I want to engage in struggle with the leadership of this organization. I think it's time to change the name and change the mission. That's a stand I'm taking and I'll fight for that. Don't try to change my mind. It won't happen.

Sara: OK, that's very clear. Thank you, *and*—I'm deciding right now that you can't work here anymore. We need people who are a match for our mission. We can't be fighting internally while trying to negotiate consensus in the community. Our work is super-challenging, and we need a coherent team.

Will: Wow, that feels sad all of a sudden.

Sara: For me, too. We need fighters in this community. We need you in this community. You've got so much to offer. I just can't see how you can make the difference you want to make through the Consensus Project. So do you want to talk about how you're going to leave?

Will: Is that really the only choice?

Sara: The choices are these: one, you get on our team and stay with us; two, you choose to move on to a place that's a match for you; or three, we let you go. It's not an option to stay here and fight with us and do your own thing. If you want to think about it overnight and tell me tomorrow if you'd like to resign, that's fine with me. But your staying here and not being a match for us—that's not going to happen.

Will: OK, I'll sleep on it.

Source: Copyright © 2008 by Rich Snowdon. Reprinted by permission.

We highly encourage you to follow your organization's policies and procedures when it comes to employee separation or termination. Be sure to have the right conversations along the way and document as much as needed so the final arrangement causes fewer issues. Separation or termination is probably the least pleasant thing you have to do as a manager. The goal is to make the process as clean as possible. At the same time, coaching can take a lot of the fear out of a firing and put the manager on very solid ground. First, if people do coaching all along, then there are, as we've mentioned, no surprises. And so when things get to termination time, there's less chance of an explosion because the staff person, if he's been paying attention at all, has been able to see this coming.

What we like about this kind of firing is that if it's done well, the person feels respected. You are taking a stand as the person's advocate. If he is not a match for this mission and this nonprofit, then you want him to get a job that is a match so he can be happy.

When there is a feeling of advocacy in the air (even if the person is hurt or angry), and there is no judgment, the chances of a lawsuit for wrongful termination are very much diminished, along with the chances of retaliation or bad-mouthing out in the community.

COACHING TOP PERFORMERS

Question: Should I Use the Coaching Approach with My Best Performers?

Yes, indeed. We've already mentioned that a manager should put the most attention on top performers—those who provide the most service, produce the most work, are best at their skills, and are ahead of the crowd. Reward them with more of what they want and need. Be available to these people because they can take an inch and run a mile. Coaching is perfect for your best performers. Your top performers may want coaching in order to

- Think about a leading-edge way of doing something

- Think more strategically about a program or project

- Stay focused under pressure

- Influence others

- Establish new goals and action plans

- Negotiate with their team

- Practice team leadership

- Achieve life-work balance

- Explore an idea about how to improve something

- Discuss how to help others

- Discuss becoming better at their piece of the work

- Expand their role

- Manage more challenging situations they may not have faced before

Coaching is for anyone who is at point A and wants to be at point B. Coaching puts you in the facilitator role, supporting the person to think through ways to make something more and different happen. You do not have to be ahead of the person's game to help him get ahead in his game. You are a neutral party in service to his possibility.

Questions to Use When Coaching a Top Performer

What do you want most from this conversation?

What should we focus on foremost?

What bigger picture do you see?

How far can we go with this?

What is at the top of your mind when dealing with this?

What's the stretch for you in this?

What do you know people need and you can give?

What do you want to take out of this opportunity?

How can we go further with less effort?

What do you want most from this opportunity?

How do you think this would best be dealt with?

What's most concerning that we can turn around?

Question: How Can I Use Coaching to Leverage My Staff Person's Strengths and Get Her Ready for a Larger Leadership Role?

This is a perfect time to coach. Coaching is the approach to use to help people move forward, to grow and stretch. In many nonprofits we do not have additional positions to offer, yet we do need more leadership. This is a great time to create the opportunity for someone to take on more leadership qualities and duties without having to wait for a promotion. Perhaps it's a short-term program lead role—a chance to be the coordinator for a particular event or a chance to lead a strategic-planning committee.

Before you meet with your staff person, get clear about the type of leadership role you need to fill. Identify the types of tasks you want this person to take on. Think through how much authority and decision-making power the person has or whom the two of you need to consult with or inform along the way. When you meet, discuss what aspirations this person has and state your own aspirations for this person. Talk about how the additional leadership duties link to those aspirations and how the duties will aid the organization and its mission. Determine what skills, strengths, and talents the person already has and any that need additional emphasis or growth.

Remember to use supportive feedback to celebrate what the person has already achieved, and don't be afraid to use developmental feedback too, if it will help the person identify what more she can achieve. (See the discussion of giving feedback in Chapter Two.) This is a time of opportunity and possibility. Make requests that stretch the person while being reasonable. (See "Make Requests" in Chapter Three.) Be open to concerns. She may want to negotiate her position.

COACHING TO LEVERAGE SOMEONE'S STRENGTHS

Melanie: Eloise, thanks for meeting today. I'd like us to discuss an opportunity for you take a lead in supporting the Children First project. First, I'd like to say you have been providing excellent administrative and substantive support to our directors for nearly a year now. Your attention to detail and your ability to keep everyone and everything organized has significantly improved our ability to stay on top of all the programs.

Eloise: Thanks. I like my work with the directors. It's easy for me. What do you want me to do with this new project?

Melanie: This project involves coordinating fifteen different organizations with three focus areas. There are more than fifty

---

people involved, including eight consultants. With your organizational skills and talent for keeping things in order, I thought this might be a great opportunity for you to take more of a lead coordinating the external partners, bringing together all their research for Saul, who's the new lead on this, and planning and organizing all the conferences up to and including the trip to Israel. What do you think?

Eloise: Wow, that's enormous. I don't think I would have time for that. [*Melanie wants to help Eloise share all her thoughts and concerns first.*]

Melanie: What other thoughts do you have?

Eloise: Well, it's a great opportunity to do something bigger, but I'm not sure where I'd start.

Melanie: What else?

Eloise: I don't really know all the players, and I feel a bit overwhelmed.

Melanie: What I hear you saying is that you would need to know where to start, how to fit this into your current work, who the players are—and you need help thinking through this. If we take time to work through those, would this be of interest to you? [*Melanie checks for motivation before moving on.*]

Eloise: Well, yes. I'd love to do something like this, but I'm worried about Anshul , Kateland, and Yael. They need me, too.

Melanie: How would you feel if we diverted the administrative support tasks you do for your directors over to Rebecca, while you work on this project?

Eloise: If she's up for it. We'd have to ask the directors though. [*Melanie explains she's already spoken to the directors. They will work with Rebecca during this time. Eloise feels relieved and somewhat excited.*]

Melanie: Out of all your other concerns, which one should we talk through first?

Eloise: I'd like to understand who everyone is and what I'd be doing. Oh, and when is Saul coming back to take over? [*Melanie and Eloise discuss the key players and how Eloise will work with Saul. They discuss how Eloise will be introduced to everyone. Then they start to talk about the tasks that Eloise will need to perform and the breadth of the job.*]

Eloise: This seems like an awful lot of stuff to deal with. I've never done anything on such a scale before.

Melanie: What strengths and skills do you have that will support you?

Eloise: Well, I keep people on track even in stressful situations. I love keeping things organized. People do say that I lay out things simply when I explain how everything will be coordinated. Actually, I'm pretty good at taking control of things, even if I'm not ultimately in charge.

Melanie: This is exactly why you are the perfect fit for this. How can we leverage these strengths to manage the size of this project?

Melanie continues to lay out key duties and tasks for Eloise. She coaches Eloise to transfer and leverage her skills to manage the magnitude of the project. Melanie reminds and appreciates Eloise for her talents. Eloise comes away with a plan that she knows she can handle. She has decided to turn the whole project into phases to make it easier for her to manage.

Questions to Use When Coaching Someone to Take on More Leadership

What do you feel you are ready for?

If we offered you an opportunity to take charge of this, how would you feel?

What's most concerning about taking the lead on this?

Even though we don't have a new title, would you be interested in this opportunity?

What do you bring to the table that you can use on this project?

What skills or strengths do you want to use more?

Which tasks do you like doing, and which ones would you like to do less of?

What do you feel will be the greatest stretch for you?

How can we best support you as you move forward?

How can you best manage your time, given your new opportunity?

How might you need to come across if you have a greater lead role?

What tools or structures do you need to take this on?

Question: I Want to Use Coaching to Develop the Leadership of My Staff, But How Do I Start?

We get this question a lot. You may have identified an individual (or several) you would like to invest in, and now the question is how to accomplish that. Leadership is such a broad topic, and there is rarely agreement even on what it means. Keeping in mind that leadership may be defined differently in your organization or community, we offer you a framework of leadership competencies for consideration (see Figure 6.1).

Figure 6.1 has been adapted from the work of the Center for Creative Leadership, Grantmakers for Effective Organizations, and David Day. This diagram reflects what we feel are areas to emphasize when stepping into a leadership role (regardless of your title). Please note that this is not a comprehensive list of leadership competencies.

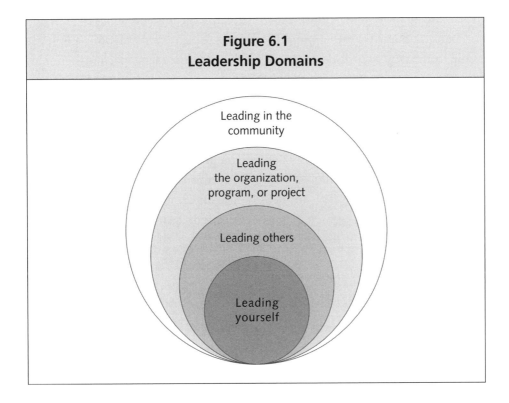

**Figure 6.1
Leadership Domains**

Leading in the community

Leading the organization, program, or project

Leading others

Leading yourself

The first domain (leading yourself) focuses on what is often referred to as *intra*personal skills. It means having personal purpose, self-awareness, and self-management. People with a strong ability to lead themselves can monitor their own thoughts, actions, and behaviors. They can also sense their own strengths and weaknesses and tend to feel comfortable enough with themselves to be able to relate to others. (We addressed some of this in Chapter Four, "The Coaching Mind-Set.")

The second domain (leading others) emphasizes *inter*personal skills. This is the ability to relate to and understand others, develop them, coordinate their efforts, and build commitments.

The third domain (leading the organization, program, or project) is entirely focused on setting vision and strategy, problem solving and decision making, and managing change.

The fourth domain (leading in the community) emphasizes the capacity to connect to and work with others outside the organization in order to advance the organization's mission.

Notice that all these domains overlap. In fact, several of these competencies are necessary across all the domains. Also notice that these domains live within the context of the organizational mission, because the mission drives the work.

There are many ways to approach coaching someone's development in leadership competencies, including by identifying one leadership competency to focus on with the staff person or by creating a personal development plan that addresses several competencies.

Identifying one leadership competency to focus on is the easiest approach and can help focus a conversation. The first step is to identify a leadership competency you would like to see this staff person grow into (for example, problem solving) and ask yourself some questions about his ability, capacity, confidence, and so on. This will help you to identify how much coaching he will need or whether he needs training, mentoring, or education of some other kind. You may even want to spend some time observing him in this particular area. Specifically:

Is this person new to problem solving?

Does he have the skills to problem solve? How do you know?

How does he feel about problem solving in various situations? Is he confident?

Has he demonstrated ownership of problem solving before?

What training or support might he need to take this on?

From there, you can engage him in a conversation. See the prior scenario on leveraging a staff person's strengths for some ideas of types of questions to ask. Remember, if you want to develop a person's leadership and he has not come to you to request this, then this conversation is your agenda. (Refer back to Chapter Five for more information on agenda-driven coaching.)

It may be that you have identified an area leadership role you would like someone to step more fully into that requires a plan for addressing multiple competencies. For example, a project manager has just been promoted and needs to develop competencies in leading others. Refer to the scenario for helping new people succeed for some sample dialogue and steps to create a development plan.

Questions You Might Consider Asking

What's your experience with . . . ?

Which of these do you already feel most comfortable with?

Which areas do you feel the least comfortable with?

What do you feel will be the greatest stretch for you?

How can I best support you to step into this area?

What training or support might you need to take this on?

What will help you get up to speed?

What do you already know you'll need to get going in this area?

What are you having the most challenge with?

We hope you use these questions, responses, and scenarios to illuminate, enrich, and inform your coaching activities with others. Although they may not match your situation exactly, the themes are universal and can be easily applied to a variety of organizational and personal situations.

We're almost done! Chapters One through Six provided you with strong grounding on all the pieces you need to skillfully coach the people you manage. Chapter Seven takes the discussion to the next level: how to move the skill of coaching from the person-to-person level in individual coaching to an institutional level, or in other words, how to create a culture of coaching in your workplace.

What's Next

Developing a Coaching Culture in Your Organization

In this book, you have explored how to become a coaching manager. This means that you have decided to bring certain skills to your work. You have decided to work more closely with those who report to you to help them develop. This will clearly have an impact on your organization. By modeling this approach, you will influence those people whom you manage—the people on the receiving end of coaching. Those who experience your coaching may be more likely to follow suit when they find themselves supervising others. You will also be modeling this for your peers, who may begin to observe your interactions or hear you use coaching to develop others.

By simply engaging in this approach, you are taking the first steps toward changing the culture in your organization. So, what if you would like to do more? Indeed, as you master this work, we would encourage you to think beyond your own relationships. Think about what this could do for your organization if all its people were to learn how to coach each other.

237

Although this book is one tool to help you become a coaching manager, we'd like to share with you some suggestions for improving your coaching skills and perhaps even to taking coaching one step further—to develop a coaching culture within your organization. In this chapter, we cover the following:

- What is a coaching culture, and why bother with it?
- Factors to consider in creating a coaching culture

WHAT IS A COACHING CULTURE, AND WHY BOTHER WITH IT?

We all want an organizational environment that provides for learning and growing, with sustainable constructs that support high performance. An emerging organizational development model that establishes such an environment is a coaching culture. So what is a coaching culture?

> A coaching culture is present when all members of the culture engage in candid, respectful coaching conversations, unrestricted by reporting relationships, about how they can improve their working relationships and individual and collective work performance. All have learned to value and effectively use feedback as a powerful learning tool to produce higher levels of personal accountability, professional development, and high-trust working relationships. The impact is improved job performance and client impact [adapted from Crane, 2005].

One of the reasons we like this definition so much is that it emphasizes the investment in coaching as an ongoing practice, as opposed to a one-time event; therefore, it supports sustainable coaching cultures in organizations. We also like the fact that it suggests engaging all members of an organization, regardless of reporting relationships.

The concept of a coaching culture may seem a little pie in the sky, especially when you are likely to be busy engaging in the ongoing demands of fundraising and client services. However, if you're committed to growing your organization, then we suggest a parallel commitment to growing the people in the organization as well. As we discussed earlier in this book, this is just what coaching does. When a coaching culture exists:

- Staff feel valued, seen, and appreciated.
- Relationships with boards are more effective (since coaching is happening there as well).
- Clearer requests and better agreements are made.
- A climate of personal responsibility exists.
- Coaching is embraced top down and bottom up, from all directions.
- There are more effective working relationships.
- All constituencies are empowered to get their needs met more effectively.
- The result is a better work environment, less stress, and more retention.
- The pressure is off the manager to be the only one who can help to find solutions.

In a 2004 *Harvard Business Review* article, Sherman and Freas argue the case for a coaching culture this way:

> When you create a culture of coaching, the result may not be directly measurable in dollars. But we have yet to find [an organization] that can't benefit from more candor, less denial, richer communication, conscious development of talent, and disciplined leaders who show compassion for people [p. 90].

As the definition offers, a coaching culture promotes open communication and high-trust working relationships. An organization that embraces a coaching culture values ongoing learning and staff development, and each individual in that organization recognizes that he or she plays a role in facilitating the development of others. The impact is improved job performance, which can affect client services and delivery of mission.

FACTORS TO CONSIDER IN CREATING A COACHING CULTURE

In this section, we present the three primary areas of focus that together contribute to creating an organizational coaching culture. First, consider how any of these might fit into your own organization. Next, think about which organizational dimensions you must address in order to implement a culture change.

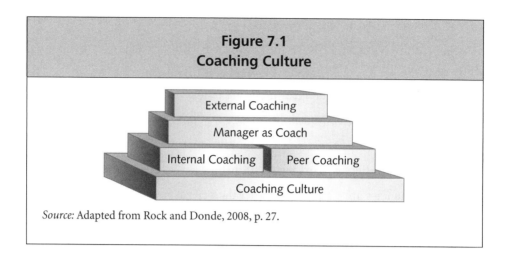

Figure 7.1
Coaching Culture

External Coaching

Manager as Coach

Internal Coaching   Peer Coaching

Coaching Culture

Source: Adapted from Rock and Donde, 2008, p. 27.

Finally, focus on the things you have an influence over. Let's start with the four different types of coaching.

The Four Types of Coaching That Build a Coaching Culture

Figure 7.1 presents the four types of coaching that make up a coaching culture. Let's look at each of these a little more closely, starting with external coaching. Along with this discussion, we provide some real-world examples of nonprofits that have incorporated these tools into their own organizations.

External Coaching
Real-World Example

- At the Institute for Human and Social Development, Inc., eight or more of the organization's managers were funded to receive professional coaching support to help them expand and grow leadership, planning, and communication skills.

External coaching is provided by a professionally trained leadership coach for key members of an organization. As we mentioned earlier in the book, this type of coaching can be very useful to and suitable for executive directors, CEOs, and board members, or when there is a need for specialized skills, experience, or confidentiality. The reality of its being "lonely at the top" is often a reason positional leaders reach outside their organizations for a coach—they need a forum where they can be completely honest about their concerns and may feel less comfortable sharing such information with staff, board, or funders.

Another reason to consider external coaching is that if you're using a coaching approach to manage others, it can be very useful to experience what it feels like to be coached yourself. Some organizations bring in external coaching to trigger what is called *cascading coaching*. Here, an external coach works with positional leaders who then coach their own team (BlessingWhite, 2008). External coaching is often used simply to help develop managers as they develop others. This type of coaching is often provided one on one, though it may also be used to coach teams or groups.

The International Coach Federation (http://www.coachfederation.org) can provide referrals to external coaches. Search for coaches with nonprofit, organizational, and leadership expertise. We have also included resources for pro bono coaching in Resource D. For resources on selecting the right coach, visit http://www.compasspoint.org/coaching.

The Coaching Manager
Real-World Examples

- Partners in School Innovation created an internal follow-up program to a coaching skills training that incorporates using what they learned and includes practice coaching sessions during monthly staff meetings.

- Bay Area Local Initiative Support Corporation (LISC) incorporated coaching skills training into its Community Development Leadership Institute for second-tier community development managers. Each manager participates in an initial coaching skills training and in monthly peer-coaching sessions to practice and reinforce the skills.

We've already given you a good deal of information about the manager as coach in this book. This type of leader and manager in an organization provides coaching to other staff on an ongoing basis as a means to develop staff members' skills and effectiveness. These individuals also use coaching to support many other managerial aspects of their job: clarifying goals, reviewing performance, holding team meetings, and so on.

Although we acknowledge that it takes some time to transition from being a working manager to a coaching manager (we'll share more about this later in this section), we do want to reinforce that it is a critical building block in creating a coaching culture.

Many agencies have opted for one of several plans for training managers to gain coaching skills. Individual leaders and managers can attend a workshop, such as our Coaching Skills for Nonprofit Managers class in the San Francisco Bay area. Organizations can also bring in a private trainer to provide a curriculum of coaching skills tailored to their particular group. After training, a follow-on program can be developed internally or with the trainer for continued learning for the managers and leaders. Finally, many leadership programs (like the LISC program mentioned earlier) are beginning to incorporate coaching skills training into their curriculum.

Internal Coaching
Real-World Example

- Park Nicollet Health Services is a large nonprofit health care organization that implemented an internal leadership coaching program less than a year ago and has already experienced qualitative results that include leader retention, job satisfaction, awareness, renewal, and increased performance. Eighteen staff members received formal training from a national coaching program to provide ongoing coaching to leaders at various levels of the organization. The internal coaches are doctors, vice presidents, directors, and managers.

Internal coaching involves identifying and developing a dedicated leader (or many leaders) within an organization to provide formal coaching to other staff on an ongoing basis. In larger nonprofits, this coach usually comes from the human resource staff or the management team. This type of coaching may be out of reach or not appropriate for smaller organizations. Medium-size and large companies in the for-profit sector have begun to implement internal coaching programs because they've realized that internal coaches create the same positive results as external coaches, but at a much lower cost (Rock and Donde, 2008).

An internal leader usually receives formal training at one of the professional schools of coaching. Once qualified, this person becomes the internal coach resource and is available to staff throughout the organization, not just to the people he or she directly manages as is the case for coaching managers. The internal leader supports the human resource and leadership function. The average professional training program takes six months to two years to complete. (See Resource D for resource recommendations.)

Peer Coaching

Real-World Examples

- The Lighthouse for the Blind, Inc., is a regional, midsized nonprofit that started using peer-coaching groups for its internal leadership development three years ago. Since then, it has expanded the use of the groups to include work on internal culture change.

- College Summit is a national nonprofit that has established peer-coaching groups for internal staff development, as well as for networking.

- Blue Cross and Blue Shield of Minnesota is an example of a very large nonprofit that uses peer-coaching groups for internal leadership and supervisory development.

Peer coaching involves bringing peers together to coach each other. It usually involves providing foundational coaching skills training to each member, as well as a structure for meeting on an ongoing basis. Each peer is equally dedicated to the other's learning and development. They can coach in pairs or in larger peer-coaching groups. There are many uses for peer coaching, especially because it makes coaching highly accessible and cost-effective. It can provide a space for people to practice and reinforce their own coaching skills. Through this type of process, peers can also share accountability and support to apply concepts and materials from traditional training sessions or address their current problems and goals. It also can be used to cultivate strong, authentic relationships among peers. As the examples show, peer coaching can be incorporated into organizations of varying sizes. (For help in incorporating peer coaching into an organization, see Resource D.)

A coaching culture is created by strategically integrating coaching skills into the organization. It is not enough to provide coaching only from an external source. It takes managers using the coaching approach, one or several people becoming internal coaching resources, or all the staff members learning to coach each other, regardless of position.

Your organization may choose one (or many) of these types of coaching to incorporate into its processes. We recognize that, depending on the size of your organization, all of these may not be necessary (or realistic). However, we are presenting the full framework to share what's possible.

Pay Attention to Skills, Systems, and Culture

If you do decide to integrate one (or several) of the coaching approaches we discuss into your organization, it's important to understand the steps you'll need to take to make this change take root. As with any major organizational change, it may not work merely to suggest that you all start coaching one another and then wait for it to happen (unless you have an extremely small and nimble staff, of course). Changing behavior or integrating a new approach into an organizational culture requires that you look at three organizational dimensions: skills, systems, and culture (Figure 7.2).

You can learn new skills and just stop there. The culture of the organization could affect your ability to apply skills. It's possible your organization may need systems in place to support and operationalize those skills successfully. Do the values and practices inherent in the culture of your organization support you in using your coaching skills? Or do they make it more difficult? Here are some things to consider when addressing change at each stage.

Skills   This book is one way to build your skills as a coaching manager. And as we mentioned in the Introduction, people learn differently. Some people are quite visual and respond well to reading information in order to learn. If you fall into this category, we've provided lots of additional reading material for you in Resource D. However, some learn best by listening or by experiencing something firsthand. In addition to reading this book, you may want to experience being

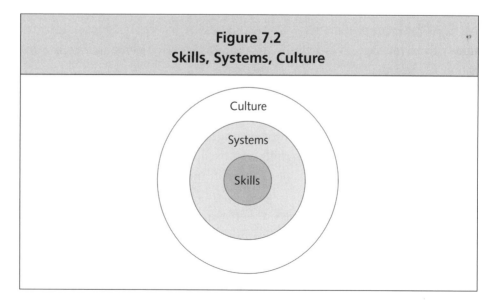

Figure 7.2
Skills, Systems, Culture

Culture

Systems

Skills

coached yourself so that you know what it's like to be on the receiving end of coaching. Consider hiring an executive or leadership coach.

Although external one-on-one coaching is clearly a powerful leadership resource for nonprofits, we understand that not every nonprofit can commit to the financial investment required by hourly coaching services. You can investigate coaches who offer pro bono services. You may also want to consider participating in a coaching skills workshop to prepare yourself to coach others in your organization, or you can go even further by getting more formal coaching training from a number of coach training organizations. Or you could consider peer coaching in order to get support on your own goals or issues and to further your own coaching skills. Again, check Resource D for resources on each of these.

Now, you can stop with just skills and that can be plenty. However, to create a true coaching culture, next you will want to pay attention to systems.

Systems   It can be easy for some to learn a new skill. It's an entirely different thing to integrate those skills into a new way of managing others. Behavior change takes time and support. To create a culture change, work to align your systems to your cultural goals. Some simple ways to create systems that support your coaching include establishing regular and ongoing coaching meetings with your staff (both formal and informal). Some managers put these formal meetings on the calendar so that they don't forget to meet regularly. Other managers incorporate skills practice into other staff trainings.

Organizations that have been successful in incorporating a coaching culture have tied coaching into organizational systems such as performance expectations, performance reviews, and compensation. They also invest in ongoing coaching training or establish peer coaching to reinforce coaching skills. Here are some other ways to integrate coaching into your systems:

- Use coaching to support learning after staff training. This can help people identify key learning and put it to work.
- Consider creating internal coaches (such as HR managers).
- Hire staff who are open to learning and growing. When interviewing, ask how candidates feel about being challenged and learning new skills.

Culture   In order for coaching to be fully integrated into the culture of an organization, it needs to come from the top down and the bottom up.

Top down means that buy-in is required from organizational decision makers. If the executive director or management team does not support an investment in a coaching approach, it can be extremely challenging to implement. At the same time, a top-down approach alone won't do the trick. Staff need to feel that coaching is worthwhile, and they need to feel they can trust their manager enough to engage in coaching. As we mentioned in Chapter Four, "The Coaching Mind-Set," a high level of confidentiality and transparency is important.

Let's not kid ourselves. The reality is that even though most staff and managers say they love coaching and even though there is evidence that when it happens, it can have a substantial impact on performance and engagement, it is not a common practice (BlessingWhite, 2008). Even with the best of intentions, some things can get in the way. Nonprofits are under-resourced and overtaxed, so it's no surprise that lack of time or competing priorities may interfere with investing in coaching. And change can be extremely difficult (if not impossible) to implement if the organizational culture is contrary to what you're trying to change. In other words, if your organization's culture doesn't already value learning and developing others, you may have a bit of an uphill climb. However, there are some things you can do.

Focus on Your Area of Influence

Everyone grapples with how to manage change in an organization, introduce new information, or galvanize support for a new idea. In these situations, you may be concerned with or about many things that you might not be able to influence (O'Connor and Lages, 2007), especially if you're faced with competing values in an organization where not everyone values coaching or development the way you do. But here's the thing: organizational culture is composed of the individual actions of every person in an organization (Kinicki, 2007). In other words, our behaviors constitute the culture. There may be many things that you personally are able to respond to or can directly affect. So, if you want to create a coaching culture, then start by behaving in a way that supports that. For example, although you may not have the direct influence to make your management team adopt a coaching approach with staff, you *can* consider any or all of the following activities as a part of your own organizational role:

- Request an investment in your own professional development so you can use a coaching approach with your team.
- Be a role model to other managers or peers by using a coaching approach on an ongoing basis (as mentioned earlier).
- Acknowledge and reward your own staff when they use a coaching approach with the people *they* manage.
- Share stories with people in the organization about how coaching has supported you as a manager and the people you manage.

As I model open-ended questions, I see the people I supervise use the skills as well. The conversations are enriched, and possible solutions to problems appear that would not have otherwise done so.

—Pat Swartz, program manager, Girls Inc. of Alameda County

As Ryan Healy, cofounder of a career site for Gen Y men and women, puts it, "It's up to individual managers to break the pattern [of too little coaching]. It's a personal thing. Coaching needs to start as conversations between managers and their employees and work its way into the culture" (BlessingWhite, 2008, p. 24).

We hope this book has helped make the case for shifting to a mind-set of ongoing staff engagement in coaching rather than seeing coaching as a one-time event. In this way, coaching is happening all the time even though taking very little time. Five minutes here and there to ask a good question or two can have a tremendous impact. And investing in staff engagement has a direct impact on retention and productivity, so the reality is that coaching *can have* a financial impact.

If you picked up this book, you have already made an investment in your personal development as a coaching manager. And we're guessing you are also invested in developing those you work with. This is a wonderful first step that can have tremendous impact. In her book chapter "What Is Our Role in Creating Change," Margaret Wheatley (2009) shares that even great and famous change initiatives begin with the actions of just a few people. Where do you have both concern *and* influence? Focus the majority of your efforts in those areas. And see what happens. You may spark something.

CONCLUSION

This book has presented coaching skills and a framework that have been taught to thousands of nonprofit managers around the country. We hope it has offered you a framework in which to work with your staff in a different and even more valuable way.

In our work, we see people trying to go it alone all the time. Our personal goal is to help you move away from this traditional solo or heroic model of leadership and help you shift your leadership approach to create a culture in which everyone "leads from his or her own chair" and shares the work, the responsibility, the learning, and the accolades! Our hope is that all leaders and managers will move away from a scarcity model to one that values ongoing staff development and invests in strengths.

We congratulate you for taking this important step in developing your coaching skills, and we wish you much success as a coaching manager in your nonprofit organization.

RESOURCE A

COACHING MANAGER SELF-ASSESSMENT

Instructions

- Read each line.
- Circle the score that best describes your perception of yourself and your approach.

    A score of 1 = Mostly not true

    A score of 2 = Sometimes true

    A score of 3 = Often true

    A score of 4 = Very often true

    A score of 5 = Always true

To score

- Count up the number of circles in each column.
- Multiply the number of circles in each section of each column with the number directly below that column section.
- Total the section scores for each column and then add the column totals together to get your final score. You may score between 48 and 240.
- Read the Coach Readiness score review below the assessment. This will guide you as you read the remainder of this book.

Coaching Self-Assessment

	Mostly Not True	Sometimes True	Often True	Very Often True	Always True
Skills					
I use language that is welcoming and inclusive.	1	2	3	4	5
I pay attention to the impact my body language has on others.	1	2	3	4	5
I am comfortable giving feedback.	1	2	3	4	5
I listen attentively, not allowing my own thoughts to get in the way.	1	2	3	4	5
I let others share their thinking before I give my advice.	1	2	3	4	5
I listen first, then speak.	1	2	3	4	5
I am able to suspend my opinions in most situations.	1	2	3	4	5
I stay objective when I work with others.	1	2	3	4	5
I ask probing open-ended questions to help people expose their best thinking.	1	2	3	4	5
I make sure people are heard and understood.	1	2	3	4	5
I acknowledge what people care about, not just what I care about.	1	2	3	4	5

	Mostly Not True	Sometimes True	Often True	Very Often True	Always True
I acknowledge things well done as much as opportunities to grow.	1	2	3	4	5
I am comfortable with being forthright when necessary.	1	2	3	4	5
I am comfortable with silence in a conversation.	1	2	3	4	5
I facilitate problem solving rather than take charge of the answers myself.	1	2	3	4	5
I allow others to discover new ways of solving problems.	1	2	3	4	5
Add up the number of circles you marked in each column.					
Multiply the number of circles by the following:	×1	×2	×3	×4	×5
Subtotals					

Mind-Set

	Mostly Not True	Sometimes True	Often True	Very Often True	Always True
I believe in people's potential.					
My words are congruent with my actions.	1	2	3	4	5
I am patient with most people.	1	2	3	4	5
I stay in touch with my people regularly.	1	2	3	4	5

Coaching Self-Assessment (*Continued*)

	Mostly Not True	Sometimes True	Often True	Very Often True	Always True
I make space for people to express themselves.	1	2	3	4	5
I show that I care, even when I am under stress myself.	1	2	3	4	5
I am trusted by most or all.	1	2	3	4	5
I realize and honor that people have different perspectives.	1	2	3	4	5
I put time aside for people-development conversations.	1	2	3	4	5
I am known as a good communicator.	1	2	3	4	5
I build connection with those I work with.	1	2	3	4	5
I manage my emotions, even under duress.	1	2	3	4	5
I forgive easily and get on with the moment.					
I find it easy to stay detached from outcomes when helping people grow.	1	2	3	4	5
I know the values and belief systems of culturally diverse people on my team.	1	2	3	4	5

Coaching Self-Assessment (*Continued*)

	Mostly Not True	Sometimes True	Often True	Very Often True	Always True
I show appropriate levels of empathy toward others.	1	2	3	4	5
Add up the number of circles you marked in each column.					
Multiply the number of circles by the following:	×1	×2	×3	×4	×5
Subtotals					

Framework

	Mostly Not True	Sometimes True	Often True	Very Often True	Always True
I am a good facilitator in conversations.	1	2	3	4	5
I help people have a vision of the end result.					
I am good at setting goals and clarifying expectations.	1	2	3	4	5
I guide people to be clear about what they are saying.					
I keep conversations and meetings focused and on track.	1	2	3	4	5
I help others drill down to what's most important.					
I often ask myself, What does this person need?	1	2	3	4	5

Coaching Self-Assessment (*Continued*)

	Mostly Not True	Sometimes True	Often True	Very Often True	Always True
I help people leverage their talents and strengths.	1	2	3	4	5
I remind people about what they are good at.	1	2	3	4	5
I am good at brainstorming and finding new options.	1	2	3	4	5
I help people use information and knowledge they have gained.	1	2	3	4	5
I am able to talk with people about their motivations.	1	2	3	4	5
I help people expand their choices when they seem stuck.	1	2	3	4	5
I make sure there are clear agreements at the end of conversations.	1	2	3	4	5
I hold people accountable for their commitments.	1	2	3	4	5
Add up the number of circles you marked in each column.					
Multiply the number of circles by the following:	×1	×2	×3	×4	×5
Subtotals					

	Mostly Not True	Sometimes True	Often True	Very Often True	Always True
Totals: Add up column section subtotals for each column.	+	+	+	+	+
Final score: Add column totals together	=				

My Coach Readiness Score

If you scored 220–240: You may be familiar with what it takes to provide great coaching. You probably possess many of the key characteristics of an effective coach. You are experienced in developing others. You are able to provide a solid framework for valuable conversations. You use the coaching approach to help people learn and grow. You are a good communicator. You understand why and how people think, and you are open to different perspectives. You practice the skills of coaching as a foundation for managing others. Which additional strengths can you leverage to optimize your coaching approach?

If you scored 160–219: You may be fairly familiar with the coaching approach. You may possess quite a lot of the key characteristics of a skilled coach. You probably partner quite well when developing others. Continue to strengthen this partnership. You communicate well in most situations with most people. You may include a coaching approach when you work with others. You are aware that people come from different perspectives, and you are learning how to stay open to those perspectives. You use many of the skills of a good coach. What will help you optimize your coaching approach? Where do you need to focus your energy and attention?

If you scored 100–159: You may be learning about what it takes to provide good coaching. You possibly possess some characteristics of a coach. You are still learning about how to best manage and develop others. You know people may need help thinking through things. Continue to grow and expand your coaching skills to help them do that. You may use the coaching approach on some occasions. Your communication is probably reliable and sound. You accept that people are unique. Continue to leverage people's differences. Which skills do you need to concentrate on first to strengthen yourself as a good coaching manager?

If you scored 48–99: The coaching approach to managing others may be new to you. You will need to strengthen your foundational coaching skills and approach. Keep expanding your understanding of what it takes to develop others. Stay open to people's unique strengths. Encourage people to share their thinking with you and others. Listen more, hold back your advice, and ask more questions when helping others. Stay open to different approaches to problems. Include others in problem solving as much as possible. Ask yourself how you can embrace what it means to be an effective coach. What part of the approach needs most attention?

Although there is no definitive list of great questions to ask when coaching, useful questions are the backbone of successful coaching. Many participants in our workshops have requested that we include in this book as many questions as possible. Here is an extended list. Also see Chapter Three, "The Coaching Framework," which includes many useful questions to guide you through a coaching conversation, and Chapter Six, "Coaching in the Nonprofit Workplace," which provides questions for specific workplace situations. We encourage you to create your own list, too. (Special thanks to Carter McNamara of Authenticity Consulting, LLC, for contributing to this list of questions.)

QUESTIONS FOR THE COACHING FRAMEWORK
To Clarify the Focus

What do you want or need to focus on?

What do you want or need to get out of this conversation?

What's going on right now that's important for us to talk about?

What should we be talking about that will help this situation?

What's going on right now?

What are you currently experiencing?

How does what you are saying relate to this issue?

What is this conversation really about?

I've heard you mention different things. Which one do you want to work on right now?

What is the bottom line here?

What's most important out of everything you are saying?

How is this issue important?

Where do you feel stuck?

What is the intent of what you're saying?

What are you hoping to achieve?

What do you really want from this situation?

What do you mean by that? What are you really saying?

What impact do you desire?

What's most important out of everything you are saying?

What's the real point?

What's the bottom line?

How can I be of most use to you in this conversation?

To Identify the Goal

Where are you now in relation to what you need to achieve?

What is currently happening that you want to change?

What other perspectives could there be?

How would someone else see this situation?

What do you need to do to shift your perspective?

What could you not be seeing yet?

What is the desired end goal?

What does success look like?

What are you hoping to achieve?

Where are you really heading with this?

What will it look like when you . . . ?

If you could set a goal around this, what would it be?

What is the end result that you are trying to get to?

Have you experienced anything like this before? What did you do? How did it work out?

To Develop Solutions

Where must you start with this situation?

Which option seems best right now?

What are the options? What else?

Which option seems to be more relevant?

Which option seems to be less obvious but might actually work out?

How can you break that into manageable chunks?

How do you see the path to where you want to go?

What needs to shift for something different to happen?

What have you not yet tried that might help?

What are other ways to get there?

What must happen in order to get that/there/it?

What support or resources do you need?

What are the obstacles in the path? How will you move beyond them?

If you meet this goal, how will it benefit you, us, our organization?

What other paths could you take?

If everything were available to you, what's possible for this situation?

Where are you coming from as you look at this situation?

What's your greatest wish about this situation?

What would you choose to do about this if anything were possible?

What is driving your choice?

How are you making this decision?

What other factors come into play as you choose to act the way you do?

What other way is there?

What if there were another way? Would you take it?

What if you came from outside the box? Where would that be from?

Where are you now in relation to what you need to achieve?

What stands between you and the future?

What are you allowing to hinder the situation that must now be changed?

What do you need to get going on to move this along?

If you get to the other side of this, what will you gain?

What have you not yet tried that would help in this situation?

What must happen in order to get that/there/it?

What options can we look at? Which option looks best?

What if you could . . . ?

How would it look if you tried that?

What do you need to shift for something different to happen?

What are we missing here?

How can you break that into manageable chunks?

To Create Accountability

What can you do before the next meeting?

What are you going to do?

Who will do that action?

By when will you do this?

What will it look like when it's done?

How will we know it's done?

What else might you need as you move forward?

What's next?

What steps are necessary to move the program forward?

What steps will you or the team assume responsibility for?

What is the best way to bridge the current disparity?

Who else needs to be involved to ensure the project's success?

What obstacles to success need to be eliminated? What will you do first/next?

What will be distinctly different from prior attempts?

How will you know it's working/succeeding?

What will we see you doing differently?

What support do you need to make this happen/to succeed?

When's a good time to get back together on this?

What, if anything, may we have left out?

What's one thing you can do right away?

What's the most strategic thing to do next?

How sure do you feel that this is going to work?

How confident are you feeling about your next steps?

QUESTIONS FOR SPECIFIC AREAS OF FOCUS

Information and Knowledge

What other information do you need or want?

Have you got all the information you need?

How well versed are you in this situation?

How familiar are you with what needs to happen?

What do you need to know?

Where can you get more information?

What information do you feel you still need?

How much do you know about this?

What data do you think are still needed?

How can we leverage what you know to help us here?

How aware are you of this situation?

What do you need to do with what you have learned so far?

What does all this information tell us?

Capacity, Proficiency, and Standards

What will help you become even more proficient with this task?

What skills do you bring to the table related to this?

How can we use your gifts to benefit this situation?

What strengths can you leverage in this situation?

How much capacity do you have to do this task?

What other training or books might be helpful?

What role can you play?

What's the scope of your ability?

How much room do you have to work on this?

How proficient do you feel you are given what we are dealing with?

How adept do you feel?

What else do you need to learn?

How ready do you feel to run with this yourself?

What do you need to learn in order to accomplish this?

What practice will you need?

What are your personal measures for this project?

What is most important to the clients?

What criteria do you need to take into consideration?

How do your benchmarks compare with other agencies?

How will we get everyone's full effort to maintain or exceed these levels?

How will performance be measured?

Relationships and Associations

What do you want in this relationship?

What will make this relationship work very well?

What value do you bring and do they bring to this relationship?

How well are things going between you and them?

What does *together* really look like?

Who else do you need to know or include in this?

What do you need from this other person?

Whom do you relate to easily and whom do you not?

What causes you to get on well with one group or another?

What is going well with your team?

How would the other person describe this same issue to you?

What is your role in this issue?

What would a successful relationship look like?

What have you not said to this person?

Leadership

What leadership strengths are you using here?

What's your normal approach when leading in this situation?

How do you feel taking the lead?

How do you like to lead?

What support do you need as the leader?

What can you do to empower others as much as possible?

What's most important to you as you lead on this?

What expectations do you need to set?

What voice should you speak in?

How available are you to others, given the situation?

How ready are you to deliver that message?

How are you sharing leadership on this project?

How much control makes sense for you to take or for you to give?

How will you guide others while standing back?

How can you give direction and coach at the same time?

Is this a matter of leading differently?

Which leaders do you admire?

How will you guide others while standing back?

How can you give direction and coach at the same time?

What's your normal approach when leading in this situation?

How do you feel taking the lead?

How do you like to lead?

What support do you need as the leader?

How are you sharing leadership on this project?

Is this a matter of leading differently?

Talents and Strengths

What part of your job description most excites you?

What work activities do you most look forward to?

What do you love about your work?

If you could work on anything here, what would it be?

What interests you most about this project?

When is a time that you were really successful at this?

What is a job you have loved? What made you love it?

When have you met or exceeded a goal like this?

When have you taken the lead on something?

When have you taken the initiative on something? What was that like?

How do you convince people to see things your way?

How do you go about solving difficult problems?

If you could spend tomorrow doing anything you wanted, what would it be?

When does time pass quickly for you? What are you working on when that happens?

What would you most like to contribute here?

What are some things you've been recognized for in the past?

Ownership, Motivation, Readiness, and Confidence

How confident do you feel about this task?

How motivated do you feel about this task?

How familiar are you with this situation?

You've done something similar before. What did you do that worked?

What will it take for you to own the whole thing?

What does this truly mean to you?

What do you want in this situation?

How would this need to look to be really valuable for you?

How can we refocus on the mission here?

What do you actually feel you want to accomplish here?

What does it really mean to achieve?

What are you tolerating that makes you less enthusiastic about this work?

How can you build on how well you did this before?

What do you want to achieve in this situation?

What would make you feel fully ready to go?

When will you be ready?

What will help you gain full commitment to the project?

How optimistic are you about the outcome?

How confident do you feel about doing this?

What possibilities are you most excited about?

What's holding you back now?

What's your uncertainty about?

How would you like to be more involved?

What would help you enjoy your work?

What's preventing this from happening?

What is really going on here?

How much support do you think you'll need, or how much can you do on your own?

What do you need?

Where are we going with this?

What do you need to know before you start this task?

What's most important for you to think through first?

Where will you start?

What do you understand the goal to be? How should it look on the other side?

What's your comfort level with doing this assignment?

How will you fit this assignment into your already busy schedule?

What's next?

What might get in the way?

Behavior, Self-Discovery, and Self-Management

What's new for you?

What's different, based on what you've learned?

What lies between where you are and where you are aiming to be?

What's your current feeling about this?

What's the unspoken truth for you?

What's possible for you?

What result does your attitude and behavior get you?

How can you balance how much you speak and how much you listen?

What do your people really want from you?

How important is it to get along with people, as well as get results?

How can you leverage your strengths to support you here?

What does it mean to really . . . ?

How do you think others perceive you?

What is working and what is not concerning your behavior?

What is working about how you are handling this and what is not?

How does speaking to others that way work for them?

How can you enhance your conversations to work for everyone?

What tone of voice might work for others?

How does your impact align with your intent?

What do you need to work on to be an even better coworker?

What is one thing you can work on that will help you grow this year?

Support, Structure, and Tools

What would make the biggest impact and help to ensure your success?

What resources are you missing that would make a difference?

What help will you need in making those contacts?

What will help you succeed?

What do you need to proceed?

How can you enroll others to help you out?

How are you doing with the equipment/technology program?

What other equipment do you need?

Do you have all the tools you need?

Whom do you need to support you?

What can you do to make sure the system supports your work?

What do you need to proceed smoothly?

How well are those templates working for you?

What other templates would make your job easier?

How does your work space support or hinder your getting the work done?

What arrangements do you need to make to get what you need to get the job done?

How does the current environment support you?

What obstacles seem to be in your way?

Planning and Time

What is your plan?

What is the timeline?

How did you come up with this plan?

Why have you ordered things this way?

How is this plan supporting the rest of your work?

How can you fit this project in with all the other work you have?

What timing makes most sense?

How will you schedule this?

What do you need to set up to help you succeed?

What else needs attention before you get going?

What else is taking up your time?

How much preparation will this need?

What preparation have you done or do you need to do?

What is your forecast?

Vision and Strategy

What do you see working here?

What is your highest vision of this?

What do you see as the best outcome?

How do you want to see this unfold?

What do you want in this situation?

What do you need to make this happen?

How do you see your strategy aligning with that of the organization?

How can we improve our strategy?

What possible strategies can you think of to meet this challenge?

What will make it most effective?

What is the next level for you?

If you could design a response with no constraints whatsoever, what would it be?

What is your or your team's vision that can be aligned with that of the organization?

Disagreement, Confusion, or Misalignment

What is your theory about how this can work?

What leads you to conclude that?

What assumptions might be getting in your way?

Where did this come from?

What do you really mean by that?

What are you really saying?

How would your proposal affect this?

What does that look like?

What do we know for a fact?

What do you think about what I just said?

What can you add to what I just said?

How do you see it differently?

What data do you have for that?

What causes you to say that?

What is the significance of that?

How does this relate to your other concerns?

Where does your reasoning go next?

Can you help us understand your thinking here?

How did you arrive at this view?

Awareness and Understanding

What is your perception of the current situation?

What do you see as the biggest challenge?

What will it take to address the challenge?

What do you know?

How well do you understand this?

What do you make of this information?

How familiar are you with this?

What's your biggest question about this?

What don't we know yet?

What's still up in the air?

What are our performance strengths?

Where are the needs around information, skills, attitudes, or behaviors?

Where do you see the opportunity in this?

What opportunity might we want to take advantage of?

Differences Between People

What should I know about you?

What do you want to know about me?

How are we the same?

How can I best work with you?

How are we different?

What similarities do we have?

What is important for me to pay attention to when working with you?

What makes you who you are?

What is it that you never want to hear me say again?

What is it that I should never say or do again when I'm with you?

What is important that I honor about your heritage?

How does where you come from influence how you think and what you do?

What is sacred in your eyes?

How do you see it differently than others do?

What questions do you not want me to ask?

What bothers you about people like me?

Improvement

What did you originally set out to achieve?

What did you want the most?

How well do you think you're doing?

What's the evidence to support what you're saying?

How well do you feel you've done in the eyes of our clients?

How well did you understand the goals and expectations?

How could we have done a better job with goals and expectations?

What support did you receive that worked or didn't work to help you progress?

What else can be achieved here?

What do we need to do if this doesn't work?

What do we need to make sure of?

What is in the best interest of the clients?

What is in everyone's best interest here?

How are you really going to change the outcome?

How quickly can we expect real change?

How would you describe path A, a path that leads to success, and path B, if success isn't reached?

Given the constraints of the organization and the work we need done, how much improvement can we expect?

What does this mean?

What do you think is fair in this situation?

What do you see as an alternative to success?

What do you see as inevitable?

Where does not succeeding leave us?

Where should we go with this?

What does this all mean or add up to?

Challenging Situations

How do you think you are achieving the required results?

What's your greatest wish about this situation?

What do you need more of?

How do you see it differently?

What leads you to that conclusion?

What information is that based on?

What causes you to say that?

What is the significance of that?

How does this relate to your other concerns?

Where does your reasoning go next?

What assumptions are you making about the other person or people?

What other factors come into play here?

What if there was another way, would you take it?

What are the options? What else?

Which option seems to be more relevant?

If this moment could be different, how would you design it?

What is really going on between us in this conversation?

What if there were other alternatives?

The way you are thinking about this situation, what effect is this having on you?

What have you not yet asked for?

What do you want here more than anything?

What must you request?

What action must you take, even if things don't go your way?

What do you feel about all of this?

What's driving your passion?

What impact are you having on other people?

What impact do you want to have?

How do your emotional outbursts affect you or others?

How can you better manage your response to disappointment?

How did you arrive at this view?

What causes you to be more emotional when you speak about a particular issue?

What's easy, and what do you have more of a hard time with?

Back-Pocket Questions

What's important for us to focus on?

What do you really want?

What do you mean by that?

Where should we go with this?

What are you aiming for?

What's the bottom line?

What options are you looking at?

Which option do you know you can go for?

What have you not yet tried that might work?

What else? What else?

What's next then?

What support will you need?

PRACTICING CULTURALLY AWARE COACHING

Chapter Four provides a perspective on culturally aware coaching but there is always more to learn, so here we provide additional information about culture, cultural awareness, and the ways culture and values are understood in the workplace. (Special thanks to Prism Coaching, Laurin Mayeno, and Contra Costa Health Services and VISIONS, Inc., for contributing to this section.)

Culturally aware coaching acknowledges a lineage of culture in every human being. How, then, can supervisors obtain the necessary foundation for culturally aware coaching? Although some cultural aspects can be learned by reading or attending workshops, they cannot guarantee the achievement of cultural awareness. This is because cultural awareness is not a distinct skill that can be achieved. It is a lifelong process of trying to "see" from other perspectives or cultural lenses. That being said, this resource offers suggestions and exercises for growing cultural awareness in yourself as an individual and within an organization.

Phase 1 involves participating in programs that help people unlearn racism, sexism, ageism, and other *isms* in our society. Phase 2 requires examining how culture and values are understood in the workplace. Phase 3 involves understanding the ways that culture affects leadership and is systematized in the governance of the workplace. Finally, we have included guidelines to consider for multicultural interactions.

PHASE 1: STRIVING TO UNLEARN *ISMS*

Culturally aware coach-managers need to be willing to commit to *undoing* deeply held assumptions that promote a singular cultural point of view in their lives. This involves engaging in such processes as unlearning racism, dealing with whiteness (understanding how being white gives a person certain automatic rights and privileges), and dealing with internalized oppression (a circumstance in which "an oppressed group uses the methods of the oppressor against itself . . . or starts to believe in negative stereotypes of itself or its group," Wikipedia, 2009) in order to prepare oneself for culturally aware coaching. Participating in such training programs helps individuals to prepare for culturally aware coaching and to build an ongoing foundation for that coaching.

PHASE 2: EXAMINING HOW CULTURE AND VALUES ARE UNDERSTOOD IN THE WORKPLACE

To begin your involvement in Phase 2, complete Exercise C.1.

EXERCISE C.1
How Are Culture and Values Understood in Your Workplace?

Reflect on and discuss the following questions with your peers:

1. What is culture?

2. What is race and what is racism? What are ageism, classism, ableism, and homophobia?

3. How does a coach-manager ask questions that allow a staff member to surface his or her own values?

4. What are the values of the board members and of staff members, and are they conflicting?

5. How do these cultural values express themselves in the workplace? How do they express themselves in the staff members' own cultural worlds?

6. What creates an environment in which *cultural competence* is mentioned but power dynamics and imbalances, especially racism, are not discussed or addressed?

7. How do coaches ensure that the racism "elephant in the room" is not ignored?

PHASE 3: EXPLORING HOW CULTURE AFFECTS LEADERSHIP AND IS INGRAINED IN ORGANIZATIONAL SYSTEMS

To begin your involvement in Phase 3, complete Exercise C.2.

EXERCISE C.2
How Does Culture Affect Leadership and Get Ingrained in Systems?

Reflect on and discuss the following questions with your peers:

1. How does culture affect leadership?

2. How does culture play a part in the dynamics between the staff, board members, and other stakeholders, including the community and other constituencies?

3. How does culture affect decision making in nonprofit organizations?

4. How does culture affect who has more power and who has less?

5. How does culture affect who is a staff member, a board member, a donor, and a volunteer in a nonprofit?

6. How does culture play a part in the management of an organization between staff leaders and others?

7. What are the characteristics of the dominant leadership style in our society? What are some different cultural leadership styles, and what are their strengths? How do they contrast with the dominant style?

8. How can raising your awareness about larger social and structural issues—power dynamics, racism, and other oppressions—be of benefit to your work as a nonprofit leader?

Then apply what you have discussed to your own organization:

1. Pull out your organizational chart and perform a demographic analysis.

2. Determine whether there is a history of conflicts between those of different cultures in your organization.

3. Determine whether there are currently issues related to culture between staff and managers in your organization.

GUIDELINES TO CONSIDER FOR MULTICULTURAL INTERACTIONS

Here are some guidelines for addressing issues of cultural competence, diversity, and inclusion:

Try on new ideas and perspectives, concepts, and experiences. Be willing to open up to new territory and break through old patterns. Remember, "try on" is not the same as "take on."

Intent is different from impact. Both are important. We need to own our ability to have a negative impact in another person's life despite our best intention. In generous listening, if we assume positive intent rather than judging or blaming, we can respond rather than react or attack.

Speaking from the "I" is speaking from one's personal experience. Rather than saying "we," using "I" allows us to take ownership of thoughts, feelings, and actions.

Confidentiality is often defined as "what you say in the room stays in the room" and we agree not to discuss what happens in this conversation in a way that would identify any individual. There is another dimension to confidentiality that includes "asking permission" to share or discuss any statement another person makes of a personal nature. It helps to remember that the story belongs to the teller—not the listener.

Both/and thinking means making room for more than one idea and point of view at a time, appreciating and valuing multiple realities—your own and others. While either/or thinking has its place, it can often be a barrier to human communication.

It's OK to disagree. Avoid attacking, discounting, or judging the beliefs and views of yourself or others—verbally or nonverbally. Instead, welcome disagreement as an opportunity to expand your world. Ask questions to understand the other person's perspective.

Be present. Let go of anything that might be a distraction (deadlines, paperwork, and so on) and be intentional about your purpose in this moment. Bring your full attention to the process. Acknowledge anything that you need to let go of in order to be present.

Listen with respect. Encourage and respect different points of view. Be aware of and respect different ways of communicating.

Listen deeply. Listen with intent to hear beyond the words for the entire content and what is behind the words. Engage heart and mind—beyond "hearing." Listen with alert compassion.

Self-awareness. Respect and connect to the authenticity of your true self. Be aware of your thoughts, feelings, and reactions. Be aware of your inner voice and own where you are by asking questions about why you are reacting, thinking, and feeling as you do. Monitor your content, your process, and yourself.

Check out assumptions. This is an opportunity to learn more about yourself and others. Do not "assume" you know what is meant by a communication, especially when it triggers your emotions. Ask questions.

Source: Guidelines reprinted with permission from Contra Costa Health Services and VISIONS, Inc.

This section presents resources for additional information and assistance in five categories: publications, training and workshops, peer coaching, external coaching, and pro bono coaching. This is of course not a complete list and is also not meant to endorse any one person or organization. Please consider which of these resources may be of use to you based on your own personal needs.

PUBLICATIONS
Coaching

The CCL Handbook of Coaching: A Guide for the Leader Coach, by Sharon Ting and Peter Scisco (San Francisco: Jossey-Bass, 2006); a rich review of the field of coaching.

Coaching: Evoking Excellence in Others (2nd ed.), by James Flaherty (Burlington, Mass: Elsevier/Butterworth-Heinemann, 2005); an excellent foundation piece on coaching from the founder of New Ventures West, with application of theory to real-life situations.

Coaching for Performance (3rd ed.), by John Whitmore (Boston: Brealey, 2002); considered the "grandfather" of coaching books.

Co-Active Coaching: New Skills for Coaching People Toward Success in Work and Life (2nd ed.), by Laura Whitworth, Henry Kimsey-House, and Phil Sandahl

(Mountain View, CA, Davies-Black Publishing, 2007); a useful reference book for coaching tools and techniques.

Executive Coaching Project: Evaluation of Findings, by Harder + Company for CompassPoint (San Francisco: CompassPoint Nonprofit Services, 2003) [http://www.compasspoint.org]; a report on new executive directors who worked one on one with executive coaches who helped them navigate life issues and organizational leadership matters.

Coaching Culture

The Coaching Conundrum: Building a Coaching Culture That Drives Organizational Success, by BlessingWhite (Princeton, N.J.: BlessingWhite, 2008); an executive summary that focuses on challenges and recommendations for creating a coaching culture

Driving Change with Internal Coaching Programs, by David Rock and Ruth Donde (Sydney: Results Coaching Systems, 2008); a white paper that outlines ways to use coaching to drive wide-scale organizational change.

Communication

Crucial Conversations: Tools for Talking When Stakes Are High, by Kerry Patterson, Joseph Grenny, Ron McMillan, Al Switzler, and Stephen Covey (New York: McGraw-Hill, 2002); offers a wealth of principles and skills for interpersonal exchanges at work.

Fierce Conversations: Achieving Success at Work and in Life, One Conversation at a Time, by Susan Scott (New York: Berkley Trade, 2004); an inspiring book about the power of speaking directly from the truth in a kind, but no-nonsense way.

Nonviolent Communication: A Language of Compassion, by Marshall B. Rosenberg, 2003); A system of communication that focuses on needs rather than on strategies and on heart-to-heart communications rather than making people do things you want them to do.

Point B: A Short Guide to Leading a Big Change, by Peter Bregman (New York: Space for Change, 2007); provides key elements for managing change in a straightforward way, albeit through a corporate lens.

Culture

These publications delve deeper into some of the topics raised in this book.

"A Capacity Building Approach to Cultural Competency," by Anushka Fernandopulle, and "Culturally-Based Capacity Building: An Approach to Working in Communities of Color for Social Change," by Frank Satterwhite and Shiree Teng, in *Organizational Development & Capacity in Cultural Competence: Building Knowledge and Practice*, Part 2: *Cultural Competency in Capacity Building* (San Francisco: California Endowment and CompassPoint Nonprofit Services, 2007) [http://www.compasspoint .org]; two monographs that make up Part 2 of a three-part series that is a collaboration between CompassPoint and the California Endowment. These explore a variety of frameworks for organizational development or capacity building and their implications for practice, taking in a number of issues that arise in real-world practice.

Generations: The Challenge of a Lifetime for Your Nonprofit, by Peter C. Brinckerhoff (St. Paul, Minn.: Fieldstone Alliance, 2007); addresses generational trends to keep nonprofit organizations relevant and able to meet the changing needs of staff, volunteers, donors, and the communities they serve.

Multicultural Organizational Development: A Resource for Health Equity, by Laurin Mayeno, Part 1 of *Organizational Development & Capacity in Cultural Competence: Building Knowledge and Practice* (San Francisco: California Endowment and CompassPoint Nonprofit Services, 2007); explores the applicability of multicultural organizational development for building the multicultural capacity of health organizations, positing that multicultural capacity and equity are interconnected; see also [http://www.mayenoconsulting.com].

Racial Equity Tools [http://www.racialequitytools.org], by Center for Assessment & Policy Development and MP Associates; a Web site designed for people and groups across sectors and at all levels in the work of promoting racial equity; intended to support transformative change within communities, organizations, systems, and individuals.

Understanding Whiteness: Unraveling Racism, by Judy Helfand and Laurie Lippin (Cincinnati, Ohio: Thomson Learning Custom, 2001); a workbook and reader providing tools for examining what it is to be white in the United States, for addressing fear and guilt as barriers to dismantling racism, and for identifying the small daily acts and larger organized movements that further the struggle for social justice and equality.

Leadership

Creating Leaderful Organizations: How to Bring Out Leadership in Everyone, by Joseph Raelin (San Francisco: Berrett-Koehler, 2003); provides a framework for sharing leadership in organizations.

Daring to Lead 2006: A National Study of Nonprofit Executive Leadership, by Jeanne Bell, Richard Moyers, and Timothy Wolfred (San Francisco: CompassPoint Nonprofit Services and the Meyer Foundation, 2006) [http://www.compasspoint.org]; three surprising findings from CompassPoint's new national study on executive directors: (1) 30 percent of executives leave their jobs involuntarily (either fired or forced out), (2) executive directors plan to leave their jobs but will stay active in the nonprofit sector, and (3) a key driver of executive burnout is frustration with funders.

Leadership and the One Minute Manager, by Ken Blanchard, Patricia Zigarmi, and Drea Zigarmi (New York: Morrow, 1985); teaches managers the art of Situational Leadership, a simple system that tailors management styles to individual employees.

Learning as a Way of Leading: Lessons from the Struggle for Social Justice, by Stephen Preskill and Stephen Brookfield (San Francisco: Jossey-Bass, 2009); offers a systematic look at the connections between learning and leading and the use of learning to inspire and organize for change.

Ready to Lead? Next Generation Leaders Speak Out, by Maria Cornelius, Patrick Corvington, and Albert Ruesga (San Francisco: CompassPoint Nonprofit Services, 2008) [http://www.compasspoint.org]; a survey of over 5,700 nonprofits that suggests indicators of strength in the leadership pipeline, as well as significant barriers to pursuing executive positions.

Strengths

Soar with Your Strengths, by Donald O. Clifton and Paula Nelson (New York: Bantam Doubleday Dell, 1992); a quick read about building on strengths rather than spending energy trying to fix limitations.

First, Break All the Rules: What the World's Greatest Managers Do Differently, by Marcus Buckingham and Curt Coffman (New York: Simon & Schuster, 1999);

a follow-up to *Soar with Your Strengths*, this study of eighty thousand managers (the largest management study ever done) comes up with remarkably simple, yet challenging conclusions, which are in synch with nonprofit values.

Now, Discover Your Strengths, by Marcus Buckingham and Donald O. Clifton (New York: Free Press, 2001); a follow-up to *First, Break All the Rules*, discussing one way to discover your talents and strengths and to deepen your understanding of them.

Strengths Finder 2.0, by Tom Rath (Washington, D.C.: Gallup Press, 2007); includes a new and upgraded edition of the online test from *Now, Discover Your Strengths*.

Supervision

Effective Phrases for Performance Appraisals: A Guide to Successful Evaluations (11th ed.), by James E. Neal Jr. (Perrysburg, Ohio: Neal Publications, 2006); useful tool for writing end-of-year reviews and assessments.

FYI: For Your Improvement: A Guide for Development and Coaching (4th ed.), by Michael M. Lombardo and Robert W. Eichinger (Minneapolis, Minn.: Lominger, 2004); sixty-seven key leadership competencies clearly defined by underused, overused, and most useful; includes maps for growth and many resources.

100 Things You Need To Know: Best People Practices for Managers & HR, by Robert W. Eichinger, Michael M. Lombardo, and Dave Ulrich (Minneapolis, Minn.: Lominger, 2004); covers topics such as selection, HR law, leadership, culture, training, and recruiting.

Teams

Mastering the Art of Creative Collaboration, by Robert Hargrove (New York: McGraw-Hill, 1997); shows how creative collaboration is much more effective in reaching desired goals than confrontation and mere cooperation (teamwork).

The Wisdom of Teams, by Jon R. Katzenbach and Douglas K. Smith (New York: HarperCollins, 2003); focuses on tackling and surmounting specific "outcome-based" challenges.

TRAININGS AND WORKSHOPS

Association of Coach Training Organizations: this association provides a directory of organizations that offer professional coach training around the country [http://www.acto1.com].

CompassPoint Nonprofit Services: this agency provides Coaching Skills for Nonprofit Managers and Leaders and other public workshops and contract training in the San Francisco Bay Area [http://www.compasspoint.org] or [http://www.judithwilson.com].

Judith Wilson & Associates: this service offers Coaching Skills for Nonprofit Managers and Leaders and other on-site training and workshops nationally and in the Asia/Pacific region [http://www.judithwilson.com].

Leadership that Works, Inc.: this service offers custom-designed coaching skills and leadership training programs based on codesigned outcomes, through on-site and public courses worldwide [http://www.LeadershipthatWorks.com].

PEER COACHING

Authenticity Consulting: this group provides customized peer-learning and peer-coaching programs for nonprofit organizations [http://www.authenticityconsulting.com].

EXTERNAL COACHING

At the time of this book's publication, a national listing of coaches serving the nonprofit sector does not exist. The following resources list a few providers of coaching for nonprofits. Coaches have varying backgrounds and experience. For resources on selecting the coach that is right for you, visit [http://www.compasspoint.org/coaching].

CompassPoint Executive Coaching Referral Service: this service matches individuals working in nonprofits with organizational leadership coaches in the San Francisco Bay Area; coaches can also be provided for individuals considering long-distance telephone coaching [http://www.compasspoint.org/coaching].

International Coach Federation: this professional organization offers information on external professional coaching [http://www.coachfederation.org and use the search word "nonprofit"].

Judith Wilson & Associates: this service offers individual coaching in the nonprofit sector nationally [650-341-1171 or http://www.judithwilson.com].

Leadership that Works: this organization provides individual and group coaching for visionary leaders, social activists, and affinity groups or as part of training and leadership development programs [http://www.LeadershipthatWorks.com].

Prism Coaching: this collective of coaches of color working in the nonprofit sector has developed a "culturally aware coaching approach" that recognizes potential assets and influences of race, class, and culture on the professional and personal lives of those being coached; it provides culturally aware coaching and the concept that understanding cultural experiences profoundly affects and strengthens clients in the coaching process [http://www.prismcoaching.org].

PRO BONO COACHING

There are many wonderful organizations dedicated to providing pro bono coaching to nonprofit organizations or individuals who may not otherwise be able to afford coaching. As with any capacity-building resource, we encourage you to interview and check references for those coaches you are interested in working with to ensure a good fit. For resources on selecting the coach who is right for you, visit [http://www.compasspoint.org/coaching].

A Hand UP Coaching: this international nonprofit organization is dedicated to providing individuals with career success coaching and life skills training programs to create economic self-sufficiency and meet career goals [http://www.ahandupcoaching.org].

The Coach Approach, Inc.: this 501(c)(3) nonprofit offers support services from coaches to individuals in the helping professions. The purpose of the work is to aid executive directors and program coordinators and also frontline staff in their personal or professional lives, or both [http://www.coachapproachinc.org].

The Coach Initiative: the mission of this group is to be the central gathering point where professional coaches can volunteer experience and expertise in support of global projects that focus on bettering the human condition and uplifting the human spirit [http://www.coachinitiative.org].

Coaching the Global Village: through this organization, world-class coaches and consultants partner with nongovernmental organizations and nonprofit social agencies to incorporate coaching skills into their work so they can reach target outcomes [http://www.coachingtheglobalvillage.org].

REFERENCES

Amman Howard, K., and Kellogg, V. *Coaching as a Tool for Building Leadership and Effective Organizations in the Nonprofit Sector.* Berkeley, Calif.: BTW Informing Change, 2006.

Argyris, C. *Overcoming Organizational Defenses: Facilitating Organizational Learning.* Upper Saddle River, N.J.: Pearson Education, 1990.

Argyris, C. *Overcoming Organizational Defenses.* New York: Prentice Hall, 1992.

Bell, J., Moyers, R., and Wolfred, T. *Daring to Lead 2006: A National Study of Nonprofit Executive Leadership.* San Francisco: CompassPoint Nonprofit Services, 2006.

Bell, J., and Schaffer, E. *Financial Leadership.* St. Paul, Minn.: Fieldstone Alliance, 2006.

Blair, G. *Learning Organisations: People Behaviour.* Edinburgh: The University of Edinburgh School of Engineering and Electronics, 1996. [http://www.see .ed.ac.uk/~gerard/MENG/MEAB/learning_organisation/people_behaviour .html#RTFToC2]. Accessed November 24, 2008.

Blanchard, K. H., Carlos, J. P., and Randolph, W. A. *The Three Keys to Empowerment.* San Francisco: Berrett-Koehler, 1999.

Blanchard, K. H., Zigarmi, P., and Zigarmi, D. *Leadership and the One Minute Manager.* New York: Morrow, 1985.

BlessingWhite. *The Coaching Conundrum: Building a Coaching Culture That Drives Organizational Success.* Princeton, N.J.: BlessingWhite, 2008.

Brinckerhoff, P. *Generations: The Challenge of a Lifetime for Your Nonprofit.* St. Paul, Minn.: Fieldstone Alliance, 2007.

Buckingham, M. "What Great Managers Do." *Harvard Business Review*, March 2005.

Buckingham, M., and Clifton, D. O. *Now, Discover Your Strengths.* New York: Free Press, 2001.

Buckingham, M., and Coffman, C. *First, Break All the Rules: What the World's Greatest Managers Do Differently.* New York: Simon & Schuster, 1999.

Coach U. "Coaching Manager Chart." Coach U, Inc., 2008. [http://www.coachu.com].

Coleman, J. S. *Foundations of Social Theory.* Cambridge, Mass.: Harvard University Press, 1990.

Collins, J. *Good to Great and the Social Sectors: A Monograph to Accompany "Good to Great."* New York: HarperCollins, 2005.

Collins, J., and Porras, J. *Built to Last: Successful Habits of Visionary Companies.* New York: HarperCollins, 1994.

Commongood Careers. *The Voice of Nonprofit Talent in 2008.* Boston, 2008. [http://www.cgcareers.org/downloads/CGC_2008TalentSurveyReport.pdf].

CompassPoint Nonprofit Services, and Snowdon, R. Exercise from CompassPoint Nonprofit Services workshop "Thriving as an Executive Director." San Francisco: CompassPoint Nonprofit Services, 2003. [http://www.CompassPoint.org].

CompassPoint Nonprofit Services, and Snowdon, R. Exercise from CompassPoint Nonprofit Services workshop "Thriving as an Executive Director." San Francisco: CompassPoint Nonprofit Services, 2008. [http://www.CompassPoint.org].

Cornelius, M., Corvington, P., and Ruesga, A. *Ready to Lead: Next Generation Leaders Speak Out.* San Francisco: CompassPoint Nonprofit Services, 2008.

Crane, T. "Creating a Coaching Culture," *Worldwide Association of Business Coaches,* 2005, *1*(1). [http://www.wabccoaches.com/bcw/2005_v1_i1/feature.html].

Deloitte & Touche USA LLP. "Catching the Coaching Wave: What Business Leaders Need to Know About Coaching in the Workplace." *Talent Market Series,* 2006, *3.*

Duxbury, S. "Looming Leadership Deficit." *San Francisco Business Times.* November 14, 2008. [http://www.bizjournals.com/sanfrancisco/stories/2008/11/17/focus1.html].

Earle, A. M. *Sun Dials and Roses of Yesterday.* New York: Macmillan, 1902.

Eikenberry, K. "The Three Sources of Coaching and Feedback." *Unleash Your Remarkable Potential,* March 20, 2006, *3*(12).

Enright, K. *Investing in Leadership.* Vol. 2: *Inspiration and Ideas from Philanthropy's Latest Frontier.* Washington, D.C.: GEO, 2006.

Finger, M., and Asun, J. *Adult Education at the Crossroads: Learning Our Way Out.* New York: Zed Books, 2001.

Gross, S., Mohamed, I., Katcher, R., and Master, N. *Advancing Your Cause Through the People You Manage: A Guidebook for Busy Leaders.* Washington, D.C.: Management Assistance Group, 2007.

Halpern, R. P. *Workforce Issues in the Nonprofit Sector Generational Leadership Change and Diversity.* Kansas City, Mo.: American Humanics, 2006.

Hammond, J., Keeney, R., and Raiffa, H. *Smart Choices: A Practical Guide to Making Better Life Decisions.* Boston: Harvard Business School Press, 1999.

Hesselbein, F., Goldsmith, M., Somerville, I., and Drucker, P. *Leading Beyond the Walls.* San Francisco: Jossey-Bass, 1999.

Hubbard, B. *Investing in Leadership,* Vol. 1: *A Grantmaker's Framework for Understanding Nonprofit Leadership Development.* Washington, D.C.: GEO, 2005.

Hunt, J., and Weintraub, J. *The Coaching Manager: Developing Top Talent in Business.* Thousand Oaks, Calif.: Sage, 2002.

Interchange Group. *7 Secrets to Working with Millennials.* Los Angeles: Interchange Group, 2006.

International Coach Federation. "What Is Coaching?" 2008. [http://www.coachfederation
.org/find-a-coach/what-is-coaching]. Accessed November 10, 2008.

Kaplan, J. *Coaching vs Therapy: An Inside Look*. Jeff Kaplan, 2007.

Kaye, B., and Jordan-Evans, S. *Love 'Em or Lose 'Em: Getting Good People to Stay*. San Francisco: Berrett-Koehler, 2008.

Kinicki, A. "Culture Eats Strategy for Breakfast." *Knowledge@W. P. Carey*, 2007. [http://knowledge.wpcarey.asu.edu/article.cfm?articleid=1506]. Accessed November 21, 2007.

Knowles, M., Holton, E., and Swanson, R. *The Adult Learner*. Burlington, Mass.: Elsevier/Butterworth-Heinemann, 2005.

Kouzes, J., and Posner, B. *The Leadership Challenge*. (4th ed.) San Francisco: Jossey-Bass, 2007.

Krishnamurti, J. *Observing Without the "Me."* First public talk given by J. Krishnamurti, Brockwood Park, England, September 5, 1970.

Kunreuther, F., and Corvington, P. A. *Next Shift: Beyond the Nonprofit Leadership Crisis*. Baltimore: Annie E. Casey Foundation, 2007.

Kunreuther, F., Kim, H., and Rodriguez, R. *Working Across Generations*. San Francisco: Jossey-Bass, 2008.

Kuypers, J. PresentLiving.com Web site, 2009. [http://presentliving.com]. Accessed February 14, 2009.

Latham, G., and Lock, E. "Building a Practically Useful Theory of Goal Setting and Task Motivation." *American Psychologist*, 2002, *57*, 705–717.

Light, P. "The Content of Their Character: The State of the Nonprofit Workforce." *The Nonprofit Quarterly*, Fall 2002, *9*(3).

Marshall, L. J., and Freedman, L. D. *Smart Work: The Syntax Guide for Mutual Understanding in the Workplace*. Dubuque, Iowa: Kendall/Hunt, 1995.

McNamara, C. *Authenticity Circles Facilitator's Guide*. Minneapolis, Minn.: Authenticity Consulting, 2001.

McNamara, C. *Field Guide to Consulting and Organizational Development with Nonprofits*. Minneapolis, Minn.: Authenticity Consulting, 2005.

Miller, F. A., and Katz, J. H. *The Inclusion Breakthrough: Unleashing the Real Power of Diversity*. San Francisco: Berrett-Koehler, 2002.

Miller, L., and Holman, M. *Coaching in Organizations: Best Coaching Practices from Ken Blanchard Companies*. Escondido, Calif.: Ken Blanchard Companies, 2008.

Mind Tools. "The Conscious Competence Ladder." 2008. [http://www.mindtools.com/pages/article/newISS_96.htm]. Accessed November 10, 2008.

Morgan, H., Harkins, P., and Goldsmith, M. *The Art and Practice of Leadership Coaching*. San Francisco: Jossey-Bass, 2004.

O'Connor, J., and Lages, A. *How Coaching Works: The Essential Guide to the History and Practice of Effective Coaching*. London: A&C Black, 2007.

Office of Human Resources, Princeton University. "Learning & Development." 2009. [http://www.princeton.edu/hr/l&d]. Accessed March 6, 2009.

O'Neill, M. *Executive Coaching with Backbone and Heart: A Systems Approach to Engaging Leaders with Their Challenges*. San Francisco: Jossey-Bass, 2000.

Preskill, S., and Brookfield, S. *Learning as a Way of Leading: Lessons from the Struggle for Social Justice.* San Francisco: Jossey-Bass, 2009.

Raelin, J. A. *Creating Leaderful Organizations.* San Francisco: Berrett-Koehler, 2003.

Raines, C., and Ewing, L. *The Art of Connecting.* New York: AMACOM, 2006.

Rath, T. *Vital Friends.* Washington, D.C.: Gallup Press, August 2006.

Rath, T. *Strengths Finder 2.0.* Washington, D.C.: Gallup Press, 2007.

Rath, T., and Clifton, D. O. *How Full Is Your Bucket?* Washington, D.C.: Gallup Press, 2004.

Rock, D. *Quiet Leadership: Help People Think Better—Don't Tell Them What to Do!* New York: HarperCollins, 2006.

Rock, D., and Donde, R. *Driving Change with Internal Coaching Programs.* Sydney: Results Coaching Systems, 2008.

Rosenberg, M. *Nonviolent Communication: A Language of Life.* Encinitas, Calif.: PuddleDancer Press, 2003.

Rosenthal, R., and Jacobson, L. *Pygmalion in the Classroom: Teacher Expectation and Pupils' Intellectual Development.* (Expanded edition.) New York: Irvington, 1992. (Originally published 1968.)

Rothwell, W. *Adult Learning Basics.* Baltimore: American Society for Training & Development, 2008.

Scott, S. *Fierce Conversations: Achieving Success at Work and in Life, One Conversation at a Time.* New York: Berkley Trade, 2004.

Seashore, C. N., Seashore, E. W., and Weinberg, G. M. *What Did You Say? The Art of Giving and Receiving Feedback.* North Attleboro, Mass.: Douglas Charles, 1992.

Senge, P. *The Fifth Discipline.* New York: Doubleday, 1990.

Senge, P. *Leadership in Living Organizations.* San Francisco: Jossey-Bass, 1999.

Senge, P. *The Fifth Discipline.* New York: Doubleday, 2006.

Shafir, R. *The Zen of Listening.* Wheaton, Ill.: Quest Books, 2000.

Shepard, J. *Strengthening Leadership and Human Resources Capacity in the Nonprofit Sector: Pro Bono as a Powerful Solution.* San Francisco: Taproot Foundation, 2008.

Sherman, S., and Freas, A. "The Wild West of Coaching." *Harvard Business Review,* November 2004.

Taylor, W. C. "The Leader of the Future," *Fast Company,* 2007. [http://www.fastcompany.com/magazine/25/heifetz.html]. Accessed December 19, 2007.

Tierney, T. J. *The Nonprofit Sector's Leadership Deficit.* San Francisco: Bridgespan Group, 2006.

University of Pennsylvania Positive Psychology Center. *Frequently Asked Questions.* Philadelphia: University of Pennsylvania, 2007. [http://www.ppc.sas.upenn.edu/faqs.htm]. Accessed November 4, 2008.

Wheatley, J. *Turning to One Another.* (2nd ed.) San Francisco: Berrett-Koehler, 2009.

Whitmore, J. *Coaching for Performance.* (3rd ed.) Boston: Brealey, 2002.

Wikipedia. "Internalized Oppression." 2009. [http://en.wikipedia.org/wiki/Oppression#Internalized_oppression]. Accessed March 13, 2009.

INDEX

Buckingham, M., 8, 64
Budesilich, C. R., 47

C

Carroll, L., 52, 100
Cascading coaching, 241
Center for Creative Leadership, 233
Clarify the focus: of the coaching conversation, 161–162; example of coaching when manager sets the focus, 162–163; importance of effective approach to, 95–96; process of clarifying funnel to, 98–99; questions to, 96, 99; what you need to know in order to, 95
Clifton, D. O., 8, 74
Closed-ended questions: continuum of, 51; description of, 41; effective use of, 49–50, 52
Coaches Training Institute (CTI), 45
Coaching: cascading, 241; combining coaching framework/foundational skills for, 113–118; confidentiality element of, 149; defining process of, 1; in difficult situations, 194–211; external, 240–241; facilitating success of new staff, 174–177; following up developmental feedback with strong, 78–81; foundational tools for, 89–90; handling delicate matters during, 108–109; how ladder of inference affects, 124–126; internal, 242; opportunities for, 18–19; organizational benefits of, 2; peer, 243; questions on readiness for, 159; requests for, 1–2; self-reliance fostered by, 13; taking unique approach to each individual, 16; what it is not, 14–16; what to do when it isn't working, 163–167. *See also* Coaching managers; Staff development
Coaching and Philanthropy Project, 302
Coaching approach: in difficult situations, 194–211; used to manage others, 10–14; problem solving encouragement of, 6–8; reflection and learning support of, 4–6; support of accountability by, 9–10; supporting others' strengths through, 8–9; as unique leadership approach, 3–4; when to use, 151–168. *See also* Coaching model; Coaching scenarios
Coaching approach applications: examples of activities open to, 167–168; familiar with task but barrier situation, 155–156; familiar with task but hesitant situation, 156–157; understanding timing for, 152–153; what to do when coaching is not working, 163–167; when the manager sets the focus, 158–163; when someone is new to a task situation, 157–158; when someone is seasoned at a task situation, 154–155; when a staff member is not improving, 165–167
Coaching conversations: acknowledging the tough stuff, 87; agenda for clarifying the focus of, 161–162; earning trust during, 135–137; handling delicate matters during, 108–109; handling emotional, 134; preparing for the resistant individual, 206–207; self-assessment questions to prepare for, 160–161; showing empathy during, 108, 135; showing respect during, 137–139; staying connected foundation of, 139–149. *See also* Communication; Giving feedback; Language
Coaching culture: definition of, 238; factors to consider in creating, 239–248; focusing on your area of influence for building, 246–248; four types of coaching that build, 240–243; organizational benefits of, 238–239; skills, systems, and culture components of, 244–246; top-down and bottom-up process of building, 245–246. *See also* Culture
Coaching former peers: coaching scenario on, 182–183; issues to clarify when, 181; questions to use when, 183–184. *See also* Peer coaching
Coaching framework: clarify the focus, 95–99; comparison of two coaching scenarios, 93–94; create accountability, 110–113; develop solutions, 104–109; identify the goal, 100–104; incorporating foundational skills and, 113–118; overview of, 91–92; short version of, 92–93
Coaching in nonprofit workplace: coaching and self-management, 170, 190–194; coaching top performers, 171, 228–235; coaching up, down, and across organization, 170, 171–189; in difficult situations, 170–171, 194–228
Coaching in Organizations (Miller and Holman), 146
The Coaching Manager: Developing Top Talent in Business (Hunt and Weintraub), 14
Coaching managers: coaching approach when focus is set by, 158–163; competency and

commitment of, 153; credibility of, 136–137; culturally aware, 137–139, 188–189; handling delicate matters, 108–109; how inquiry benefits, 40; inquiry self-assessment by, 55–57; making effective requests, 111; real-world examples of, 241–242; self-management by, 190–191; servant leader role of, 132; supervisory manager versus, 11–12; thought partner role of, 14. *See also* Coaching; Managers; Self-assessment questions; Staff

Coaching mind-set: believing in others component of, 123–130; confidentiality component of, 149; description of, 121–123; earning trust and showing respect component of, 135–139; managing needs component of, 130–135; staying connected component of, 139–149

Coaching model: on coaching framework, 91–119; description and diagram of, 21–22, 24, 92, 122; on foundational coaching skills, 23–89; on mind-set, 121–149. *See also* Coaching approach

Coaching moments: a moment in the hallway example of, 19–20; opportunities for informal, 191–194. *See also* Coaching scenarios

Coaching other coaches: coaching scenario on, 211–213; how to, 211; questions to use for, 214

Coaching scenarios: being a culturally aware coaching manager, 188–189; coaching a former peer, 182–183; coaching while delegating, 179–180; the constant complainer, 199–201; giving last chance to someone not improving, 220–224; helping new people succeed, 175–177; individual who's lost interest (part 1), 215–216; individual who's lost interest (part 2), 217; letting someone go, 224–227; to leverage someone's strengths, 230–232; someone to be better coach, 211–213; someone who doesn't report to you, 184–186; someone who explodes, 202–205; someone who is resistant, 208–210; someone with know-it-all attitude, 195–197; staying in questioning mode, 172–173; when you have only a few minutes, 192–193. *See also* Coaching approach; Coaching moments; Self-assessment questions

Coaching skills: coaching culture building by improving, 244–245; giving feedback as,

58–81; incorporating coaching framework and, 113–118; inquiring (the skill of inquiry) as, 39–57; listening as, 25–42; overview of foundational, 23–24; sharing as, 82–90. *See also* Ability (coaching)

Coaching staff not reporting to you: coaching scenario on, 184–186; questions to use when, 186

Coaching up: managing up compared to, 186–187; recommendations for, 187–188

Coffman, C., 8, 64

Coleman, J., 135

College Summit, 243

Commitment (coaching), 153

Communication: anger self-management for nonviolent, 190–191; body language for nonverbal, 147–148; giving effective feedback, 58–81; using inclusive language in, 143–147. *See also* Coaching conversations

Community Health Academy, 138

CompassPoint, 165, 301, 302

Competency: coaching, 153; identifying leadership, 234–235; from unconscious incompetency to conscious, 163–164

Complainers: coaching scenario on the constant, 199–201; how to supervise, 198–199; questions to ask for coaching, 201

Confidentiality, 149

Connections. *See* Staying connected

Contracting for action, 110

Craig, C., 154

Create Your Own Back-Pocket Questions (worksheet), 56

Credibility, 136–137

Cultural lens, 137–139

Culturally aware coaching managers: characteristics of, 137–139, 188; coaching scenario on, 188–189

Culture: being sensitive and respectful of, 137–139; definition of, 139. *See also* Coaching culture

D

Day, D., 233

Delegating roles/tasks: coaching scenario while, 179–180; how to coach during process of, 178–179; questions to facilitate, 177–178; questions to use when, 180

Limiting belief, 126–128

LISC (Bay Area Local Initiatives Support Corporation), 154, 241

Listening: four modes of, 25–35, 38; questions to ask yourself about, 38–39; silent, 35–37

Listening modes: engaged listening as, 25, 26, 32–35, 38, 141–142; fix-it listening as, 25, 26, 30–32; overview of four, 25–27; self-referential listening as, 25, 26, 28–30; superficial listening as, 25, 26, 27–28

Locke, E., 100

M

Maeterlinck, M., 35

Making requests: suggestions for, 110–111; three responses following, 111–112

Mampilly, S. R., 136

Managers: credibility of, 136–137; supervisory versus coaching, 11–12; "working manager" self-perception of, 10. *See also* Coaching managers

Managing needs: aligning needs of others with organization, 131–133; balancing coaching with, 130–131; coaching when things get emotional, 134; handling your personal needs, 133–134; showing empathy as part of, 108–109, 135

Managing up, 186–187

Marshall, L. J., 111

Mayeno, L., 138

McNamara, C., 6, 17

Mentoring, 17–18

Mid-Peninsula Housing Corporation, 240

Miller, L., 146

Mind Tools, 163, 164

Mind-set: coaching, 121–149; disinterested person, 214–218; questions about work, 218

Missing talent issue, 164–165

Morgan, H., 132

N

National Public Radio, 141

Needs. *See* Managing needs

Nonverbal communication, 147–148

Nonviolent Communication: A Language of Life (Rosenberg), 191

Now, Discover Your Strengths (Buckingham and Clifton), 8, 165

O

Oak School experiment, 124

Objective observation: description of effective, 59; evaluating versus observing behavior for, 62; evaluation component of effective, 59–61; exercise for, 63; giving feedback using, 61

Observation sharing, 83–85

Observer-expectancy effect, 124

O'Connor, J., 246

Office of Human Resources (Princeton University), 17

Open-ended questions: continuum of, 44; description of, 41; exercise on using, 48–49; inquiry using, 43, 45–46; suggestions for effective use of, 45–49

Organizations: aligning needs of others with, 131–133; coaching benefits to, 2; coaching not meant to replace good HR of, 16; coaching up, down, and across, 170, 171–189; developing coaching culture in your, 237–248; incorporating coaching skills into systems of, 245; keeping focus on mission of, 133; termination policies and procedures of, 228

Osage, P., 66, 106

Overconfident individuals: coaching scenario on, 195–197; issues related to coaching, 195–197; questions to use when coaching, 197–198

P

Park Nicollet Health Services, 242

Partners in School Innovation, 241

Peer coaching, 243. *See also* Coaching former peers

Performance problems, 15. *See also* Lack of improvement

Personal counseling issues, 218–219

Posner, B., 65, 133, 136

Present Living, Inc., 142

Preskill, S., 2, 39

Pritchard, J., 131

Problem solving: accountability as facilitated through, 10; coaching facilitating others' empowered, 6–8; identifying the goal of, 100–104. *See also* Solutions

Problems: clarifying the focus of the, 95–99; good solutions to well-posed, 97; "jumping in the hole" by overly focusing on, 106

Pygmalion effect, 124
Pygmalion in the Classroom: Teacher Expectation and Pupils' Intellectual Development (Rosenthal and Jacobson), 124

Q

Questions: for clarifying the focus, 99; closed-ended, 41, 49–52; for coaching complainers, 201; for coaching other coaches, 214; for coaching overconfident individual, 197–198; for coaching people about their work mindset, 218; for coaching someone who explodes, 205–206; for coaching top performer, 229; for coaching when you don't have much time, 193–194; for creating accountability, 112; for developing solutions, 109; for identifying goals, 104; for identifying leadership competency, 235; open-ended, 41, 43–49; for resistant individual, 210–211; why, 41, 52–55. *See also* Self-assessment questions
Quiet Leadership: Help People Think Better— Don't Tell Them What to Do! (Rock), 63

R

Raiffa, H., 97
Raines, C., 141
Rath, T., 74, 134, 174
Razavi, S., 32
Reflection, 4–6
Request making: suggestions for effective, 111; three options for responding to, 111–112
Resistant individuals: coaching scenario on the, 208–210; how to coach the, 206–207; questions to use when coaching, 210–211
Respect: cultural awareness and, 137–139; examples of showing, 138; importance of showing, 137–139
Rivera, S. M., 10, 45
Rock, D., 6–7, 63, 240, 242
Rodriguez, R., 17
Rosenberg, M., 191
Rosenthal, R., 124

S

Scenarios. *See* Coaching scenarios
Scott, S., 134
Seashore, C. N., 58

Seashore, E. W., 58
Self-assessment questions: before you coach, 123; for coaching up, 187; about connecting with others, 140–141; determining when to coach and when to tell, 173–174; about giving appreciative feedback, 70–71; about giving developmental feedback, 80–81; about inquiring (skill of inquiry), 55–57; about listening, 38–39; to prepare for coaching conversation, 160–161; on readiness for coaching, 159; about sharing, 88–89; when coaching a former peer, 181, 183–184; when coaching someone who doesn't report to you, 186; when delegating new roles, 177–178, 180. *See also* Coaching managers; Coaching scenarios; Questions
Self-fulfilling prophecies, 124
Self-referential listening: in action example of, 29–30; description of, 25, 26; as ineffective coaching skill, 28–29
Self-reliance: coaching as fostering, 13; coaching to facilitate problem solving, 6–8, 10; how inquiry encourages, 40. *See also* Accountability
Senge, P. M., 5, 125
Servant leader role, 133
Shafir, R., 28, 35
Sharing: description and value of, 82–83; four basic steps to, 83; a hunch, 85–86; ideas, information, and examples, 86–88; observations, 83–85; questions to ask yourself about, 88–89
Sherman, S., 239
Silent listening, 35–37
Situational leadership, 153
Smart Work: The Syntax Guide to Mutual Understanding in the Workplace (Marshall and Friedman), 111
Snowdon, R., 205, 227
Solutions: figuring out how to reach, 104–106; identifying what's needed for, 104; questions for developing, 109; well-posed problems required for good, 97. *See also* Goal identification; Problem solving
Staff: coaching to facilitate success of new, 174–177; coaching facilitating problem solving by, 6–8; coaching as fostering self-reliance of, 13; coaching supporting accountability of, 9–10; coaching which

supports strengths of, 8–9; credibility perceptions of managers by, 136–137; delegating new roles to, 177–180; how inquiry benefits your, 40; ladder of inference role in coaching, 124–126; ongoing performance problems of, 15; turnarounds made by, 220; unconscious incompetency of, 163–164; who needs therapy or personal counseling, 218–219. *See also* Coaching managers; Talent

Staff development: benefits of investing in, 16; handling lack of improvement, 165–167, 219–224; helping new staff to success, 174–177; matching leadership style to, 153; mentoring as resource for, 17–18; missing talent issue of, 164–165; to take on new delegated role, 177–180; training component of, 17. *See also* Coaching

Staying connected: being available for, 148–149; being present required for, 141–142; deciding and making the choice for, 143; engaged listening required for, 141; focusing the other person for, 145–147; importance of, 139; using inclusive language for, 143–145; Kara's story on, 139–140; letting go of distracting thoughts for, 142; paying attention and noticing for, 142; questions to ask yourself about, 140–141

Strengths Finder (Rath), 174

Success: coaching to facilitate new staff, 174–175; coaching scenario for helping new staff, 175–177

Superficial listening: in action example of, 27–28; description of, 25, 26; as ineffective coaching skills, 27

Supervisory managers, 11–12

Swanson, R., 4

Swartz, P., 4, 247

T

Talent: coaching top performing, 228–235; description of, 164; issue of missing, 164–165. *See also* Staff

Termination: following policies and procedures for, 228; scenario for friendly exit, 224–226; scenario for involuntary firing, 224–225, 226–227. *See also* Lack of improvement

Therapy: coaching not replacement for, 14–15; when individual requires professional, 218–219

Thomas, M., 64

Thought partner, 14

The Three Keys to Empowerment (Blanchard, Carlos, and Randolph), 153

Top performers: coaching approach for, 228–229; coaching to take on more leadership, 232–235; leveraging strengths of, 229–232; questions to use when coaching, 229

Trust: confidentiality and, 149; earning, 135–137

Turnarounds, 220

U

Unconscious incompetency: coaching approach when facing, 163; moving to conscious competency from, 164

W

Weinberg, G. M., 58

Weintraub, J., 14, 138

What Did You Say? The Art of Giving and Receiving Feedback (Seashore, Seashore, and Weinberg), 58

"What Is Our Role in Creating Change" (Wheatley), 247

Wheatley, M., 247

Whitmore, J., 3

Why questions: continuum of, 53; description of, 41; effective use of, 52, 54–55; Judith's back-pocket, 55

Willingness (coaching), 153

Wilson, J., 9, 13, 300–301

Working across Generations (Kunreuther, Kim, and Rodriguez), 17

Working managers, 10

Worksheets: Appreciative Feedback Preparation, 70–71; Create Your Own Back-Pocket Questions, 56; Developmental Feedback Preparation, 77; Inquiry Self-Assessment, 57

Z

The Zen of Listening (Shafir), 35

Zigarmi, D., 153

Zigarmi, P., 153

ABOUT THE AUTHORS

 Judith Wilson, M.C.C., one of the original adopters of professional coaching, was professionally trained at the Coaches Training Institute in San Rafael, California, and is one of only six hundred practicing International Coach Federation master certified coaches. Judith brings fifteen years of organizational leadership and workforce development to individuals and organizations worldwide and specializes in leadership and staff development in the nonprofit, government, and for-profit sectors. Educated in England, Judith is the author of the Coaching Skills for Managers and Leaders program and has taught at John F. Kennedy University and currently teaches managers to coach around the world.

Judith assists many types of organizations, including nonprofit and social services agencies and educational, health and human services, municipal government, financial, biotech, and consulting organizations. Among her past and present clients are the Academy for Educational Development, Partners for School Innovation, Kaiser Permanente Educational Department, Bureau of Jewish Education, Haas School of Business, Asian Pacific Islander Health Foundation, Support for Families with Disabilities, Partners in School Innovation, Child Care Coordinating Council of San Mateo, University of California at Davis, YMCA, San Francisco Foundation, Mid-Peninsula Housing Coalition, Goodwill, City of Oakland, Genentech, Adobe, Deloitte US Firms, Varian, Pfizer, Gilead Sciences, and American Express. Judith is regularly called on to provide executive coaching and training for the Ken Blanchard Companies and CompassPoint Nonprofit Services.

Judith has lived in, worked in, or visited fifty-four countries in areas from South America to the Middle East. She has served as a board member for the Professional and Personal Coaching Association and is cofounder of the Black Professional Coaching Association. She lives in California with her husband, Eiji.

Michelle Gislason is a senior project director at CompassPoint Nonprofit Services. She is responsible for the program creation, management, and delivery of CompassPoint's core leadership programs, including the Coaching and Philanthropy Project, Leadership Circles peer-coaching program, and the Leadership Development Program for Executives Serving Transition-Age Youth. In addition, she provides peer-coaching facilitation and skills training in both coaching and people management for leadership initiatives and organizational clients. Michelle is also a lead trainer and coach for CompassPoint's leadership series, "Thriving as an Executive Director," and the Bay Area Local Initiative Support Corporation's (LISC) Community Development Leadership Institute.

Her past and present clients include Alameda County Foster Youth Alliance, California Pan-Ethnic Health Network, Emerge California, Exhale, GAP Foundation, Immigrant Legal Right Center, KIPP Foundation, LISC, Public Interest Clearinghouse, and California Wellness Foundation.

Michelle is a trainer, consultant, and certified organizational coach. She is also an occasional guest lecturer for University of California at Berkeley Haas School of Business. She graduated from UCLA with a bachelor of arts degree and completed her master's degree in organizational psychology in 2007.

CompassPoint
NONPROFIT SERVICES

ABOUT COMPASSPOINT NONPROFIT SERVICES

CompassPoint Nonprofit Services is a consulting, research, and training organization providing nonprofits with management tools, strategies, and resources to lead change in their communities. With offices in San Francisco and Silicon Valley, we work with community-based nonprofits in executive transitions, leadership development, nonprofit finance, fund development, governance, management of people, and technology. Our mission is to increase the impact of community nonprofits and the people who work and volunteer in them.

ABOUT THE COACHING AND PHILANTHROPY PROJECT

The Coaching and Philanthropy (CAP) project was created to assess and advance the application of coaching as a strategy for building effective nonprofit organizations. In partnership with Grantmakers for Effective Organizations, BTW Informing Change, and Leadership that Works, CompassPoint Nonprofit Services launched a project to

- Help nonprofits become conscious consumers by making the best use of coaching as a means for leadership development and organizational effectiveness
- Help foundations understand how coaching fits as a strategy for leadership development and organizational effectiveness
- Develop the coaching profession to most effectively support the needs of nonprofit organizations, leadership development, and organizational effectiveness and engage nonprofits in a healthy way

This project is funded by the W. K. Kellogg Foundation, the James Irvine Foundation, the David & Lucile Packard Foundation, and the Harnisch Family Foundation.